Poor Circulation

Ashes to Boonville

Geoff G. Thomas

For Hannah and
George and Barbara Thomas

Forward

Riding around the world on a budget of just £20 a day? Delve into this gripping adventure and you'll find that against all odds, it really is possible.

Following this journey through Europe and Asia, across the wilds of Siberia and onwards into North America, you'll find yourself standing in some of the most beautiful places on earth, and riding roads that have fearsome reputations. Geoff Thomas introduces you to the lands and people along the way with vivid descriptions and a refreshingly openhearted manner. You'll discover a warm and unique thread woven through this story, a thread that will constantly tug at your heart strings.

At times you'll laugh and at others, you'll feel the depth of the challenges. On a daily basis, Thomas and his riding companion face unexpected hurdles that will have you turning the pages even faster. What happens next?

Anyone interested in travel, motorcycles, stretching boundaries and the beauty of this world will love this book.

Sam Manicom

Introduction

Traditionally speaking, this is where you'd expect to find an introduction to the author and a literary tease that tempts you to keep on turning the pages. However, within the first few pages of this book you'll discover that I'm anything but 'traditional' and that I certainly don't consider myself to be an 'author'. But, where necessary, I'll try my best to conform.

I'm just a motorcycle despatch rider from the fine city of London, a middle-aged man who got incredibly lucky. With a little massaging of circumstances and a rude amount of alcohol, in 2008 I developed a half-baked plan to ride around the world on a motorcycle. In this day and age such mid-life adventures are certainly not uncommon, but I think you'll find that this adventure is a little more unusual than most. The fact that I'm here to tell this story is evidence that the journey didn't kill me, but I hope that my avoidance of death doesn't detract from your vicarious enjoyment of this adventure.

It all started out quite innocently, but as with so many other things in my life, my plans have a tendency to change. A twenty week shoestring journey around the world, a journey to realise the unfulfilled wishes of my late mother, Barbara Thomas, unexpectedly morphed into an adventure without a foreseeable ending. I could point the finger of blame at others: My parents George and Barbara Thomas for first introducing me to motorcycles, my good friend Steve Corby for encouraging me to read Jupiter's Travels and at Ted Simon for writing that book in the first place. I could easily point the finger of blame at any of them, or all of them, but I won't. Everything that follows, the good and the bad, happened as a direct result of my own actions.

Aside from being amazingly rude, reading a stranger's diary would probably be quite boring, so I hope that Ashes to Boonville will read more like a novel than a hastily written travel journal. However, this is not a work of fiction. Everything that follows is a reflection of actual events, a record of the many things that happened on the overland journey between England and California. However, in order to protect the innocent, and in many cases the guilty, certain names and descriptions have been changed. The editor's pen has shown little mercy, and in the process of condensing several months of adventure into just a few hours of entertaining reading, certain events have been simplified and others have simply disappeared. These alterations should in no way change the substance of Ashes to Boonville, only the narrative.

Acknowledgements

I'd like to thank my daughter Hannah for allowing me to become an absent father and for her endless encouragement while writing this manuscript. I also need to thank Alan and Torrey and Sam and Willow for inviting me to Boonville and for helping to make that initial journey possible. I say a special thank you to Torrey Douglass, Timo Schmidt, Sam Manicom, Bernard & Cathy Smith, Ted Simon and all of the advisers at the Ted Simon Foundation for transforming my shoddy manuscript into a genuine book.

For their support and generous donations, I must also thank CitySprint, P&O Ferries, WeMoto, Triumph-on-Line, MotoHaus, The Riders Digest, Revolution Signs and the amazing people from Boxertrix and Horizons Unlimited. I must add to those names the countless people who reached out and helped me along the road, all of whom gave so generously and asked for absolutely nothing in return.

Many people, some of whom have chosen to remain anonymous, have made generous donations to my chosen charity, St Teresa's Hospice in Darlington. To all of those people, I offer my sincere thanks and gratitude.

I offer special and belated thanks to Ted Simon for writing Jupiter's Travel's, and to Steve Corby for introducing me to it at a very impressionable age.

Most importantly, I'll say thank you to George and Barbara Thomas, for accompanying me on the long journey to Boonville and for being the best parents in the world.

Bangkok, Klong Toey District

If the Elephant Bar had a clock, it would be telling me that it's time to go home. The battery in my laptop is exhausted, the bar's almost empty and apart from Sunthon, the remainder of the guests have ridden away into Bangkok's neon sunset. The two unnamed girls are huddled together in the far corner of the bar, chatting, examining mirrors and re-painting synthetic nails. Sunthon's asleep beside me, his arse pushed back on the patio chair and his head resting on folded arms. I should really tell him to go home, back to his wife and children where he belongs, but I don't have the heart to wake him. I've settled the reasonable bar-bill and the bar owner, Sunthon's eldest brother, seems happy for us to linger. It's just as well because I don't have a bed to go to tonight and for all of its faults, the Elephant Bar's plastic seats are far more comfortable than the cold steel benches of Bangkok's Suvarnabhumi Airport. I've got an early morning flight to Seattle and it seems pointless spending money that I don't have on a bedroom that I'll probably never remember. The Elephant Bar is my home for tonight, and I've certainly slept in worse places than this.

I hadn't seen the young man entering the bar. Maybe I'd dozed off for a moment or perhaps he's a stealthy ninja assassin who dropped in through the ceiling. Regardless of how or when he'd entered, he's certainly making his presence felt now. Screams are ringing out and echoing back from the shabby tin roof. Wild animal screams that sound too highly pitched to be human. Fists and feet are furiously flying. The shorter of the two girls is already lying on the floor, perfectly still and worryingly silent. The taller girl is bravely standing her ground. Her head bowed defensively low, black silken hair performing an amazing fan dance, arms and fingernails wind-milling wildly. Despite the valiant effort, her slender frame and plastic talons are no match for the short but strapping ninja. She's lashing out like an anxious cat and he's grinning back at her like a loaded junkie. He's dodging her random blows and playing with his quarry. But then, he just seems to get bored with the game.

Punch. Punch. Kick. It's all over in three swift moves. Checkmate. She's down on the floor, lying next to her friend and there's nothing to be heard but the chilling sound of defeat: Silence. The battle has lasted just a few seconds but it feels more like minutes. I'd wanted to shout out for him to stop the assault, but the words just hadn't left my mouth. I don't know why I didn't move earlier. Perhaps it all happened so quickly that there was no earlier to mention. Now I'm moving, but it might be too late. His brutal mission is complete. He's making for the exit and there's no time to think.

The Elephant Bar is narrow, one way in and the same way out. As the ninja approaches my table, he scowls and points an angry finger towards me. He's probably telling me that it's none of my bloody business, and he's absolutely right. But he's also too late. I really don't mean to do it. I'm not a brave man, but I'm reasonably drunk and it's just something that instinctively happens. I swing around towards him and the edge of the closed laptop lands squarely on his chin. No warning shots. No opportunity for surrender. All that I hear is a satisfying 'crack' as two kilograms of plastic encased technology strikes hard against brittle bone. A knockout blow by Fujitsu Siemens and the girl beating ninja is finished.

Sunthon looks worried. He's leaning over me and saying something that I really don't understand. I've got a hundred different questions and no immediate answers. 'Why's he speaking Thai? Is he Thai? Can I speak Thai? Why is his tee shirt so red?'

There's a second man standing here and he looks an awful lot like Sunthon. I'm not seeing double, it's definitely two different men. Slowly the fog begins to clear and reality creeps in. I hurt so much that I couldn't tell you exactly where I hurt. The pain is just extreme and universal. Sunthon's not really helping and the whiskey that he's using to cleanse my mouth is stinging like hell. I stop him from playing nurse for a moment, and ask him to enlighten me.

Sunthon can't really answer my questions, he'd slept through the entire disturbance, but his brother can fill in some of the blanks. Apparently the ninja is a well known local thug, a full-time hoodlum and part-time lover of the tallest girl. Earlier in the evening they'd had a lover's quarrel, but I'm not to worry about that, because everything's going to be alright. Shortly after the battle she'd regained her composure, followed her violent boyfriend out of the Elephant Bar and was last seen at the end of the street sucking on his face and making all chummy. 'Good for them'.

Apparently, my confidence in delivering the perfect technical knockout had been slightly misplaced. The laptop had certainly struck its target, but the target had stood his ground and instantly retaliated. He'd knocked me to the floor and kicked me until I'd finally stopped bleating. Oh how I wish that I'd stopped bleating an awful lot earlier and saved myself some pain. But, much more than that, I wish that I'd finally learn to simply walk away from other people's shit.

I take the lint cloth from Sunthon and dab the area that hurts the most. It's my mouth. I must have bitten my tongue when the ninja hit me. It's throbbing like crazy and won't stop bleeding. Sunthon offers me the bottle of whiskey, insisting that it will help, so I take a reluctant mouthful and discover an entirely new level of pain.

I press a comforting palm to the side of my cheek and sense that the contours have changed. I've lost a bloody tooth. He's kicked one of my lower teeth clean out of its socket and my tongue probes the newly formed hole.

My temporary nurses look towards the floor, but the missing tooth is nowhere to be seen. I must have swallowed it. I start cursing the ninja for costing me a potential fortune in dental expenses, but Sunthon's brother jumps in to correct me. It probably wasn't the ninja but his tall and slender lover who caused my dental damage. Seemingly upset by my intervention, on her way out of the bar in pursuit of him, she'd paused and aimed several kicks at my body and face. It's not news that I'd expected to hear and recognising my new feeling of discomfort, mental not physical, Sunthon leaps to the defence of my waning masculinity.

Talking with the confidence of a man with some experience, he suggests that given the girl's ample bosom and unusual height, it's quite possible that she wasn't a 'Girl' at all. His brother's nodding along with the statement. I understand that they're only trying to help, giving me an opportunity to save face, but it's the kind of help that I really don't need right now.

Having my teeth kicked out by a girl would be embarrassing, but in my defence I'd been unconscious when she'd attacked me. On the other hand, if Sunthon's claim is true, then earlier this evening while fully conscious and relatively sober, I'd thoroughly enjoyed being partially pleasured by an attractive man wearing a frock. All things considered, I've enjoyed more comfortable endings to an evening.

Tonight has taught me a valuable lesson, but I'm not entirely sure what that lesson is. Day one hundred and fifteen of this journey is now behind me, a fresh day is dawning and it's probably time for yet another new beginning. 'Mai pen rai kap' as they like to say here in Thailand: 'Go with the flow'.

Chapter 1:
The Beginning

I'd wasted far too much time searching for the right place to begin. By opening my diary at a random page, I'd found an appropriate place to start writing; 'Bangkok', the one hundred and fifteenth day of an around the world journey, but that certainly wasn't where it started.

In desperation, I sought advice from friends and family and they all told me roughly the same thing: 'I should start at the beginning and keep on writing until I came to the end'. It was obvious really, but the 'End' hadn't been reached and exactly which 'Beginning' did they mean?

I've written paragraph after dreary paragraph and concluded each of them with the 'Delete' key. My recycle bin is overflowing with literary garbage and the right combination of words has continued to elude me. Now, in an act of sheer desperation, I can only hope that plagiarism will be my saviour:

Dear Mrs Thomas,

Will you please meet me at Hope Dene, Gloucester Road, Newcastle -on-Tyne on Wed, for a very nice baby boy. This is the Salvation Army Mother & Baby Home.

I would like you there at 2-30p.m. and I will be there to meet you. He is nine weeks old, baby of a very nice girl, he has not been Christened.

The girl is very anxious to get back to her own home, as no one knows about this, she is supposedly away working, also she is in the Women's Territorial Army, and if she does not report next Sat, will lose her stripes.

He will have clothes to travel in and you will be given a tin of food, and his routine. Sorry for the short notice.

Yours sincerely
Miss M Hedley, Welfare Worker

I suspect that Miss M. Hedley, Welfare Worker, didn't win too many school prizes for English Composition, but in the context of my life, hers are without doubt the finest words ever written. Reading her letter almost fifty years after it was written, I'm left with the distinct impression that back in the early nineteen sixties the adoption of children wasn't optional. Miss Hedley's letter reads more like a summons than a request, but thankfully for me, her summons was answered. I can only assume that on the appropriate day in 1962, George and Barbara Thomas had arrived at the Salvation Army Mother and Baby Home and whisked me back to their small rented house in the market town of Darlington, County Durham.

My adoption happened long before the arrival of digital photography and I've absolutely no memories or mementos to mark that life changing day. In fact, my first real memories are as a toddler, growing up in a happy home with a farm labourer father, a full time mother and Alan, a brother who was several lifetimes older than me. My new family didn't have much money, but that wasn't necessarily a bad thing for me. Back in the days when 'Credit' was only granted to those with the ability to repay it, an expensive motorcar would have been beyond our financial reach, so instead, we owned a motorcycle and sidecar.

I can clearly remember the blue twin cylinder Triumph Thunderbird, a motorcycle that growled like an angry tiger and flew like the wind. Attached to the motorcycle was the largest sidecar you could possibly imagine. It was a vast space, half the size of my bedroom and twice as exciting. It came complete with a front seat for Alan and a rear seat for me. Above our heads was a folding sun roof for summer days and to the side, a magazine rack that overflowed with pencils, wax crayons and colourful sheets of drawing paper. In my young eyes, that motorcycle was more than just an economical means of family transportation, it was something far more magical. It was a mobile adventure playground that took us to amazing places: Family holidays in Scotland, Wales and the South of England. Weekend trips to the seaside and camping on the North Yorkshire moors.

Every time I'd heard that Triumph Thunderbird cough into life and the sidecar door close behind me, I'd known that another new adventure was about to begin.

Without doubt, I was the luckiest kid in the world. I'd been adopted by a family who showered me with love on an unconditional basis, and thanks to a simple letter written by Miss M. Hedley, at the tender age of nine weeks, my love affair with an amazing family and motorcycles had begun.

Throughout my happy days from childhood into adolescence, there was just one small blot on an otherwise perfectly formed landscape. That small blot was called school. It wasn't 'all' of school that I disliked, just the parts that involved reading and writing. It wasn't that I couldn't read, because I could, I just wasn't very good at it. It was almost as if talking and reading were two very different languages and I was much more fluent in one than the other. Needless to say, I left secondary school with limited qualifications and absolutely no idea of what I wanted to do with my life. With an academic record favouring the letters 'E' and 'F', I had the options of taking a dead end job in an anonymous factory, applying for an engineering appritiship or enrolling at the local catering college. It wasn't an easy choice to make, and I knew that it might not lead to the career that I really wanted, but at least I'd never go hungry.

In comparison to school, catering college was a very different world. At college they treated me like an adult and the tutors seemed to know things that school teachers simply didn't. Within the first few weeks of attending, they'd added two very important words to my limited vocabulary: 'Profoundly' and 'Dyslexic'. Another major difference was that colleges seemed to have far more resources than schools. At school I'd probably been categorised as a problem child and largely ignored by the teachers, but at college I was singled out for special attention. I was discreetly assigned to a personal tutor, a man who seemed to understand my problem, and within a short space of time my reading and writing had dramatically improved. It was slow progress at first, and certain words still seemed like complicated puzzles, but at least they were teaching me how to solve them.

It's hard to explain the difference that learning to read and write with confidence made to my life. It was almost as if I'd waited seventeen years before discovering that I also had a right hand. Everything in life suddenly became much easier. I was devoting less time to disguising my problem and that seemed to leave far more time for the more important things in life. I was a typical teenager, full of piss and vinegar with a life to live and a determination to live every minute to the full. There were certain things that I loved, and high upon that list were several varieties of beer, motorcycles of every kind, cigarettes of the dubious kind and girls of obliging virtue.

All of these teenage discoveries required money, but hard work wasn't something that scared me. I took every part-time job that I could find. Most of those jobs involved working behind bars and all of them involved payments in cash. It didn't make me rich, but it did allow me to ride motorcycles and to make the most of my teenage freedom. Through summers of seemingly endless sunshine, I rode an increasingly bizarre range of motorcycles to places that were both new and exciting. Discomfort and distance were irrelevant. I was young, I was cocky, and unlike the rusting wrecks that my student budget afforded me, I was invincible. Every journey was an adventure involving mishaps and mechanical breakdowns, but I was on a voyage of discovery and all of those challenges simply added to the richness of my days.

Then, on the day that I finally graduated from the Darlington College of Technology, my good friend Steve Corby handed me a book. It was a hefty paperback with a photograph of a motorcycle on its cover and he delivered it with a very personal message. He warned me, quite seriously, that reading it would probably change my life.

Intrigued, as much by the warning as by the book itself, I'd immediately started reading. It was the first book that I'd ever read on a voluntary basis, cover to cover and not a single word missed. From the very first paragraph I'd been hooked and in the author of that book I'd found a genuine hero, an explorer who'd ridden around the world on his motorcycle, a Triumph Tiger. Steve Corby had introduced me to Ted Simon and his now iconic book Jupiter's Travels.

It took me a little time to read it, but as I'd turned the final page I'd realised that my destiny had changed. One book had transformed a myriad of random teenage dreams into one single desire, an overwhelming urge to pack up my acne cream, mount my own motorcycle and follow in Ted Simon's tyre tracks. The seeds of adventure had been sewn onto amazingly fertile ground, but at the age of nineteen my desire to ride around the world on a motorcycle had been far stronger than my ability to finance such a journey. As a student I'd been in no position to set out on my own great adventure, but I'd known with a strange degree of certainty that one day it would happen. So, in the absence of any real money, I'd bought a second-hand copy of The Readers Digest World Atlas and begun dreaming of a different future, a future where such an adventure would be possible.

As a teenager it had seemed that a lack of money had been the only thing holding me back. But, as college morphed into university and university led to an unconventional career path, it became abundantly clear that the passage of time would leave an alarming number of new responsibilities in its wake. The years rolled-on and my earnings slowly increased, but every increase in income arrived with new obligations attached to it; marriage, mortgage, motorcar, divorce, a little more marriage and then the arrival of my daughter Hannah. The unavoidable consequences of life, some good and some not so good, joined forces and silently conspired to keep me from realising my teenage dream.

At the tender age of nine weeks, George and Barbara Thomas had accidentally introduced me to the enduring love of my life: Motorcycles. At the age of sixteen, the arrival of my first driving license had kick-started a journey of a million motorcycle miles and reading Jupiter's Travels had inspired me to dream of one day starting out on my own global adventure.

Then, at the age of forty-five, the randomly orbiting planets of Opportunity and Circumstance finally moved into alignment. Unplanned, unexpected, and certainly undeserved, after almost thirty years of waiting the time came for me to set out on the journey of my life. It would be an accidental odyssey adopting the title 'Poor Circulation' and a journey that would dramatically change my life.

This is the story of that journey.

The first photograph of me. Taken in 1963
aboard the family's Triumph Thunderbird
with its trailer and sidecar

Chapter 2:
The Decision

In October of 2007, dressed in the distinctive blue jacket of a London despatch rider working for CitySprint, because that's exactly what I was, I'd ridden away from Darlington, the hometown of my parents. I'd passed from County Durham into North Yorkshire and through the busy market town of Richmond. The picturesque village of Reeth had slipped behind me in a blur of empty tea rooms and I'd just kept on riding. With no particular destination in mind, I'd enjoyed the freedom of the empty moorland roads and headed wherever my heart dictated.

On that day, there'd been no need for a map. They were roads that I'd known since childhood in an area that we'd explored together as a family so many times before. Every mile had brought with it a different memory. There'd been the small bridge across the fast flowing stream where Mom had watched as we'd unsuccessfully fished for brown trout using nothing more than our tickling fingers, the high grassy hill where I'd learned how to fly a kite and the road junction where Dad had taught me how to fix a flat tyre using nothing more than fresh milk and a foot pump. There were so many family memories out there, and all of them were good.

The family's Triumph Thunderbird was long gone, everything in life had moved on, times and technology had changed. I was riding my rental Honda and if ever a soulless motorcycle had existed, then that was certainly it. The Honda CBF600 had been my working companion for a little more than six months, but unlike any of the other motorcycles that I'd previously ridden, we'd never experienced a single moment of connection.

Working in London as a despatch rider, on a daily basis that Honda had done everything within its power to suck the enjoyment of riding a motorcycle right out of me. It was the exact opposite of what any motorcycle should be. It was a machine devoid of both character and soul. But on that day everything had changed. The Honda CBF600 had miraculously transformed, the prissy prom queen had vanished and in her place had been the kind of girl who should never be introduced to your parents. The rev counter had found a new home in the upper reaches of the dial and the tyres had discovered the art of speech. At every opportunity, the small hero spikes at the base of the footpegs had kissed the surface of the road and the throttle had lost its elasticity. I'd twisted my right wrist and out of every turn the little Honda had stood upright and chased towards the next vanishing point on the winding road ahead. I'd squeezed the front brake with two gentle fingers and the bike had lost exactly the right amount of speed without ever shaking its ass in protest. The gear selector had become redundant and the six ratios in the gearbox had become hard-wired directly to my thoughts. I hadn't been physically riding the motorcycle so much as mentally wringing it's neck, and the soundtrack to the journey had changed. Gone was the usual daily dose of easy listening garbage and in its place, 'Paint it Black' by the Rolling Stones. Full volume.

During almost a million miles of riding, I'd never felt so totally connected to a motorcycle. I'd never ridden so smoothly nor smiled so widely in surroundings quite as perfect as those. For sixty glorious minutes, I'd enjoyed what I can only describe as the most perfect journey of my life. It was almost as if that Honda CBF600 had known what cargo it was carrying.

At Tan Hill, the highest public house in England, I'd stopped to relax and catch my breath. Tan Hill was a good place to think, and thinking was exactly what I'd needed to do. A few meters behind me, the Honda's tortured engine had 'Pinged' and 'Cracked' as it cooled down in the chilling late afternoon breeze. It had been a spirited ride and the motorcycle probably deserved the rest far more than me.

Sitting next to me on the spongy moorland grass had been the contents of the Honda's rear panniers. Two simple metal urns from the bargain pages of the funeral directors catalogue, each urn engraved with the name of its occupant. From the first urn I swear that I'd heard Mom 'tutting'. Perhaps she hadn't appreciated the swiftness of the journey, or maybe it was the cigarette hanging from my lower lip that she'd disapproved of. I really wasn't sure which element would have vexed her the most, but from Dad's urn I'm certain that I'd heard nothing but chuckling.

Following Mom's death, Alan had found Dad's engraved urn at the bottom of her wardrobe and with it had been two small photographs, pictures that must have been taken just before their wedding in 1948. The ride across the Yorkshire Moors and Dales had filled me with happy family memories, but sitting there on the grass, ignoring the magnificent views and looking at those two small black and white photographs, my thoughts had turned to their passing. My emotions were in conflict, the happy memories of those earlier family days were fighting with the vision of their final days and my own feelings of guilt. 'Had I been a good son? Why hadn't I shown more appreciation for their love and generosity? Why hadn't I told them more often, or even at all, that I loved them? How could I survive in this crazy world without their continuing support?'

In 1998, Dad had lost his long running battle with prostate cancer and nine years later Mom had lost her own shorter but no less painful battle with cancer of the pancreas. Although each of them had fully appreciated the severity of their conditions, they'd remained strong and cheerful to the bitter end. Shunning the sense numbing pain relief that was available in their final days, they'd each chosen to remain lucid and all of their words and thoughts had been in support of family and close friends, the loved ones they'd be leaving behind. At their time of greatest need, a time when I'd be crying out for double doses of morphine, they'd each chosen the bravest possible option and spent their final days helping those around them. They'd been painful times for all of us, mentally and physically, but Mom and Dad's amazing strength had simply highlighted my own inner weakness and I'd known for certain, that under such circumstance, I could never be so brave or selfless.

There was a bitter wind blowing across Tan Hill that October afternoon, a wind that could easily bring a tear to the eye, but my tears owed absolutely nothing to the weather.

Midway through my own personal pity party, I remembered a conversation that I'd had with Mom in Ward 32 of Darlington's Memorial Hospital. It was one of the last long conversations that we'd had. Her voice had been weak and her words laboured and slow. She'd held my hand as tightly as she could and told me that she'd had the happiest life imaginable and that she'd leave it without any regrets. However, there were two special things that she'd wished might have happened during her lifetime.

The first wish was really quite straight forward, perhaps even obvious. She'd wished that Dad could have lived long enough to meet his new grandchildren, Sam and Willow, who lived in Northern California. Shortly after Dad's death, my brother Alan had moved to Northern California where he'd met and married his American wife Torrey. A few years later, first Sam and then Willow had arrived. Overcoming her lifelong fear of flying, Mom had travelled to America and stayed with them at their new home in the rural community of Boonville in Mendocino County. She'd fallen in love with the grandchildren, and the town of Boonville, and she'd wished that Dad could have been there to share those experiences with her.

Mom's second wish had been a little more surprising, something that I really hadn't expected. While visiting California, she'd driven a little way down the Pacific Coast Highway, in particular the road known as California Highway 1 in Mendocino County. In all of the years spent riding their Triumph motorcycles throughout the dampness of England, Mom wished that just once they could have ridden together down that beautiful road. No rain or snow to dampen their mood, just a perfect ribbon of tarmac winding its way alongside the Pacific Ocean and down through the enchanting Redwood Forests of Mendocino County.

I'd visited Boonville earlier in the year and I'd known the road that Mom had dreamed of riding together with Dad, and of course I'd known Sam and Willow, so I'd understood exactly what she'd meant. I'd also known that although it was impossible to rewind the passage of time, there was still something that I could do to help.

Sitting quietly on the grass at Tan Hill, the randomly orbiting planets of Circumstance and Opportunity had finally moved into alignment. A thousand pieces of a complicated jigsaw had fallen neatly into place. The individual pieces to that jigsaw had been circling in my mind since the age of nineteen, but recalling Mom's words had finally painted the picture that would help me to solve that thirty year puzzle.

With the pair of urns securely packed inside the Honda's panniers, and feeling alive with excitement, I'd left Tan Hill and headed south, back towards London. My mind had been juggling with endless possibilities and there were a million things that I'd needed to do.

Maybe it would be an act of pure self indulgence, an extreme remedy for midlife mediocrity and an act that I would justify by constantly referring to Mom's two unfulfilled wishes, but the time had come to realize my teenage dream of riding around the world on a motorcycle. I was finally going to follow Ted Simon's shining example and undertake the motorcycle journey of my life, but unlike Jupiter, I wouldn't be travelling alone. I'd be carrying with me the most important package of my despatch riding career, the ashes of my adopted parents, George and Barbara Thomas.

They'd get to ride together down the beautiful Pacific Coast Highway on a motorcycle, Dad would discover the wonders of Boonville and get to meet the grandchildren he'd never seen, and Mom's final wishes would be granted.

Chapter 3:
The Planning

Google Earth is an amazing tool. With the cursor hovering above London, I took a deep breath and 'clicked' the mouse. For thirty minutes, I scrolled in an easterly direction around the world and arrived back in London unscathed. It all looked surprisingly easy, and why shouldn't it? I'm sure that in the now famous motorcycle adventure Long Way Round, Ewan McGregor and Charlie Boorman made everything look slightly more difficult that it really was. After all, drama makes for better television and even in the most challenging of situations Claudio Von Planta, their novice riding cameraman, had always managed to keep up with them. If they could do it, then so far as the physical riding was concerned, surely I could do it too?

Brimming with equal measures of excitement and confidence, I sat down with my old copy of The Readers Digest World Atlas and a new A4 notepad, and worked on a simple plan. Starting in London, I could ride a motorcycle east until I ran out of land somewhere in the far east of Russia. From there, I could fly or sail to Alaska or Vancouver in North America. Then, I'd ride south down the Pacific Coast Highway to Boonville in California, California Highway 1, the road that Mom wished she could have ridden with Dad.

After an appropriate break with the family in Boonville, I'd continue heading east until I reached either New York or Toronto. From there, it would be a simple case of finding safe passage back to London. Once around the world, a Special Package delivered to my brother and his family in Boonville and home in time for tea. Just how difficult could that be?

I calculated that the most direct route would involve riding twenty thousand miles through twenty different countries and should take me no more than twenty weeks to complete. On the face of it, I had enough money in my bank account to fund those twenty weeks on the road, but I also had debts that would have to be settled before leaving England. With some hesitation, I listed my outstanding liabilities and deducted the total from the money that I had in my bank account. Thankfully I was still in the black, but the final balance wasn't quite as much as I'd hoped for.

If my arithmetic was correct, I'd be left with the princely sum of just £2,880. If I divided that amount by twenty weeks, or 140 Days, it would leave me with a budget of around £20 per day. The plan seemed to be very neat and tidy, riding around the world following the newly discovered Rule of Twenty: Twenty thousand miles across twenty countries in twenty weeks spending £20 a day. The only thorn in the side of this otherwise beautifully symmetrical plan was a rather painful one. I didn't own a motorcycle capable of making the journey and there wasn't enough money in the budget to buy one.

For the purchase of a suitable motorcycle, camping and cooking equipment, various insurances and passage across the Pacific and Atlantic Oceans, I calculated that I'd need to find at least another £5,000. It was money that I didn't have, but what I did have was an underused eBay account and lots of things to sell. Over the years I'd accumulated many things that no longer seemed important to my life; a selection of broken motorcycles, hundreds of books, a television, furniture, old music systems and the vinyl LP's that they played. I made a list of those things and began advertising them for auction on eBay. I had absolutely no idea if anybody would want to buy another man's unwanted debris, but I was strangely confident that come the day of departure, whenever that might be, the money that I needed would be there.

When it came to choosing an official starting point, there'd only ever been one serious contender, the iconic Mecca of British motorcycling, the Ace Cafe in Northwest London. The remainder of my proposed route was dictated primarily by cost and conflict: I wouldn't have much money and I honestly didn't relish the idea of getting shot. So, I needed to avoid wars and any countries where the temporary importation of motorcycles was either prohibitively expensive or legally forbidden. For those reasons, Iran, Afghanistan, India, Myanmar, China, Vietnam and the entire continent of Africa would all be off limits for the journey. They were all sadly too expensive, too dangerous, or in many cases, a little too much of both.

Along the way there were certain places that I really wanted to visit, specific places that had been important to Mom and Dad. After Mom's death I'd discovered that they'd actually enjoyed a life of their own, a personal life beyond the trials and tribulations of volunteer parenthood. In a small suitcase belonging to Mom and Dad, I'd found a large album that chronicled their fifty years of married life together. It was an album filled with mementos and photographs, things that had meant a great deal to them, but things that probably would have been discarded by anybody from a younger generation.

The notes written in Mom's spidery hand alongside photographs and press clippings, all pointed to places that had held a special place in their hearts. I began adding those place names to my route, places that I'd visit along the way: Whitby in North Yorkshire, their favourite town in England, Darlington in County Durham, their home town and the location of St Teresa's Hospice, the organisation that had cared for them in their final days and the charity that I'd like to support. Oberammergau in Austria, a town they'd visited for the famous 'Passion Play', an experience that they'd both thoroughly enjoyed. I'd then ride down the Adriatic Coast to Dubrovnik, a town where they'd had their most memorable holiday together just a few short years before conflict had torn the historical town and its people apart.

Leaving Dubrovnik, I'd continue riding south into Greece and then turn east towards Turkey. I'd cross into Asia through Istanbul, a city they'd hoped to visit, a plan they'd abandoned when Dad had been diagnosed with prostate cancer, a dream that was never to be realised. From Istanbul, I'd follow the Black Sea coast across northern Turkey and through Georgia before entering the vastness of Russia. It would be nice to inject the Russian experience with additional adventures down into Kazakhstan and Mongolia but that would mean additional visas, additional costs, and headaches that should probably be avoided on such a limited budget.

From Magadan in far eastern Russia, I'd fly or sail to Anchorage in Alaska and follow the Pacific Coast Highway down through Canada to Boonville in Northern California. In Boonville, the Special Package would be delivered to my brother and his family, the package containing the ashes of our parents, George and Barbara Thomas. I'd no idea where their ashes would be scattered, but it would certainly be in a place that was special to the family and my homeward journey would be solo.

After spending a little time in Boonville, I'd probably just keep heading east towards the Atlantic seaboard and find the cheapest possible means of getting back to England. I'd keep the whole journey as simple as I possibly could. There'd be no satellite telephone or GPS navigation systems, no expensive hotels and certainly no support crew. It would be one man on his motorcycle with a map and a compass, discovering the world and in the process going some way towards fulfilling his parent's unfulfilled dreams.

Up until that point, the journey had only really existed within my mind. The 'to-do list' pinned to my rented wall and the auctioning of my life's possessions on eBay were the only physical evidence of my plan. At any time I could have cancelled, changed my mind, abandoned the entire journey and nobody would ever have known that I'd failed.

I was aware that the planning process could drag on for months and that no matter how much preparation I did, or how much research I undertook, I'd never feel fully prepared to set out. Given my penchant for procrastination and extreme laziness, I knew that if the journey was ever to begin there were two important things that I really needed to do. The first was to set a departure date that I couldn't avoid, and secondly, I'd have to start telling people about it.

But, before telling people, I needed to find a name that would encapsulate the journey. Jupiter's Travels, One Man Caravan, Long Way Round, Mondo Enduro, all of the great motorcycle adventures had great names attached to them. In comparison to those journeys, my own ride would be adventure-lite, but I still felt that it needed to have a name. I was a single man of a certain age, riding around the world on a motorcycle with a very limited budget. For such a journey, there could only ever be one possible name: 'Poor Circulation'.

First to receive the news about Poor Circulation was my teenage daughter, Hannah. The prospect of telling her probably scared me far more than the journey itself, but it was something that had to be done. I'm not sure how I'd expected Hannah to react, but I really needn't have spent so much time worrying about how she'd take the news. In her teenage eyes, Poor Circulation was quite simply the coolest thing that any Dad could possibly do. Hannah's only real concern was that I didn't embarrass her by saying stupid things in my blog, or by acting like an idiot. I promised to do my best, and Hannah proceeded to give me my first geography lesson in almost thirty years: 'Dad, Yugoslavia is so last century'.

Because of my geographical ignorance, and my failure to replace my 1970's Readers Digest World Atlas with a more up to date version, in the blink of an eye Poor Circulation had increased to twenty-five Countries. The Rule of Twenty had fallen at the first hurdle and I'd identified the need to buy an accurate set of maps.

Having broken the ice and conquered my fear of telling others about Poor Circulation, next in line for the news was my brother Alan and his family in Boonville. When you're growing up in a small town such as Darlington, older brothers can be an unavoidable burden to bare. But thankfully, the passing of time seems to have a way of changing such relationships for the better. Being four years apart and having absolutely no interests in common, as kids we'd never been particularly close and as adults our lives had moved in very different directions.

However, in recent years the aging process of parents had drawn us closer together and we'd become brothers with a common interest, the interests of Mom and Dad. At first Alan had thought that I was joking about the journey, or that I was drunk, or stoned, possibly even both. I'd told him that I was coming to visit them in California and he'd suggested a website where I'd find the cheapest possible flights. I'd told him that I wouldn't need an airline ticket because I'd be riding to Boonville on a motorcycle with Mom and Dad's ashes, and that seemed to be the end of our conversation.

Overnight, Alan must have thought about what I'd said and realised that I was serious. The following morning, he was back in touch. I explained Poor Circulation as clearly as I could and suggested that if I set out from London on April 23rd 2008, St George's Day, then I'd probably arrive in California towards the end of August. As I'd talked my way through the journey Alan had been quiet, listening to everything I'd had to say and aside from the occasional offering of 'ok' and 'I'm still here', he'd said nothing at all to interrupt me. He could have stopped me at any time and pointed towards the many dangers or obvious flaws in my plan, but he hadn't. He'd simply listened to everything and when I'd finally finished had asked one simple question: 'Is there anything that we can do to help you?'

With the departure date set, it was time to start adding flesh to the skeleton of the plan. Aside from watching Ewan McGregor and Charlie Boorman in Long Way Round; a production that made their journey seem all but impossible for any individual to achieve, I knew absolutely nothing about riding around the world in the twenty-first century. I registered with the website Horizons Unlimited, an internet forum for long distance two-wheeled travellers. Browsing the website, I was immediately shocked by the number of ordinary people who'd already earned their 'Round the World' tee-shirts. It seemed that everybody had already done it and all of the information that I needed was right there. It was a one stop free shop for would-be world travellers like me.

A few evenings spent browsing the website reaped a harvest of riches that undoubtedly saved me months of preparation time. I quickly learned how to sort the wheat from the chaff and discovered that the armchair travellers with their dusty passports enjoyed using words such as; mustn't, couldn't, wouldn't and impossible. On the other hand, those who'd already sent the postcards simply wished me luck and warned me to ignore the doubters. The advice seemed to be that as long as I approached the journey with the right attitude and an open mind, then it would be an awful lot easier than I could ever imagine. The only real note of concern, which was expressed several times by various experienced people, was that I'd seriously underestimated the costs.

A budget of £20 per day was apparently far too low, and although it might be theoretically possible to complete the journey on such a small amount of money, one significant mechanical breakdown would be an expense too far, an absolute show stopper for Poor Circulation. Those experienced travellers weren't telling me what I wanted to hear, but their budgetary advice didn't really worry me. Lots of the elements within Poor Circulation were flexible, or to be more precise unplanned, but the budget wasn't one of them. I'd leave London on the 23rd of April with as much money as I had, and that amount of money would somehow get me safely back to London. Rich Circulation simply wasn't an option.

The auctioning of my life's possessions had gone well, but with everything of any possible value already sold, I'd raised only half of the money that I'd hoped for. I still had no motorcycle and no credibility, but Poor Circulation had gone public and I had no option but to push on. I really needed some external financial help, but I'd been warned that any form of corporate sponsorship would be out of the question. Apparently there was a recession looming and financial support that was scarce in times of plenty, would now be virtually non-existent. I didn't expect to receive offers of a free motorcycle from major manufacturers, but I figured that if I didn't ask for anything then I'd definitely get nothing.

So, I made a list of everything that I might possibly need for the journey and composed a range of appropriate begging letters. My plan was to ask various retailers for small items, low value products that to me would add up to a great deal but to each individual supplier would be of little financial consequence. I'd never done anything like that before and had absolutely no idea if it would work, but I hoped that if I asked for a simple light bulb or a single sparkplug, then it would be just as easy for the supplier to send me the item requested as it would be to compose and mail a rejection letter.

In an attempt to broaden my list of potential donors, I sought the assistance of Adam, a local biking friend who I'd met four years earlier on the first day of an event called Moto Challenge GB. In July of 2004, geographically lost and mentally confused, we'd come together as strangers on a bridge above the M4 Motorway in deepest Gloucestershire. Two more lost souls had also been on that bridge, Mark Wallis and Lee Crahart, and together we'd accidentally become 'Team Haphazard'. For the next seven days, we'd hill climbed, raced and navigated our assortment of motorcycles across England, Wales and Scotland. Together we'd shared three thousand road miles of laughter, three racing circuits of deep adrenaline joy and the occasional night time beer. By comparison, the other twenty teams competing in the annual event had all been far more professional and better prepared for the challenges. We'd been none of those things, just an accidental team of strangers and clearly only there for the fun.

The other teams hadn't taken us seriously, but that's hardly surprising, because neither had we. We'd probably looked like nothing more than four clowns riding an assortment of rusty old nails, but beneath that comedy façade there'd been a determination to get things done. We'd attacked every challenge with stealth, laughter and only a minor amount of crashing.

The week long competition had ended in the Scottish town of Kelso, and when the final scores had been calculated Team Haphazard had ridden away with a rich embarrassment of trophies. During that amazing week I'd discovered that Adam had read every book that had ever been written, by any person who'd ever ridden a motorcycle, to absolutely anywhere in the world. In short, I hoped that if help was available then Adam was probably the person who'd know exactly where to find it.

After bribing Adam with a serious quantity of beer at my local public house, we'd worked through my plan and developed a broad list of potential donors. Many of the items that I'd need would be determined by the make and model of motorcycle that I'd be riding, but as I'd be approaching general suppliers rather than particular motorcycle manufacturers, that wouldn't be too great a problem. It's fair to say that Adam had very little confidence in this part of my project, but he was certainly excited by the broader adventure. For the majority of his adult life he'd vicariously followed the adventures of others and by the end of the evening, Adam had decided to join me for at least part of the journey.

With Adam deciding to come along, and with absolutely no desire to carry two different sets of tools and spare parts, my own choice of motorcycle became easy. Adam already owned a Triumph Tiger 955i, all shiny and new and fully paid for. I didn't consider it to be the most appropriate motorcycle for the journey; too heavy, too tall, too complicated and even on the used market, slightly too expensive. However, it was a Triumph and in the context of this journey that was very important. It was a motorcycle that Mom and Dad would have been proud to ride themselves.

I checked the dealerships, the classified advertisements in various motorcycle magazines and the Internet. Many second hand Triumph Tigers were available, but all were slightly too rich for my budget. Through the sale of my world on eBay, long hours of despatch riding in London and a generous donation from Alan and Torrey in Boonville, my bank account had swollen, but in comparison to the budgets of more experienced travellers, it was still lingering on the shabby side of poor. In short, anything above £3,000 would start eating into my £20 per day travelling budget, so the Tiger had to come cheaply.

It was a frustrating time. I was placing bids on eBay and watching the Tigers escape me: 'Sold £4,510.00'. 'Sold £4,320.00'. 'Sold £4,725.00'. But then it happened. Perhaps there'd been a recent surge in Tiger sales and all of the would-be purchasers had already achieved their dream of Tiger ownership, or possibly the market had just reached saturation point.

'Triumph Tiger 955i. 2004 Cast Wheel Model. Lucifer Orange. Full Luggage. 3,000 Genuine Miles. Owner Selling Due to Ill Health. Low Reserve. Happy Bidding'. I watched the auction for two days; no bids, no movement, no activity at all. I crossed my fingers and placed my initial and maximum bids. The price began to move upwards: £2,500.00 - £2,550.00 - £2,600.00. In the final seconds of the auction, the price jumped to £3,300.00, an amount that was right on the limit of my maximum bid. With my heart thumping like never before, I'd refreshed my web browser and waited for what felt like an eternity: 'Congratulations Blue88, you have won the item'. It was great news, I now had a motorcycle that was capable of taking me around the world, it had come at exactly the right price and everything was falling neatly into place.

Sometimes when something good happens, it's closely followed by something even better. In response to my many begging letters, every day when I arrived home from work small packages were waiting for me; spare brake pads, chain and sprocket kits, crash bars, light bulbs, spark plugs and even a pair of complimentary ferry tickets from Dover to Calais. Cheekily, I'd also asked all of the major oil companies to provide me with free fuel, but none of them had replied to my letters.

However, I'd copied the same begging letter to Andrew Bernard, the Chief Executive Officer of CitySprint, the London based courier firm that I rode for on a daily basis, the company that had many years earlier given me the call sign 'Blue88'. Andrew Bernard was interested in my plan, a meeting was arranged and I put forward a proposal.

If CitySprint would cover the cost of my fuel, approximately £2,500, then I'd happily wear their uniform throughout the journey and carry with me a CitySprint package for delivery to my brother in Boonville, California. It would be, I believed, the world's longest ever motorcycle courier delivery and a new Guinness World Record. I hadn't really expected any support from CitySprint, but regardless of their decision I'd be carrying an important package with me and it would've been rude not to have asked them for a little help.

Two days later I'd received CitySprint's reply: 'Yes, we'll be happy to pay for your fuel and we'd like to wish you the very best of luck with your journey'.

They'd agreed to pay £100 per week directly into my bank account and the final piece of the financial jigsaw had fallen neatly into place. My journey was now fully funded and baring any major disasters, money would no longer be a problem, or an excuse.

With my confidence boosted, I'd then decided to make a direct approach to Triumph Motorcycles. I already had the motorcycle that I needed for the journey, so all that I'd asked for was a little free technical advice. However, the advice that Triumph gave me wasn't the advice that I'd expected:

'We can't help you because the Triumph Tiger won't make it across Russia. It's a street bike wearing an adventure frock, so we advise that you buy a BMW'.

The original route plan was quite sketchy. Ride east and avoid wars.

Chapter 4:
Departure Day

It's Monday the 21st of April 2008, departure day. It's a day that a few short months ago I'd thought might never arrive. But, now that it's here it seems to have come around too quickly and has almost taken me by surprise. I know that departure was originally planned for St Georges Day, the 23rd of April, but if any child could make Christmas arrive two days early, then they probably would.

The Riders Digest magazine have asked me to write a monthly column covering the journey and tonight they're celebrating the expansion of the independent motorcycle magazine with a party at the Ace Cafe, so it's a simple case of killing two birds with one stone. Anyway, today's the Queen's birthday and that's significant enough for me, but on the downside, the weather clearly hasn't been following the script. It's pouring with rain, but this is England and that's probably one of the few things that we still do reasonably well here.

Despite the weather, I've been busy all morning and the Tiger's starting to take shape. Every item has its designated place and every place has a designated item that fills it. Apart from a box containing our family history that's been safely stored with friends, and a couple of suitcases that will be stored here in the adjoining apartment, the remainder of my possessions are piled high and wide on the motorcycle. It really isn't much to show for forty-five years of existence, but it's all mine and for the first time in my adult life, absolutely everything is paid for. Well, that's not strictly true.

Apart from the motorcycle itself, most of the things hanging from it have actually arrived in response to a hundred shameless begging letters. Triumph-on-Line, WeMoto and MotoHaus have all kindly donated essential pieces of equipment that would have otherwise weakened my already anorexic budget. The petrol in my tank has been paid for by CitySprint and the ferry ticket in my pocket by P&O, and my gratitude towards these organisations is unending.

At the weekend I consolidated Mom and Dad's remaining ashes with a handful of earth from the land that Dad had farmed for more than sixty years of his life. The urns themselves are far too bulky to carry with me, so the ashes and soil have been vacuum sealed into a clear plastic sleeve. The sleeve fits neatly into an A4 manila envelope that's addressed to my brother Alan, and that envelope will fit neatly into a CitySprint waterproof wallet. To all intents and purposes it will look like a package of documents, and as such, will hopefully avoid unwanted attention.

The actual contents of the Special Package are known only to those people who need to know, and that's hopefully how it will remain until I've arrived safely in America. It would be nice to tell the world exactly what I'm carrying with me, but with twenty international frontiers to cross, that simply isn't possible. Ashes and soil are classified as 'Agricultural Products', and as such would be barred from entering certain countries on my planned route.

At the appropriate time I'll reveal the true contents of the package, and in doing so explain the real reason behind this journey, but until that time arrives I can only hope that the people who already know me, and the border officials I'm yet to meet, will all assume that it's nothing more dangerous than a folder full of dreary documents.

With everything packed, I'm ready to start rolling but there are some important things that are still missing. A passport with a Russian visa and a credit or debit card would be comforting things to have, but those items remain unchecked on my to-do list. Our passports are with a 'Fixer' in London waiting for the granting of business visas for entry into Russia, but they should arrive on the day before we're due to leave England. That's ten days from now and will hopefully prove to be perfect timing, but if they're late for any reason then we'll just have to improvise.

Unfortunately, obtaining a credit or debit card has been more of a challenge. According to credit card suppliers, of which there are many, I'm seemingly unwashed and unworthy of receiving credit. I've got one Cash Card for my basic bank account with the Nationwide Building Society, but absolutely no access to credit. In an attempt to mitigate this problem I've bought a pre-paid Credit Card from the internet and loaded £500 onto it for emergencies. If any emergencies arise that require more than £500, once again, I'll just have to get inventive and find an alternative solution to the problem.

In my waterproof jacket, in the areas normally designated for protective armour, I have lots of US Dollars and some British Pounds. This morning I've repaid all of my outstanding debts and exchanged half of the remaining contents of my bank account for US Dollars. They'd offered me two US Dollars for every one British Pound, and it seemed rude not to accept such generosity. I'd requested small bills and when I'd collected them this morning I'd felt like the richest man in the world, but it looks like an awful lot more money than it is. After I'd counted the money, the helpful cashier had asked me: 'Are you going anywhere nice Mr. Thomas?' That question had worried me. Five minutes earlier the same cashier had confidently confirmed that my Cash Card would be accepted in a long list of countries that I'd helpfully written down on a sheet of paper for her. I can only hope that she'd been joking and that I don't get robbed before I've spent all of the cash.

We're now on the road and the Tigers are much heavier than I'd expected them to be. They feel far too wide for the slender gaps in the rush-hour traffic. It's quite possible that each pannier would qualify for its own unique post code, but we can't make them any slimmer so we'll just have to get used to them. The extra weight is compressing the suspension but I still can't touch the floor, and while that's not a problem riding into London, it probably won't feel quite so comfortable on the more challenging road surfaces to come.

London's A406 North Circular Road is busy tonight, congested, cold and miserable. We're filtering line-a-stern between the stationary vehicles making our way towards the Ace Café, but progress is painfully slow. It's approaching seven in the evening, the work-a-day folks in their cars and vans are all heading home at the end of their working day. Adam and I are at odds with the mood of the road and are probably the only ones smiling out here tonight. It's Monday evening, but for us it could be absolutely any day of the week. The next one hundred and seventy five days represents the longest weekend that either of us is ever likely to enjoy. For the next six months of our lives, Mondays should feel exactly the same as Fridays, and after almost thirty years of constant working, that's an absolutely amazing feeling to have.

We ignore the rain that's pouring without mercy and concentrate on the suicidal traffic, traffic that seems intent on ending this journey before it's properly begun. The gaps that we aim for have narrowed and we draw to a claustrophobic halt. There are simply far too many vehicles for the amount of available tarmac.

Following a custom that's peculiar to major British cities, the white van ahead of me has deliberately pulled across the lane in order to block my path. I bring the flabby Tiger to a halt and balancing on tiptoes, flip open the front of my helmet. I catch the van driver's eye in his dinner plate mirror. He knows exactly what he's done but he just smirks back at me and refuses to make room. I can't stop chuckling to myself. On any other day I'd mentally if not physically be kicking the living crap out of him and his vehicle, but today along with the rain, the anger just washes straight over me.

Another driver and his rear seated family are admiring the world maps on the side of my pannier. The driver catches my eye and smiles, and I smile back. His car slowly inches backwards creating the gap required for our progress to resume. I send a wave of my hand in recognition of his generosity and a beaming smile for the kids in the rear seats. We wriggle the Tigers through ninety degree turns aiming towards the newly found daylight ahead of us. Through his mirror, I catch the swing of the van drivers head. We've changed lanes and for the briefest of moments he can't understand where we've gone. The van jumps forwards on its axles, he's engaged first gear but he's spotted us too late. His front wheel turns outwards from its arch and inches closer towards me, but he doesn't have enough space to complete his latest blocking manoeuvre. With a deliberate clip of a pannier against his front bumper, I squeeze past him. He's probably expecting me to give him 'the finger', but today I'm peddling love not anger. I turn my head and blow him a perfect kiss. Our progress resumes and I'm still head over heels in love with this world and it's many amusing people.

From the topbox behind me, I'm sure that I can hear Dad talking. I think he's suggesting that I've finally grown up, and maybe he's right, but Mom's just smiling. She hates conflict.

Finally, the unmistakable 'Ace of Spades' sign appears through the evening's grime and a traffic controller rushes to move the plastic cones that block our way into the Ace Cafe's car park, a car park that's already full to capacity with motorcycles. As we pass, he offers a smiling salute and points towards a gap at the front of the main entrance, an area that's been reserved for the Triumphs' of Poor Circulation.

The fifty yards of pavement between the road and designated parking space brings people flocking towards us. Trying to pick out recognisable faces in the crowd, I'm not concentrating on where I'm riding and stupidly clip a parked motorcycle that I simply hadn't seen. A hand reaches out and catches the small black bike mid-fall and prevents an embarrassing demonstration of domino felling along a line of at least twenty other parked motorcycles. A worried and straining face beams back at me and it's a face that I recognise. With one fleeting movement of his hand, Julian has saved my blushes, and no doubt my no claims bonus, and will forever be my hero of the Ace Cafe. I'm supposed to be riding around the world but I can't even navigate my way around a familiar car park in Northwest London. Hopefully the incident hasn't blown my cover, but I still feel like a fraudster and an idiot.

Side by side we park the Tigers in the designated area and try to dismount. We're surrounded by people who are pointing, poking, shaking hands and asking probing questions. Everybody's laughing, smiling and joking in a carnival of activity that I really hadn't expected. A sausage sandwich is thrust into my hand and somebody grabs my arm, turning me around to face an unknown photographer. An arm around my shoulder and a stranger's face beaming brightly next to mine: 'Flash', and he's gone.

A group of riders from Boxertrix, an internet based forum for BMW riders, have arrived in numbers to wish us well and make generous contributions to our respective charities. They've travelled here from all across the country and I'm sincerely moved by their kind wishes and generosity. I can see Adam, his body drowning in a sea of people, his head bobbing above them and wearing a look of total bemusement. A microphone is held alongside my sandwich and another smiling stranger is asking me questions. The business card tells me that I'm being interviewed by John Chatterton-Ross, Director of Public Affairs from the FIM (Federation Internationale de Motorcyclisme). A man with a hyphen is asking me for personal details and that's something that usually only happens after I've clipped an expensive car in traffic, but this guy is genuinely interested in what we're doing. I try to concentrate on John's questions and answer them as clearly as possible, but it's a difficult task.

My hands are filling up with gifts from unknown donors; a Mars Bar, a giant mug of steaming coffee mysteriously containing the perfect amount of sugar, some Russian money of unknown value and an inch of business cards from people offering their support. As John Chatterton-Ross moves backwards into the mass, more people move in with their questions and gifts. Mark Wilmslow, owner and saviour of the Ace Cafe, thrusts a pair of classic white biking socks into my open jacket and wishes me well for the journey. There are so many people giving so generously that I lose track of names and donations, but the feeling of genuine warmth and friendship is unexpected, undeserved and really quite amazing.

As a London despatch rider, I seem to have lived the majority of my adult life far below the recognition radar, an anonymous place where colleagues don't know my real name, nor I theirs. To other despatch riders I'm just 'Blue88', but tonight that has changed and it feels as if my entire world has been turned on its head. It's encouraging that so many people are offering us their support, but it also makes me feel like an imposter. The people here tonight seem to think that what we're doing means that we're somehow special, which of course we're not. We're absolutely no different from the people who're here to wish us well tonight, we're just fortunate enough to have the opportunity to do something that is different.

With the shutters falling on the emptying Ace Café, we're joined around the Tigers by my friends from The Riders Digest magazine. If the truth were told, most of the well wishers this evening had probably arrived for the magazine's celebrations and we've just been feeding from their ample trough, so we thank them for allowing us to share their special evening.

These are people who know the real me, the man who still gets lost on a daily basis in London, and it feels like a welcome return to normality. Paul Knight, an old despatching friend and feature writer for the magazine, makes the final offering of the evening. A small plastic duck is attached with cable ties to the side of my Tiger. It's the 'Dakar Duck', a tiny yellow mascot that saw Paul safely complete his first Dakar Rally in 2007. I'll carry Dakar Duck around the world before passing him onto another rider for his next great motorcycle adventure.

We say a final farewell to new and old friends, start our engines and prepare to set out on the first leg of the journey. I slip the Special Package into the waterproof CitySprint sleeve, tear off the sealing strip and press out the unwanted air. It's time to go.

'Blue88 ... leaving the Ace Cafe ... on board with Ashes to Boonville ... Over'

'Roger that Blue88 .... Call Empty in Boonville... Ride safe. .. Out'

Chapter 5:
England

Last night after leaving the Ace Cafe, I'd headed back to my apartment in rural Essex. That hadn't been the original plan, and the road had certainly been calling, but my bed had been screaming an awful lot louder than the tarmac. The prospect of warm shelter for one more night, a comfortable mattress and an electric kettle had been far too inviting to ignore, so I'd ridden home.

After a perfectly comfortable but sleepless night, I rose this morning long before the sun and I've drunk an unreasonable amount of coffee since then. Now I'm too excited to stand still, I need to get going, to start riding. No more delays. I called Adam an hour ago and he was almost ready to leave his home. He only lives two miles away, so we'll meet in thirty minutes time at a small petrol station standing midway between our homes. From there, we'll start heading north.

The single room that I've called home for the past five years is almost empty and I'm confident that I've got everything that I need to take with me. The Tiger's fully laden with luggage, but I'm carrying absolutely no baggage at all. This morning I've discovered an entirely new feeling, a feeling that's way beyond a sense of freedom, but I really can't put it into words, at least none that could do it justice. I'm standing looking at everything that I own in this world and from here onwards anything that happens in my life will be down to me, a direct result of the decisions that

I make. With the door locked behind me, the Tiger comes to life at the first touch of the button. It's the perfect start to the most exciting day of my life.

I beg a second mug of coffee from the owner of the small filling station and send a text message to Darryl Booker. Darryl's a good friend who I've arranged to meet at Squires Milk Bar in North Yorkshire around lunchtime, and the message is to tell him that we should arrive there on time. As I wait for Adam to arrive, I talk to the local villagers as they fill their cars with fuel. It seems that today the people who've never before spoken to me are suddenly interested in my world. Perhaps they're just being polite, or more likely they're happy to see the back of me and the old despatch bikes that have blotted the beauty of their perfectly manicured village for the past five years. Either way, I'm happy to pass the time of day with them while I shelter from the unexpected rain.

I check my mobile phone, but there's no further news from Adam. I'm impatient, I telephone him for the fourth time in as many hours and he tells me that this time he really is on his way to meet me. We're running late, and that's something that I really dislike, but it'll take more than poor punctuality and a drop of rain to spoil this day.

The rain has stopped, the sun has broken through the clouds and five hours later than promised, Adam finally potters into view. He pulls his Tiger to a halt, removes his gloves and starts toying with his recently acquired Garmin GPS unit. He knows that I've been waiting here in no man's land for five hours, and I'm waiting for an explanation, but explanations aren't uppermost in his mind right now. With a puzzled expression he presses various buttons on his GPS unit and looks to its small grey screen for answers, answers that don't seem to be there.

I've been stationary for far too long, I need to ride and I try to hurry him along. The plan is to meet Darryl at Squires and then ride on to Whitby where we'll camp for the first night and spend the evening at a pub belonging to a mutual friend. Free food and beer, life really doesn't get much better than that. But, we were due to meet Darryl an hour ago and we're still two hundred miles south of him. There's no time to lose, so I pull on my crash helmet, just as Alan removes his. It's the first full day of the journey and we're enjoying our first breakdown, but fortunately it's not the breakdown of our motorcycles, just our ability to communicate.

14, 15, 16, 17, 18, the junctions of the M11 Motorway click by as we cruise somewhere above the legal speed limit but slightly below the territory of the instant driving ban. The M11 becomes the A1 North, same tarmac but different speed enforcement cameras. Peterborough, Grantham, Newark. I look in my mirrors and see Adam standing up on the motorcycle to stretch his substantial legs. He probably wants to stop for a break, but we're late and the Tigers are good for at least another hundred miles before needing fuel.

Too much coffee has my bladder screaming for relief but Darryl is waiting patiently to meet us at Squires Milk Bar and I don't relish the idea of erecting an unfamiliar tent on a windswept cliff in total darkness. We really need to arrive in Whitby before nightfall so with a slight feeling of guilt, I ignore the sign for the service station and pull out to overtake a line of slower moving vehicles. Adam reluctantly follows my lead, but under his breath I know that he'll be cursing me.

Even before our gloves have been removed, a smiling Darryl Booker is thrusting steaming mugs of coffee into our cold and eager hands. We laugh and joke together, but as the sun is already melting into the distant hills, it's probably far too late to start heading towards Whitby.

We get permission to pitch our tents on the sloping field above the car park at Squires, but if the erection of tents is to take place in darkness, then it might as well be executed by drunkards. It seems rude to leave the lovely warm pub, so we don't. We have a great evening at Squires, a night filled with endless ribbing and laughter, but we honestly hadn't intended to get quite so drunk. The landlord had been following my blog and much of the night's beer had flowed freely. It had been hospitality at its finest and the only price to be paid will be an uncomfortable night in badly erected tents and tomorrow's inevitable hangovers.

It's now St Georges Day, Wednesday 23rd of April 2008, Day 3 of the journey. Ever since leaving Squires Milk Bar at 8am this morning, the rain has been pouring relentlessly. This is England and rain is something that we come to expect here, but we never learn to enjoy it. What we lack in the way of climate in England, we certainly make up for with weather. I can only hope that the next twenty four countries will be climatically more accommodating than this one.

Last night I'd had the bright idea of waking early and riding out to watch the sunrise from the cliffs above Whitby's harbour. It was a drunken idea that at the time hadn't been greeted with universal enthusiasm, and on peering out from my tent at 5:00 am this morning, I'd had to agree that it wasn't my finest plan. Instead of breaking camp, I'd rolled over in a perfectly warm sleeping bag and prayed that the overwhelming desire to take a piss would eventually disappear. Mom and Dad would understand, they loved Whitby but they didn't like riding in the rain any more than I do. Anyway, we can always visit Whitby on the way back down to London.

At Leaming Bar Service Station, we stop to let Adam squeeze the excess water from his brand new Frank Thomas, fully guaranteed waterproof, riding suit. Darryl's wearing a torn and battle scarred Dainese suite and I'm wearing bargain basement Army Surplus Gore-Tex, but we're both bone dry, warm as toast and seriously trying to empathise with Adam. He's not just damp or slightly wet, he's literally swimming on the inside of his suit.

Frank Thomas was one of the companies that I'd approached for free samples of their waterproof clothing, but they'd politely turned down my request. For me that wasn't a problem, I'm average height and weight and can do my clothes shopping almost anywhere, but sadly for Adam, he isn't. Measuring six feet eight inches in his size 14 boots, Adam's shopping options are limited and it seemed that Frank Thomas were the only company who made an off-the-peg waterproof riding suit in his size. So, despite their understandable reluctance to donate to our cause, Adam had been left with no alternative but to invest his own money in one of their suits. Watching Adam steaming in the warmth of the roadside café, I'm selfishly quite thankful that they'd declined our request and I'm sure that Adam will eventually dry out and start appreciating the funny side of the situation.

It would be good to hang around here and wait for the rain to stop, but we've got less than an hour to reach St Teresa's Hospice and it's still another forty miles north of us. On a brighter note, the Met Office has promised universal sunshine for the remainder of the day and that's something that we'll all appreciate. If everything goes according to plan, which is highly unlikely, we'll reach Gretna Green in Scotland by mid afternoon and be tucking into excellent pub food in Eskdale this evening. To get there, we'll be riding along some of Britain's finest roads, so despite the current rain, this could still turn out to be the most perfect of days.

At Darlington's St Teresa's Hospice everybody knows Barbara Thomas, she's an absolute legend around here. I see faces in the small crowd that I recognise, smiles coming from beneath large corporate umbrellas, friends who'd visited Mom in hospital, people who came to her funeral celebrations and even nursing staff who'd cared for Dad here almost ten years ago. St Teresa's is a building like any other, but it's the people who work in and around it that take it into a very special dimension. Any visit here is inspirational and you can't help but leave this place feeling uplifted and firmly believing in the inherent goodness of people. I feel proud to be representing Mom and Dad, who in their days of retirement had devoted much of their free time to supporting the work of this Hospice.

I'd like to mirror the actions of my parents, but I've absolutely no skills that could be of any use to the Hospice. All that I can do is to try and raise awareness and a little money to support the many services that they provide. I'll try to raise £5,000 for the Hospice within the next year. It's a sum of money that will keep those services running for a period of just twenty-four hours, which in the scheme of things isn't a great deal, but at least it's a start in repaying them for the support that they give freely to people when they need it the most.

I'm now talking with BBC Radio Tees, their microphone hovers in front of my mouth and I try to answer the questions. The reporter has asked me to turn off my engine so as not to interfere with his sound, but the newspaper photographer has asked me to leave the headlights burning for his photographs. The interview lasts for several minutes and a guard of honour has been formed for our departure. Volunteers, clients, nurses, staff and friends all line the driveway and wave for the benefit of the cameras. The BBC reporter stands back and announces to the live radio audience, the departure of Poor Circulation.

'Bollocks Bollocks Bollocks'. My Tiger refuses to start. The battery that I'd always intended to replace, but for financial reasons hadn't, is now officially dead. The good people of County Durham have just been informed that a journey of 20,000 miles around the world was about to begin, but I can't even make it out of the bloody car park. When things like this happen, all that you can do is laugh.

A push-start with the assistance of four hysterical nurses fails to bring the Tiger to life but provides the Northern Echo's photographer with an almost perfect photo opportunity. Everybody seems to be genuinely concerned. They've seen right through my veneer of false confidence and their initial doubts have become certainties. A dead battery at this stage of the journey really isn't a big problem, it's just a huge embarrassment. With a set of jump leads attached to the Tiger's resting heart, and the alarm system drawing more attention than I'd like, the bike finally splutters into life. I climb aboard, flip down my visor and the guard of honour finally gets to fulfil its duty. Waving and smiling, we file past them and out into the big world beyond.

With Triumph unable to help me at such short notice, I contact the local Honda dealership and find that they have a perfect replacement battery in stock. They immediately put the battery 'on-charge' and when I arrive to collect it they'll accept nothing more than their own trade price plus the unavoidable VAT. It's a quarter of the price that Triumph had tried to charge me when I'd first considered replacing it, and that's great news for me.

The beautiful Wast Water in the Lake District

The folks at the Honda dealership had been listening to the live report on BBC Radio Tees and had probably fallen about laughing when the Tiger had refused to start. 'Poor Circulation eh? Are you the guy who couldn't make it out of the car park?' Ten minutes later, the Tiger's good to go, and its warm handshakes and best wishes all round. To David Burrell and all of the staff at White Bro's Motorcycles in Darlington, I say a very big 'Thank You'.

In the comforting warmth of Darlington's Auntie Richard's Cafe, an establishment that hasn't changed since the days of my childhood, over chipped mugs of hot milky coffee, the kind of coffee that forms a thick chewy skin on its surface, there's been a unanimous show of hands and our plan to ride up to Scotland has been abandoned. We blame the weather and our lateness, we even blame the prospect of potential fuel shortages due to a strike by tanker drivers north of the border, but if the truth be told, we're probably just being amazingly lazy.

Instead of Scotland, we'll head directly towards the picturesque village of Hawes and then onwards to the equally beautiful village of Boot in the Lake District. At Boot, we'll find a camping ground that we'll use as a base from which to explore the Lake District over the next few days. It's

Poor Circulation

a very good plan and in celebration, the rain has stopped and the sun is breaking through the heavy clouds. We're good to go.

The roads to Hawes are almost empty of traffic and we reach the famous Penny Garth Cafe in reasonable time. Drinking mugs of coffee in the High Street, Adam suddenly realises that he can't find his mobile phone. When leaving the pub last night we'd all been quite drunk, and when packing to leave this morning very hungover, so it's possible that the phone is packed away somewhere on Adam's motorcycle.

The population of Hawes look on as we undress Adam's Tiger at the side of the road. Everything comes off the bike, every roll unrolled, every pack unpacked, but his missing phone is nowhere to be seen. It's taken half an hour to rummage through every possible hiding place and then Darryl has a sparkling idea. Why don't we call it and listen for the ringtone? I call Adam's telephone and the ringing is clearly heard, but unfortunately not by us.

The phone is answered by a member of staff back at Squires Milk Bar and the mystery is solved. Adam had left his telephone in the bar last night. Calling his phone had been the first thing that we should have done, but two guy's pretending that they can ride around the world hadn't even thought about doing it. Darryl immediately volunteers to ride back and collect it, but given Squires' record for free hospitality and his thirst for good cider, it's more than possible that we'll never see Darryl, or Adam's telephone, ever again.

We hatch an alternative plan. Adam's brother will be driving up from Essex tomorrow, so he can collect the phone from Squires and then meet us in Boot later in the day. It's only the third day of the journey and we've already missed Whitby, bypassed Scotland, replaced a battery and lost a mobile telephone. We've covered one percent of the journey, in what should be the easiest country along our route, and if this is a sign of things to come then we're certainly heading for some very interesting experiences in the months ahead.

If the roads from Hawes to Lake Windermere are interesting, then the roads from Windermere to Boot are spectacular. If there was a God and he rode a Triumph, then this is probably where you'd find him. Leaving the picturesque town of Ambleside the road climbs towards Little Langdale where we turn away from the main road and head out over the two great passes: Wryno's and Hardknott. It's ruggedly beautiful, masculine and stark with a quality of light that defies description. The ribbon of road stretches out for as far as the eye can see and not a single part of it is straight.

The Tiger feels almost perfect for these roads, the engine counters the additional weight of the luggage and the power delivery is as smooth and comforting as silk. It loves these mountains almost as much as I do and just seems to take everything in its ample stride. With the extra luggage it should feel fat, awkward and cumbersome, just as it had done in London, but here in the Lake District the additional weight seems to make absolutely no difference to how the Tiger performs. In fact, the Tiger's far more capable than I am and doesn't mind constantly reminding me. It makes me look almost competent and masks my many mistakes, but it's much too polite to take any of the credit.

Perhaps I've misjudged the Tiger? It's not a bike that I'd ever considered falling in love with but on these unforgiving roads, it seems to have shed its dowdy underwear and slipped into something far more appealing. It's not exactly Agent Provocateur, but it's definitely a move in the right direction. We're not racing, we're just enjoying these empty open roads on reasonably fast motorcycles and if we encounter any traffic, ramblers or animals, then we'll slow down and become responsible pillars of the community. But until that happens, we'll just smile and have some fun.

For three glorious days we've explored the limitations of our Tigers and enjoyed the breath taking beauty of the Lake District from our base at the Hollins Hall camping ground in the picture postcard village of Boot. Thanks to the generosity of the site's owner, our camping was free for the duration and that had left us with more money for social matters. Adam's brother and his wife have joined us, they've brought Adam's mobile phone from Squires and presented us with an exquisitely decorated cake with which to celebrate our departure. It's sad to be leaving such good friends behind, but leave them we must.

Our trip to the Lake District has served its purpose well. I've learned a lot about the Tiger and its capabilities, I've learned even more about the packing and unpacking of equipment and I've discovered that despite its name, the Lake District only has one lake. There are more than eighty 'Tarns', 'Waters' and 'Meres', but Basenthwaite is apparently the only 'Lake'. It just goes to prove that you're never too old to learn, and I'm sure that I'll learn an awful lot more over the coming months, but I still have absolutely no idea why Tarn's, Mere's and Water's aren't classified as Lakes?

Chapter 6:
France

It's Thursday the 1st of May 2008, Day 11 of the journey and it's finally stopped raining. Thankfully, Russian visas have been stamped into our passports and here in Dover, Adam and I have been joined for our first few days in Europe by our good friends Mark Wallis and Lee Crahart. For the first time since the Moto Challenge GB in 2004, the four members of Team Haphazard have been reunited and I have the feeling that this is going to be another great week to remember.

At Dover's ferry terminal, Adam and I hand over our complimentary vouchers for P&O Ferries and the attendant looks back towards the four parked motorcycles where Lee and Mark are fidgeting with gloved fingers in jacket pockets. Perhaps the attendant thinks that they're searching for their own complimentary vouchers, or maybe he's just impatient or bored. Whatever he's thinking, no money changes hands and with just two free tickets between us, four motorcycles and four lucky souls are invited to board the 9:30am ferry to Calais.

At passport control, the solitary uniformed official looks to be bored and simply waves us through. Wearing full-face crash helmets and visors we could be absolutely anybody, but nobody here cares about details like that and leaving the country seems to be an awful lot easier than entering it.

From the rear of the ferry, I look down onto the expanse of concrete.

It's a vast area covered from end to end with articulated container trucks and I can't help but wonder if any of them are carrying illicit human cargo. It's hard for me to understand the lengths that some people will go to in order to enter the UK, especially as we're so keen to be leaving. Maybe after I've seen a little more of life in the Balkan's, Asia and Russia, I'll better understand their motivations, but until that time arrives, I'll go and find out what a Euro note looks like.

Yes, I'm here as a 'Traveller' yet I've never touched nor spent a Euro in my life. The last time I was in France I was spending Francs, and in Germany Deutschmarks, it really has been that long since I've travelled anywhere in Europe. At the Bureau de Change I hand over a hundred British Pounds and they give me back more than a hundred Euros. It seems like another fantastic way to grow my money and I make a mental note to do it more often. To be honest, they could have handed me notes from a French version of Monopoly and I wouldn't have been any the wiser. I'm British, so I probably would have just smiled and said 'Thank You'.

It's a Roll-On Roll-Off ferry, and even at this early hour I suspect that many of the passengers onboard are determined to be rolling off drunk. Everybody seems to be drinking beer, but not us of course, we're clean living motorcyclists and stick to the skinny lattes. As we dock in Calais and ride down the ramps from the ferry, none of our documents are checked. We'd expected to gather at the immigration control point and develop a plan for the remainder of the day, a day that is now one hour shorter than any of us had planned for. But, there is no immigration, or any other form of control. So, with Mark in the lead we just roll off the ferry and keep on rolling into France.

I notice that we're following signs for Dunkerque, which might be part of a plan to visit places of historical military interest along the way. The truth is that there is no real plan, at least no plan that I'm aware of. Mark is our European expert, and for this part of the journey we're nothing more than his willing bitches, following his lead, relaxing, chilling, sitting back and enjoying the ever changing views. The roads are quiet, very quiet. Suspiciously quiet in fact. Since leaving the ferry terminal in Calais, we've hardly seen another moving vehicle. The shops all seem to be closed and France is apparently still sleeping.

We all need petrol, but every fuel station we've seen has been closed. Of course, what an idiot I am. In Britain we celebrate May Day on the first Monday in May, it's more convenient that way and businesses can plan for the holiday, but were no longer in Britain. This is France and today is Thursday, the first day of May. Today is their public holiday and the French take their holidays a hell of a lot more seriously than we do in England. I know that the Tiger should be capable of covering two hundred and eighty miles on a full tank of petrol, but unfortunately our tanks hadn't been full when we'd left home. I'd convinced myself, and the others, that petrol would be far cheaper in France, so we'd avoided filling up in Dover and hoped to save money by buying our fuel here in France. I now fear that my fiscal plan is about to backfire on me and we have two simple choices. We can either find somewhere to camp for the night and get drunk a little earlier than planned, or we can try and ride to the larger city of Lille where we'll hopefully find a fuel station that's open. My decision, my fault, guilty as charged. We meet at the side of the road and decide that it's still too early to camp, so we'll head on towards Lille.

With Marks GPS duly programmed for a fuel station in Lille, we set out again. On our right we pass three impressively tall chimneys belching plumes of white smoke into a cloudless lunchtime sky. The road is a dual carriageway, wide, smooth and at these fuel saving speeds, amazingly boring. Several minutes later, we pass another three equally tall chimneys belching out similar plumes of white smoke, but this time they're to our left.

We stop again to consult their three different GPS's, and after several minutes of conversation that I simply don't understand, Adam, Mark and Lee are confident that between them they now have the correct route towards fuel. We start out again and thirty-four miles into this latest stage of the journey, the three impressively tall chimneys appear once again. This time they're back on our right and I now understand why 'déjà vue' is a French term.

After a short break to consult my cumbersome but seemingly reliable map of France, hopefully we're back on track. I guide us away from the dual carriageway and waft gently along on smooth ribbons of tarmac between low lying fields bordered with tall trees and narrow canals. It's really quite beautiful and exactly how France should look. But, just as we're becoming confident about reaching Lille before our fuel supplies expire, we encounter a series of diversion signs. We follow the signs around the edge of a village, along tracks and through fields, into farm yards and then back onto the original road.

It's a public holiday, and apart from eating and drinking, what do the French people love to do on such days? Answer; they indulge in their strange passion for cycle racing and close half of their roads. Unfortunately, today they seem to have closed only those roads that we need to use.

Approaching another village, we're stopped at a road block and stand aside to watch a hundred Lycra clad men glide past in a cavalcade of fluorescent splendour. The diversions are everywhere and if we're forced to follow them all, then we'll have absolutely no chance of ever reaching Lille.

We hatch a plan, probably not a very good plan, but desperate times call for desperate measures. It might not work, but even if it doesn't succeed it'll certainly give each of us something to tell our future grandchildren. At the side of the road, I pull two bright blue CitySprint jackets from my topbox and Adam and I slip them on.

Approaching the next roadblock, instead of being turned away towards a meandering back-road by the Gendarmes, they pull aside the barrier and wave us on through. We dare not breathe lest our fortunes should change, but we do dare to smile. Through the centre of the village, the streets are lined with happy cheering people. They triumphantly wave their tricolours and take photographs as we pass. They clearly think that we're marshals for the cycle race and that we really do belong here. They must expect to see the cyclists close on our tails, but all they actually see are four smiling Englishmen waving back at them and progressing seamlessly along otherwise closed roads towards the promise of a fuel supply in Lille.

At the exit to the fuel station in Lille, we compare our petrol receipts and laugh. None of us have arrived here with any fuel to spare. In fact, if we believe the manufacturer's claims regarding the capacity of a Triumph Tiger's fuel tank, then Adam and I had already run dry. We'd all been cutting it fine, but at least we've made it and my blushes are almost saved. I'd anticipated potential fuel shortages on the journey across Siberia, but it hadn't even crossed my mind that on the first day in Europe we'd be running out of gas. Lesson number one of this journey has been learned early: Fill up with fuel whenever the opportunity arises, no matter how expensive it might appear. When compared to pushing a 300 Kg motorcycle over any distance, expensive fuel is a very small price to pay. My blushes have been saved, but our money hasn't, because the fuel here in France is actually more expensive than it is back in England. Bollocks, there goes the budget on our first day in Europe.

With our fuel tanks replenished, we've decided to head for the Belgium town of Chimay. I've never heard of it, but according to Lee there's a small but famous brewery there, an establishment that provides free tours of its facilities and endless samples of free beer. Enough said, it's time to move on before it closes.

We travel for what seems like only a few miles and suddenly out of nowhere, Chimay appears. We're back to following Mark and I must be getting lazy, because I hadn't even noticed that we'd entered Belgium, or indeed left France. Looking around this old market town, I can see that the blue white and red tricolours of France have changed to the black yellow and red flag of Belgium, but I certainly didn't notice any border crossing.

The brewery seems to be closed until Monday and the promise of free beer has vanished. But, there must be other things of interest in this quaint little town. We've passed what appears to be a suitable campsite a few hundred meters back down the road, and it's now time to seek out a venue for tonight's entertainment. Without worrying about the security of the luggage that's piled high and wide on all of our motorcycles, we walk away in different directions searching for possible venues.

When we rendezvous back at the unmolested bikes, Adam, Mark and Lee have little to report. I'm not telling them what I've found, but if they're game for a laugh then we're sure to be in for an evening of appropriate fun and frivolity.

The campsite in Chimay is absolutely fine. After experimenting with our limited command of the French language, they've only charged us for one single site and before the sun finally sets, the tents are erected and the four of us are looking up at the sign above the small and ancient building. 'The Queen Mary' - 'Bikers Welcome'. It looks to all intense and purposes like an old coaching inn that you might find in Oxford or Stratford upon Avon. It's the sort of venue that here in Europe might often be seen with a 'Watneys Red Barrel' hanging directly above its door, the kind of place that I'd ordinarily avoid at all costs.

The three of them look slightly crest fallen and suspicious. It's not the quintessential European Café-Bar that perhaps they'd hoped for, but at least if serves beer and they're yet to see what awaits them inside. Adam goes in first and I know what's about to greet him. Ducking down to avoid hitting his head on the low doorway, he enters and then quickly turns around with a huge smile on his face. He's laughing so much that he can hardly speak. 'You've got to see this'.

We sit squashed into the smallest space that was ever designed to contain four fully grown people and stare around the room in amazement. The bar tender lovingly scrapes a quantity of foam from the top of the final litre of bierre and delivers them to the table along with four small menus. All around the long narrow bar is memorabilia from motorcycle racers that we've never heard of. Everything looks suspiciously familiar, but it's just not quite right. The mannequin standing in the corner looks a little like Valentino Rossi and at the other end of the bar is the Australian rider Troy Bayliss. Around the walls are signed sets of racing leathers, fairings and belly-pans from seemingly famous racing motorcycles and riders. But again, they're not quite accurate. Either these are from local riders that we simply haven't encountered back in England, or they're homemade replicas. Bangkok specials: 'Rolex watch sir?'

While the third round of drinks is being lovingly prepared, we try to order food from the less than extensive menu. 'Non'. 'Non'. 'Non Mousier'. Nothing seems to be available. The host's menu is about as genuine as the memorabilia hanging on his walls. I can't stop laughing, I'm having a ball and this tiny little place just keeps getting better and better. Finally, I'm invited to inspect the small fridge in the kitchen and I ask the 'Chef' to cook everything that's available: Two beef burgers, three cheese burgers and four small boxes of fries, all pre-packaged for the microwave. The menu is strange, the memorabilia is distinctly odd, but all of this is nothing when compared to the people who are flowing into the bar. The fashion here, even by my poor standards, is probably best described as being 'uniquely random'. Either that, or it's fancy dress night here in Chimay and nobody's bothered to warn us. It's also karaoke night and it's clear that the local hopefuls have turned out in their droves to join in the fun. It's a joke, a wind-up, it has to be. Surely nobody can be taking this seriously?

Our table is littered with the debris of our gastronomic disaster and we're laughing uncontrollably at everything. Everything here is quite simply odd, but for me that also makes it utterly fantastic. I feel a pair of uninvited hands massaging my shoulders and hear a strange voice uncomfortably close to my left ear. Adam is laughing so much that if space allowed, he'd fall from the banquette. An alarmingly unconvincing transvestite has taken a shine to my upper body and is whispering sweet and seductive nothings into my ear. If the words were in English I'd be running for the nearest exit, but even coming from a man, the French accent is amazingly disarming. Thankfully it doesn't give me a chubby, but now he wants to hear my own sexy English accent. I tell him that 'Geordie' probably doesn't qualify as 'English', but he wants to hear it anyway. Mark is falling across the table and mouthing like an exhausted goldfish; 'fucking hell, fucking hell, fucking hell', but mostly it's just uncontrolled laughter from all of us.

The rules for the karaoke competition are announced with horrendous whining feedback from the MC's microphone; 'testing one two, ...tap tap,... one two testing', but obviously in French or Flemish, or at least some language other than English. I'm saved. The transvestite is the first to sing and he minces down towards the MC. The music starts. It's an old song that sounds familiar, possibly Edith Piaf, and it seems to suit his voice, but I won't tell him that when he's finished singing. He's actually quite good and as he hits the final high note, everyone gives him a warm and genuine round of applause. He's a big hit and he's discovered the popularity that he'd probably been seeking. He now has many new friends and thankfully for me, they're all at the far end of the bar. I'm left in peace, but I must admit that my neck and shoulders feel absolutely wonderful. It's probably close to midnight. I'm wearing my watch but it's difficult to see which hand is the long one. The bierre must be very strong here in Chimay. It's certainly reasonably cheap.

This morning there's not even a hint of a hangover, so perhaps last night had been nothing more than a dream? I'll no doubt discover the truth when the others wake from their own dreams, but right now it's time for me to check out the reasonably priced European camping facilities. I pull on my very English tourist attire of shorts, socks and sandals and head for the showers.

It feels like lunchtime, but it's only 7:00am and most of the other campers are already awake and quietly going about their business. The showers are free, spotlessly clean, lots of hot water and they smell only of scented soap. I linger beneath the warm water for a little longer than I normally would, not just because it's so refreshing, but because I'm trying to work out why I've forgotten to bring a towel with me. I didn't sell it on eBay, so if it's not hiding somewhere on the Tiger then I've absolutely no idea where it could be. It's not really a problem, just a minor inconvenience, but it does make me wonder if I've forgotten to bring anything else of importance.

Refreshed and back at the tent, a short stout German fellow with shaven head, handlebar moustache and black leather waistcoat is beckoning me towards his small caravan parked just above our tents. Not again for Christ's sake, why is it always me? He greets me at the entrance to his awning with a pot of freshly brewed coffee and tells me to take it away with me, to share it with my friends and to bring back the empty pot if we would like some more. I thank him and wander back to the tents where Adam, Mark and Lee are all beginning to rise.

The coffee is delicious, strong and aromatic with a slight hint of saltiness. They ask where it came from and I point to the stout bald German standing on the hill. He's looking directly down at us with a huge smile, standing guard at the edge of his temporary territory. 'Good ya?' Indeed it is good, and a second pot is soon being shared between us. Welcome to Europe, where individuality and generous hospitality are alive and well.

Chapter 7:
Germany

We're heading for Landau in the Black Forest where we hope to find some of Germany's best biking roads. In a small car park, we're standing consulting my map when two local guys arrive riding their Triumph Daytona 675 sport bikes. There are four of us and only two of them, so they keep their distance. A single rider will easily interact with others, but as a group we seem to be much less approachable. It's not really a 'Biker' thing but more of a 'Human' thing that we need to be aware of.

The four of us are looking at the map and three conflicting GPS units, and arguing about which will be the best road to take. We're strangers in a not so strange land but not fifty meters away from us stands the font of all local knowledge. I grab the map and a pair of Poor Circulation pin badges and approach the two Daytona riders. They don't hesitate in choosing a road, and there's absolutely no difference of opinion. The local oracles point directly across from the car park to a narrower stretch of road, the B500, in their opinion the 'Best Biking Road in the world'. With badges attached to their perfectly styled leather suits, and their reputation for friendliness glowingly endorsed, they're off. No mirror, signal, manoeuvre, and no life saving glance across their left shoulders, just the satisfying clunk of first gear engaging, a fistful of throttle and two perfectly executed wheelies out across the main road and onto the twisting B500.

Minutes later we're following their example, but without the wheelies of course. It's not that we can't lift the front wheels of our respective motorcycles, any idiot can do that, it's the landings that tend to let us down. We look right, look left, look right again and we're off.

Within a mile it becomes clear that the oracles have served us well. The mountain road that they've chosen for us is beautifully smooth, rising steeply in parts and gently in others, recently surfaced and gloriously twisty. The air in the shadows of the forest is dark, clean and cool, and the sky that we're climbing towards is cloudless and blue. Banks of snow still linger at the side of the road but it isn't cold, it's just a perfect day for riding. The road is narrow but the visibility around every one of its tight and smoothly paved bends is good. As tends to happen on such roads, we gently pick up the pace and with it, the enjoyment of the ride.

Dropping down towards a tight right hand bend across a small stone bridge, through the trees I see a flash of yellow immediately followed by a flash of red. The two local Triumph riders are coming back in our direction. With only our half of the road to use, we scrub off speed and take tighter lines for safety. Mid-corner I meet the yellow Daytona and raise my left hand in the traditional British biker salute. But he's German and has far more style than I. His left knee is balancing the bike and dragging hard against the tarmac, sparks are flying from his titanium knee-slider while his left hand is off the handlebars and pointing slightly away from his body, his fingers forming the 'V' sign. That's just far too cool for us Brit's and realising that we're actually four of the slowest kids on this particular block, we back off the pace and pretend that we were never really trying to impress.

Arriving at the summit feeling hot and alive, we unpack the food that's been distributed between the available spaces on each of our motorcycles and wander into the forest to eat lunch. I'm not sure why the food that we've purchased in various villages along the road this morning, the same food that we could easily buy in any decent market in England, tastes so much better here? It's fresh, but no fresher than the food that's available at home, so maybe it's the perfect view of an island town in the middle of the fast flowing river that makes it taste so much better. A prepared and experienced traveller would now name both the river and the island town, but unfortunately 'Experienced Traveller' isn't an accurate description of me. However, this is a lifestyle that I could easily grow accustomed to.

As evening arrives, our four tents have been pitched in front of a large and apparently deserted ski chalet overlooking the valley at Linach

Schwarzwald. Mark and I prepare dinner on our petrol burning stoves; pasta, onions, tomatoes, cheese and bread, all washed down with a substantial quantity of beer that's been chilled to perfection in the small mill-pond just a few metres behind us. The skies are clear and with no light pollution up here in the mountains we lie back on the cold dry grass and admire a perfect display of stars. By 9:00pm, the still night around the picture perfect ski lodge is disturbed only by the sound of four happy snoring campers.

This morning at 6:04am, the sun rose above the mountains to the east creating a diamond ring effect similar to that seen at the beginning and end of a solar eclipse. The birds had been singing for an hour and being chased by the rising sun, the shadow of night had raced up the valley towards me. Helios was pursuing Artemis, the sun chasing the moon and any photographs would have been a poor reflection of the reality. You simply had to be here to appreciate the splendour of it.

An hour earlier it had been cold, very cold. I'd been woken by an aching bladder and had marvelled at the amount of frost that had formed on the inside of my tent. We're well below the current snowline, but during the winter months this valley is a ski slope, so of course it's bloody cold up here. A month earlier and this lodge would have been filled with young dudes catching air on their snowboards by day and bedding every chalet girl in the neighbourhood by night, but now it's our turn to enjoy it. The changing season has taken the Ski-set to the southern hemisphere and these roads and valleys are left to the bikers who marvel at the same geography, but for very different reasons. At this time of the morning, this place is quite simply one of the most beautiful places in the world and given the power, I'd change absolutely nothing about it. Perfect mountains, perfect valley and amazing light are complimented with a rare stillness that makes the area feel strangely spiritual.

A small chapel stands beside the still pond and produces a perfect reflection of itself in the water. It's decorated with a million small wooden shingles and years of neglect seem to have made it all the more beautiful. The kettle sings on the stove and aside from the chirping of early morning birds, it's the only noise that can be heard. It's Monday morning, friends back in England will be rising and thinking only about the working week ahead of them. It's probably raining in London and while many of the less enthusiastic despatch riders will be rolling over beneath their duvets, the remaining hardcore will be rubbing their hands with glee at the prospect of making good money on a busy circuit that's short of willing despatch riders. Even on the best of maps I'd struggle to find this place here in the mountains of Germany, but my mobile phone is showing a full five bars of clear signal. At my old home, just forty five miles from the centre of London, Vodafone couldn't provide me with any level of signal, but here in the middle of nowhere they can give me a full five bars. I send an early morning text message to my old friends back at CitySprint. They'll probably hate me for it, but I really don't care. I need to share this amazing morning with somebody, and everybody else here is sleeping.

By 7:30am, everybody in camp is awake and the kettle has been boiling continuously since dawn. They talk about the cold and they laugh about snoring, but they've no idea of the sunrise that they've all missed. It's not really a mystery, the sun tends to rise and set on most days, and for me, being able to witness both events as often and in as many different places as possible, is one of the greatest pleasures of travelling. Every day is the same, but every day is amazingly different. It's one of the best things about this world and it comes to you absolutely free of charge, and that really is my kind of price. It's certainly been another beautiful start to a day, but it's a day that will be marked by the departure of our friends. Mark and Lee are returning to England, riding home, returning to work and normality.

They'll retrace the six hundred mile path that brought us here and the weather forecasts suggest that they'll return to England in the pouring rain. They don't want to leave us and we don't want them to go, but their respective responsibilities are calling them. They're adults with homes and families to support, but thankfully Adam and I are not.

It's sad to see Mark and Lee riding away, but it's something that we always knew would happen and in a way, it's another new beginning for the journey. The four of us have had an amazing week together, but the time that we've spent together has been at the expense of meeting others. As a group of four we were seen as a crowd, friends having fun, talking, laughing and interacting together, but from an outsider's point of view, we were relatively unapproachable. From this point onwards it will be just the two of us, we'll interact more with the people we encounter and hopefully, unplanned and unexpected adventures will be our daily rewards.

The small chapel and millpond at Linach Schwarzwald in Germany

Chapter 8:
Switzerland

We've kicked around in Linach for a couple of days longer than expected. It's not that we had any real reason to remain here after Mark and Lee had headed back to England, but more that we'd wanted to. I don't want to race through this journey and miss anything, so lingering isn't necessarily a bad thing to do. The chances are that I'll never be passing this way again and I intend to make the most of it now.

By day we explore the local area, rummage around in unique little markets and talk with some of the most strangely wonderful people that I've ever had the good fortune to meet. Sadly, I can't really say that I've learnt anything from many of those conversations, but I've enjoyed them all the same. It would help considerably if I could speak German, Italian or French, but how often in life do you get the opportunity to talk with a one armed alcoholic fiddle player in a bar that serves twenty-four inch long sausages and surprisingly cheap beer? Probably not many, so I figure that it's best to make the most of it while I can. Another important factor in extending our stay here on the edge of the Black Forest is the fact that we seem to be camping here without charge. It's not that we wouldn't be willing to pay for the pleasure of camping here, it's just that nobody has ever asked us for any money. Aside from the coldness of the night and early morning, this site in the mountains has turned out to be an almost perfect place to unwind before the real journey begins.

Each night as I climb into my tent, I look forward to the next morning and a sunrise that never fails to satisfy. I've encouraged Adam to wake early and witness the spectacle for himself, but he just doesn't seem to be interested. In truth, I'm worried about him and his mind seems to be anywhere but here. He's quiet, and when he does talk it's mostly about home and family, or the worries that he has about crossing Russia and the problems that he's experiencing with his Garmin GPS unit. It's probably just homesickness but I'm concerned that if Adam doesn't wake up soon and start appreciating the things that are happening all around him, then he's going to end up missing-out on much of the really good stuff. This isn't yet travelling, it's not even touring. So far, it's just been a small holiday to gently introduce us to the increasing challenges ahead.

Tomorrow we'll need to move on from here, Russia is calling and we need to reach its border in the first few days of June. We're no more than six hundred miles away from home and probably have another two thousand miles to cover in the next two weeks. We've yet to start peeling the onion of adventure, but the prospect of doing so seems to be affecting us in very different ways. Every day I feel like I'm growing in confidence, but Adam seems to be shrinking into an invisible shell where silence is a comfort to him. Hopefully it is just nothing more than homesickness, something that will quickly pass, because this is a once in a lifetime opportunity for both of us and we'd better buy now while stocks last, because it's not going to come our way again.

Consulting my map, we've agreed upon a route for the coming days that will take us through Switzerland, Liechtenstein and then on into Austria. From a base somewhere in the west of Austria, I'll travel alone to the town of Oberammergau for a couple of days. Oberammergau is where Mom and Dad twice attended the ten yearly performance of the town's famous 'Passion Play'. Their initial visit in the nineteen eighties had been their first real international holiday and had wetted their appetites for future travel. I've never been to Austria, I've even struggled to find Oberammergau on my map, but I want to go there and hopefully meet some of the people who'd made Mom and Dad feel so welcome. When I ride onto Oberammergau, Adam's going to relax for a couple of days at a campsite reading his Garmin GPS instruction manual and hopefully find a way of banishing its mysterious gremlins. In England and Wales his GPS unit had worked perfectly well, but ever since entering France it seems to have been throwing him curve balls at every turn. I've never really used GPS and when I look at Adam's system all that I see is the small icon of a motorcycle standing all alone in a world of confusion. Adam suspects that there's either a problem with the Garmin unit itself, the demands that he's making of it or the maps that are loaded into its memory. Whatever the problem is, Adam's determined to resolve it before we move east into the Balkans and feels that Austria will be the perfect place to do it.

With the Tigers packed and only bleached grass and smiles left behind us, we start riding away from Linach towards Schaffenhausen in Switzerland. We stop for breakfast in a small roadside cafe and it's all served with a broad smile and warm conversation. The folks in this part of Germany are friendly, warm, hospitable and chatty, and I love the feeling of community here. At home in England, my daily conversations with strangers generally go nowhere beyond 'print and sign here', sometimes with the addition of 'please', but here things are very different. Every meeting, no matter how brief, inevitably turns into a proper conversation about something that's important to somebody.

People here seem to have time for other people. They know their neighbours and are not afraid to share small parts of their daily lives together. I know that the atmosphere of large cities will always differ from that of smaller towns, but this style of living is something that I experienced as a child growing up in Darlington, and something that in latter years seems to have all but vanished. Sadly that sense of community isn't something that I really appreciated at the time, I was just a kid with different priorities, but it's certainly something that I'd like to see making a fashionable return in England. Sure, you've caught me wearing my rose tinted spectacles again, but in just a few short days on the road the nature of the mental-memos that I constantly write to myself have changed, hopefully for the better.

Following the signposts towards Rhinefalls, the landscape that we're riding through looks strangely familiar. The road dissects miles and miles of rolling green meadows spotted with bright yellow flowers and framed by snow capped mountains in the distance. The temperature has risen and I'm whistling a very familiar tune. I'm riding a motorcycle towards the border with Switzerland and everything around me reminds me of The Great Escape. For a few glorious minutes of my life, I'm actually Steve McQueen. Fortunately for us, our entry into neutral territory goes rather more smoothly than his did. With no fences to jump, we slide into Switzerland at 60kph with nothing more than a jaunty wave to the sole

German border official. Oh how times have changed, no border controls, no passports and not a trace of razor wire anywhere.

A few miles beyond the border we pull into the car park at Rhinefalls, Europe's largest waterfalls. It's just after midday, the car parks are already bursting with empty tour buses and the sun is scortchingly hot. Why did I always think that Switzerland would be cold? I will honestly admit that before today, I'd never heard of Rhinefalls, but they are absolutely amazing. We stand inches from millions of gallons of falling water, the noise is deafening and the organs in my body shake and echo to the thunder. Rhinefalls are beyond spectacular, they're Europe's answer to Niagara, but without the surrounding tat and tacky motels. It's very busy here, but then that shouldn't surprise me because the best stuff usually is.

There are people everywhere, coach loads of tourists from every nation on earth. At every possible vantage point, they stand alongside us in open mouthed amazement. I shoot film and take photographs but they'll never come close to capturing the immense power of these falls. These are the most spectacular waterfalls that I've ever had the good fortune to see. They're quite possibly Switzerland's best kept secret, but if you're going to pay them a visit then be sure to arrive early, because it's seems that they're only a secret to us Brit's. Everybody else in the world is already here.

Back in the dry heat of the car park, Adam goes in search of the toilet while I buy ice cream and sit idly watching the world walk by. People are milling around, posing for photographs and discussing the shared experience of the falls. A small group of Sikh tourists walk close to where I'm sitting, the men looking smart in their highly polished shoes, immaculately pressed shirts and pastel turban's, the women following closely behind in their vibrant saris, all smiles and happily chattering.

They're trying to take a group photograph but nobody wants to be left out, so I offer my assistance. With a string of strange cameras hanging around my neck, I start to point and press and hope that I don't screw it up for anybody. They're all shouting instructions in very good English, but I've absolutely no idea which particular camera each instruction refers to. It doesn't really matter, they'll probably end up sharing their photographs and it feels good to become a fleeting part of their adventure.

Happy that each of them now has a group reminder of their experience here at Rhinefalls, their cameras are now turned on me. I pose with the women and the men and from the remnants of my past life, offer them a few words of thanks in Punjabi. They know how to laugh and they're not afraid to do it in public, nobody cares who's watching or what they're thinking. They're living in the moment and making the most of the experience, enjoying life to the full, and in the process are making us European tourists look just a little bit reserved and boring, which of course by comparison, we certainly are.

With my photographic mission of mercy completed, I return to the table where Adam's now sitting. He's shaking his head and muttering something under his breath. I'm confused. I must have misheard him so I ask him to repeat it. Loud, proud and as clear as day, Adam obliges. I'd heard him correctly the first time, but repeating the statement seems to add new conviction to his words.

I want to reach across the table and rip out his throat, tear it out and spit in the resulting hole. I can't believe what I've just heard. I'm waiting for the punch-line to a joke that couldn't possibly be funny in any context. There is no punch-line, Adam's deadly serious and believes in everything that he's just said. He seems oblivious to the fact that I'm silent with rage and has absolutely no idea how close I am to killing him. I'm lost for words. I just sit still, silent, angry, disappointed and numb. What can you say when somebody you think you know, a person you consider to be close a friend, turns out to be an ardent racist?

If I'd actually slept last night, then I would have woken this morning in the beautiful surroundings of this campground at Idyll, just to the east of Lake Bodensee. But I didn't really sleep last night and therefore I didn't wake.

Last night I'd cooked dinner and we'd eaten in silence. Not a single meaningful word had passed between us. Adam had understood that I was angry, and he surely must have worked out why, but we hadn't talked about it. Throughout the sleepless night his words had been echoing through my mind and the more they'd replayed, the more confused and angry I'd become. I won't repeat his words, but Adam firmly believes that places such as Rhinefalls, and countries such as Switzerland, should be saved for the exclusive enjoyment of white people. I'd tried to mentally justify his remarks by employing, on his behalf, the defence of 'Ignorance', but that hadn't really helped. In the twenty-first century, ignorance could never be an excuse for racism. So, after rising this morning I'd made coffee and drawn clear lines on a map, lines along roads that Adam could easily follow. The first lines are drawn in Blue and lead directly back to Calais. The second are in Red, and they lead south into Italy.

Adam had slept late, but I suspect that he'd been awake for hours and was simply using his tent as a bunker to shield himself from my wrath. I'd known that he'd have to come out eventually and when his bladder could hold out no longer, he'd emerged; sheepish, apologetic and rightfully humble. On early morning campgrounds, noise travels far. I'd tried to keep my voice down, but when Adam had said that he'd meant no offence by his remarks of yesterday, I'd shot him down with both barrels.

It hadn't been pretty, and for all of the venom that I'd let out from my system, I'd felt absolutely no better for venting it. There'd been tears and apologies, Adam's not mine, and there'd been pleading too, from both of us. I'd pleaded with him to ride on alone or to return to Calais. I'd even offered to take him back there myself. Adam had pleaded to stay with me, at least for a few more days, a little more time to improve his confidence. He'd claimed that he also wanted to improve his understanding of the world, he understood that what he'd said was probably wrong and he'd wanted me to help him to become a more understanding person. A few more days, perhaps a week, that's all that he'd need and after that, we could go our separate ways.

As I'd finally submitted to Adam's tearful pleas, I'd felt as if I'd abandoned my own principles, let down the memory of my parents and I swear that I'd heard Dad muttering in disgust. But, if Adam really wanted my help in changing his outlook on this world, then maybe that's a large part of what this journey is about. Besides, what options did I really have? Despite Adam's personal views on world integration, it's a free world so I couldn't stop him from following me and I certainly couldn't force him to ride back to Calais. Adam would do what Adam wanted to do, but I wouldn't let another person's narrow opinions stop me from continuing on this journey. What's done was done, I couldn't change the world or the past, but maybe for one individual I could help to mould a much more tolerant future.

The rest of today has been something of a mystery to me. I've followed Adam along the route that I'd planned last night, the route towards Italy, letting him lead and hopefully gain some riding confidence. I've abandoned all thoughts of going to Oberammergau and after briefly entering Austria, we'd headed straight towards Liechtenstein. We'd stopped briefly at an internet café and I'd updated my blog. I hadn't known what to write, and in the end I'd written nothing of any importance to this journey. I'd mentioned the magnificence of Rhinefalls but very little else. As far as the world outside is concerned, the negative events of day sixteen of this journey, Tuesday the 6th of May 2008, simply didn't happen.

Perhaps over the next few days things will change. Maybe I'll find sufficient distractions on the road to take my mind away from its current state of anger. I certainly hope so, because life's way too short for shit like this.

Chapter 9:
Austria

Geography is much more confusing than I'd thought. At the Idyll Campground on Lake Bodensee, I'd thought that I was in Switzerland. But that wasn't the case, Idyll is actually in Germany. That means that I've been in and out of Germany three times in as many days. Today, I've been in four different countries: Germany, Switzerland, Liechtenstein and Austria. Liechtenstein had been the only physical border, but even there they hadn't asked to see my passport. Come to think of it, they hadn't even asked me to stop. Liechtenstein was never going to be anything more than a tick in a box, but even so, I feel embarrassed for not seeing more of it than I actually did. Beyond being a home for Shell Companies and discreet Private Banks, Liechtenstein is probably a very nice country, but today it was just two cigarettes and a bathroom break, a short diversion on the ride towards Austria.

Entering the small town of Prutz in the Landeck district of Austria, I couldn't find a suitable camping ground. I'd actually found some very nice sites, but every site had been full of young folks with very shiny muscles driving large vans with lots of climbing equipment on top of them. Maybe it was a special gathering, or maybe it's just a special place for adventurous young people to hangout. Whatever the reason for its popularity, I'd had no option but to move on. Heading out of Prutz in search of a rough camping opportunity on a randomly chosen route, a rock fall was blocking the road leading up into the mountains.

With time on our side, I'd decided to wait for the work crews to clear the blockage with their JCB and was joined at the front of the lengthening queue of vehicles by a two Dutch guys aboard a BMW K1100 motorcycle. I'd chatted with them for a while and they'd suggested that I try a campsite in the grounds of their hotel. They'd had no idea how good the camping facilities would be, or even if we'd be allowed to pitch our tents there at all, but they'd insisted that the journey there would be a memorable one.

With the road reopened, they'd dashed away like there were too few tomorrows with our Tigers in hot pursuit. It was a journey of twenty miles, twenty of the most perfect miles that I've ever ridden and they'd come at exactly the right time for my sanity. The road had climbed between the mountains in a perfectly smooth serpent of bliss and for a while at least, the traumas of the previous day had vanished. Forget about Prozac, Cocaine or Crystal Meth, if you ever need to outrun your demons then a fast motorcycle on a beautiful road is the surest way to do it. It works every time but be careful, because it's far more addictive.

We've arrived feeling hot and alive at the Hotel Weisseespitze in Kaunertal, an amazing palace of luxury where Royalty wouldn't feel at all out of place. The Dutch riders are staying here with their wives and they guide me into reception, where I do feel a little out of place. Dirty and tattered with dishevelled hair, any London concierge would be escorting me back towards the exit, but here I'm greeted with a welcoming smile: 'Do you have a reservation Sir?'

Of course I don't have a Reservation, I probably couldn't afford the gratuity never mind the room tariff. I bravely ask about the possibility of camping and I'm expecting a swift and negative response, but that's exactly what I don't get. I'm directed to the rear of the hotel where I find a flat piece of ground that's perfectly suitable for camping and where the views are really spectacular. We're on a small plateau nestling between tall snow capped mountains that completely encircle us and I feel dwarfed by their magnificence.

Within minutes of pitching the tents, Chris, the hotel manager arrives in an unusual four wheel-drive electric vehicle. Foolishly, he invites me to take it for a test drive. It's a fun little thing, operated by a simple joystick and for an electric vehicle is amazingly swift. I tear around the campground but shy away from investigating Chris's claims that it will climb almost vertical slopes. He tells me that it's a demonstration model and that it's actually for sale. It can be mine for only 30,000 Euros. I explain the concept of Poor Circulation, placing great emphasis on 'Poor', and Chris looks slightly crestfallen. I climb out of the richly upholstered bucket seat and with the 'low charge' light flashing on the opulent carbon-fibre dashboard, Chris returns to the hotel at a slightly more pedestrian pace. He hasn't made the sale that he wanted and that might be bad news for him, but the good news for us is that our camping here is free, no charge, compliments of Chris. Thank you very much indeed Chris, and sorry for draining your battery.

Despite the fuel that's turning out to be slightly more expensive than I'd expected, a quick check of my diary tells me that I'm actually running under budget. I'd like to think that it's all down to my amazing ability to plan ahead and make compromises, but it's not. It's all down to the generosity of people just like Chris. Wherever we go, every conversation seems to lead to some form of generous offer. The generosity of strangers in faraway lands is something that I've read about in the works of other travellers, but it's not something that I'd expected to find this close to home. Without such generosity my budget would be halfway up Shit Creek, and because of it, I will be eternally grateful.

This camping ground is quite possibly the most spectacular so far. The views are beyond comparison but the price to be paid for such beauty is the altitude at which we're camping. As the sun set last night, the temperature had fallen like a brick. There's real ice on the inside of the tent this morning and the petrol stove refuses to burn with any heat. In the absence of coffee, a freezing dash to the beautifully appointed external shower facilities wakes me up. The sheer beauty of this place encourages me to linger, but the cold encourages me to shake my ass and get moving. There's a choice of two roads to be taken this morning, so I choose left and retrace the twenty mile ribbon of heaven back towards Prutz and I have to say, the ride down is every bit as good as the ride up. I feel that my diary will soon overflow with claims of 'The World's Best Biking Road', but that's certainly not a problem for me. I choose to ride a motorcycle not for reasons of comfort, practicality or safety, I choose to ride a motorcycle for the enjoyment of riding a motorcycle. It's as simple as that, but it's roads such as this that take my enjoyment to ever higher levels, and long may that continue.

As we ride without formality into Italy, we come across a lake that's impossible to pass without stopping. I've seen photographs of this lake before, but I'd never taken the time to find out what it was or where it could be found. Now that I've accidentally found it, there are notices posted in English that tell me everything that I could possibly need to know, everything that is except for the fate of the people who once lived here. Lake Reschen is a manmade lake and the valley in which it stands was first flooded in 1950. Beneath its waters stand one hundred and sixty three homes, a sizeable village that was sacrificed to the development of the lake.

The water is flat, not a breath of wind to disturb it and the reflections of the surrounding mountains on the glass like surface demand your total attention. From the still blue water rises the tower of a fourteenth century church, the only evidence of the community that once thrived beneath its surface. Even before the forming of the lake, this must have been an idyllic place to live, so it's difficult to imagine that those villagers had left here voluntarily. The information boards talk in depth about the capacity of the lake and the cost of constructing, but the human cost seems to have been completely ignored. Did the villagers leave their homes voluntarily? If not, what was the nature of the incentive, or the stick? Where did they go? What became of them? A few days into this journey and I'm already changing. A few short weeks ago I would have accepted this lake for what it is today, a beautiful place to visit and capture forever in photographs, but now I'm starting to ask questions that delve, in this case quite literally, beneath the surface.

Unfortunately, the endless questions that are forming in my mind aren't answered by public information boards. I'll probably only find answers to my growing list of questions by talking with more people, which I guess is a natural part of travelling, but always having far more questions than answers is probably something that I'll simply have to get used to.

The road to and from Lake Reschen is a Mecca for bikers, another contender for 'World's Best Biking Road', and for the first time on the journey we come across a large group of BMW Adventure motorcycles. They wear German registration plates, shiny new and dripping with TOURATECH bling. The riders cast doubtful eyes across the Triumph Tigers and ask me questions. It seems that gaffer tape and cable ties are scarce in this part of the world, but quite clearly the availability of money isn't. They're part of an organized tour, but organized by whom I really couldn't say. They seem to have an amazingly detailed itinerary and when I suggest that they should follow the amazing road up to the hotel at Kaunertal, they tell me that the Hotel Weisseespitze will be their home for tonight. I suspect they mean rooms, not tents.

These guys are on a one week holiday, an adventure that they repeat in different parts of Europe on an annual basis, but each adventure is never more than a week in length. They follow an itinerary that packs the biggest possible punch and they clearly travel in style. They have jobs that provide them with the means to buy their beautiful machines, but those same jobs steal away the time that they'd dearly like to spend riding them.

They tell me that they'd like to do what we're doing but feel that it would be beyond their capabilities, but they're wrong. What we're doing requires absolutely no special capabilities, and we're living proof of that, it's simply a question of circumstances and choice. Their circumstances are different and so they make different choices, not better or worse, just different. It's an interesting conversation, North and South Poles meeting, but their time is short and they must be moving on. We shake hands, exchange contact details and they file out of the car park following their guide like a well trained motorcycle display team.

Moving onwards, we pass several signs for the Pass De Stelvio, but Chris the hotel manager had been right, the pass is still closed. We're a month too early and the snow that blocks it won't be cleared until the second week in June. It's a huge disappointment but the better news is that at only 6,000 feet above sea level, the Pass De Giovo is now open and passable on a motorcycle. Stelvio is more famous than Giovo, but with that lack of fame comes a lack of traffic. The Porsche and Lamborghini brigade enjoy the kudos of driving Stelvio, but thankfully for us they seem to largely ignore the Pass De Giovo. At the base of the Pass, I attached the camcorder to the engine bars of the Tiger and set off with a feeling of great anticipation.

For several minutes I enjoy the experience but even the light traffic is still something of a headache. I finally lose patience and pass the silver Mercedes SL that's been holding me back. The road ahead is clear and the Tiger surges forward finding its own comfortable pace. I feel free, nothing ahead of me and nobody in my mirrors. I play with the throttle and do just enough to increase my heart rate as the road seems to climb and climb forever. I close in behind a Porsche 911 Cabriolet and the driver's clearly looking to play. He's seen me approaching in his mirrors and quickens the pace. His passenger's long blonde hair dances wildly in the air and she tries in vain to hold it in place with one hand while waving back at me with the other. Around three blind hairpin bends I sit respectfully on their tail, but they eventually succumb to the Tigers stare and pull aside for me to pass.

They smile and wave and I reciprocate. They're not annoyed that I've passed them, but actually seem happy that I'm enjoying the road just as much as they are, and from my experience of riding a motorcycle in England, that kind of reaction is really quite rare.

I cross the snowline and immediately feel the drop in temperature, but the road remains the same. The walls of snow and ice banked high on either side send the sound of the Tiger's snarl straight back to my ears and I find myself using slightly more engine braking than is strictly necessary. A little higher and the snow bank to my right suddenly vanishes. In its place is a light Armco barrier and a worryingly magnificent view of the adjacent snow covered mountain and the deep sided valley that separates me from it. This is 'Playstation' magic for all five of the senses, and although any mistake would be disastrous, the majesty of the surroundings banishes all such thoughts from my mind.

All too soon a wooden chalet comes into view, a small café and a sign recording the height: 'Jaufenpass Passo Giovo 2094m'. I've reached the summit of a climb that I never wanted to end. I pull into the café and order coffee and Black Forest gateaux. Surrounded by snow, but shirtless and soaking up the warmth of the sun, I sit down, eat my cake and smile. Sunbathing on snow? For an Englishman that's a very weird feeling, but after a spirited ride along another contender for 'World's Best Biking Road', it's also an immensely satisfying one.

The church spire rising from the depths of Lake Reschen

Chapter 10:
Italy

People are staring at me and smiling. They're grown men, completely naked, and if this was happening back in England I'd be a very worried man. But this isn't England, this is the communal shower room at a camping ground in Grettle An See in Italy. Perhaps they're smiling because they think that I'm mad, and maybe they're right, but I'm quite happy to be brightening their day.

Over the past week I've developed a routine that's allowed me to abandon many of the clothes that I'd carried with me from England. At the end of a day's riding when a shower is available, I take one. That's quite a normal thing to do, but I actually take my clothes in with me. Not in a nice neat bundle, but physically wearing them. In private shower cubicles this activity generally goes unnoticed, but here the only available showers are open and shared. My fellow campers look on in amazement but I really don't care what they think. I'm an Englishman and therefore I'm supposed to be unusual. It's a common design fault for which there's never been an official recall and not something that I ever really worry about. Using whatever shower gel or shampoo has been left behind by earlier bathers, I wash the clothes that I'm wearing and remove them as each item is done. The wet clothes are then attached to the bike beneath an elastic cargo net and the following day, within a couple of hours of riding, they're dry, fresh and ready to be worn later that evening. To my new audience this probably looks like a mighty strange ritual, but it's a ritual that works for me and if it makes them smile, then that's got to be a good thing all round.

After the mandatory morning coffee, we leave the Grettle An See campground and buy food for breakfast on the way. One of the finest things about picnicking from a motorcycle is that for each meal you get to choose a different view. Today we've stopped a few miles beyond the sleepy town of Auer and eat breakfast beside a church in a dandelion filled meadow overlooking the picturesque village of St Lugarno. We're off the beaten track, riding along partially paved roads through villages that cling precariously to the sides of the mountains. Every village has fluttering flags, cobbled streets, tall narrow houses with brightly painted doors, hanging baskets with vibrant flowers, old men who like to sit chatting in the street and of course, at least one village church. The people that I see seem to wear the same uniform, clothes that are different in style but in colours that are mirrored from one person to the next, always black and white.

This is Italy, not the Italy that I'd expected to find, but definitely one that I can appreciate. Each village seems to share a common atmosphere of relaxed laziness, tranquil places where people clearly don't like to rush. In one such village, I stop at a small café and order a single espresso. It takes an age to prepare, but the task of preparation is nothing less than theatre. Never before have I had a coffee that's been made with such love and devotion, so much so that I hardly dare drink it. Fashion may have passed these villages by, but fashion is fleeting and style is much more permanent. Style is what these villages have in abundance and I want to sit here and enjoy it for as long as I can, but even on the loose and flexible schedule that I'm following, the time to sit and dream in places like this is all too limited. The espresso is delicious, but it's time to ride on towards Lake Garda.

With our tents erected at a campsite right on the shores of Lake Garda, the sky turns a deep shade of purple. We haven't seen rain since leaving England, but that's clearly about to change. The sun vanishes and the wind begins to bellow. I dive into the tent with a bottle of chilled beer and watch as the most violent storm takes hold of the lake, turning it into a raging ocean. The wind blows and threatens to remove the tent from the ground and then the rain begins falling. It's like a tap, on or off, no British drizzle or mild precipitates, proper stair rod rain, the kind of rain that you commonly see in the movies. Within seconds the visibility is down to zero, streams of running water are circling the tent and heading down to replenish the lake. Then the lightening begins and the thunder quickly follows. The raindrops become giant hailstones and the gap between lightening strikes and thunder closes as the storm passes directly over the campground. It's by far the most impressive storm that I've ever witnessed under canvas, but thankfully everything inside of my little tent remains perfectly dry. By 7:30pm the storm has cleared and the grass and canvas are drying beneath a perfect evening sun.

Behind my tent a group of twenty something boys are looking longingly towards a group of similarly aged giggling girls. The girls are cooking pasta on a large stove and have seemingly arrived here well prepared. The interest of the boys is further heightened when the girls produce several cases of chilled beer from the boot of their old Renault car. The courtship rituals begin in earnest and will probably continue long into the night. I was young once and I can still remember how these situations progress, so I reach for a pair of ear plugs and hope for a decent night's sleep.

It's now Sunday, and in all of the villages that we enter, all but the churches are closed. The bells call to the faithful and the faithful religiously flock to their chimes. Back in England I used to hear the bells of my village church ringing every Sunday morning, but I don't remember ever seeing too many people striding enthusiastically towards them. Here in Italy it's very different, they still seem to take their religion very seriously and wearing my filthy leathers on a Sunday makes me feel like an unwanted intruder to their weekly ritual. We're heading for a campsite close to the town of Nevegal, but it's a town that I simply can't find. It's marked on the map but there doesn't appear to be a road that will lead us directly to it. So, using the compass for guidance, I navigate along any track that seems to take us in the general direction of Nevegal.

The tarmac ended long ago and halfway up what feels like a mountain, we arrive in a village consisting of no more than twenty small houses. At a 'Y' junction, an old man sits in an even older rocking-chair, eyes closed and folded arms supporting his ample belly. I flip up the front of my helmet and ask the question: 'Nevegal?' He opens his eyes, chuckles and wobbles his belly for my amusement. He turns his head towards the right and nods. I lift a thumb and nod my head in the same direction. He just nods back and smiles.

For the next three miles we travel along increasingly rutted and washed-out gravel tracks catching occasional glimpses of the Dolomites far away in the distance. The road keeps on climbing, it's rough going and the only people that we see are serious climbers carrying ropes and crampons. We smile and they look back at us with a mixture of disdain and disbelief. I get the feeling that not many vehicles ever make it this far. I stop and show a small group of walkers the 'X' that I've marked on my map. They look slightly confused, but point along the track and all that I can do is continue riding in hope. A few torturous miles later we find that the climb was certainly worth the effort. The chalet at Nevegal appears before us and the most beautiful girl that we've seen so far points us towards a suitable place for us to camp.

Before the sun can set, we pitch our tents and retire to the fully stocked bar of the chalet for an evening of silent voyeurism. As the night progresses, cars arrive and obviously already drunken drivers wobble into the bar. A small and constantly changing group of people sit together on tall stools and talk animatedly in a language that I don't understand. It's an eclectic mix of friends; old and young, male and female, and aside from geographical proximity, I'm struggling to identify a common link between them. Jimmy James and the Vagabonds, Archie Bell and the Drells, Tavares and other assorted pop hits from the 1970's fill the room and people randomly get up to dance. A fluorescent shell-suited man arrives and joins the circle of friends on the stools. He appears to be their leader, the mayor of the circle, slightly older and dripping with gold chains and bracelets. He flirts with the beautiful girl from reception and she seems surprisingly receptive to his slavering attention. I don't know if I'm jealous or envious, but she's beautiful and every move that she makes gives me pleasantly intimate tingles. She makes me think about sex, but I think about sex quite often so that's not really unusual, the really unusual thing would be getting any. I sense that my priestly record of abstinence is unlikely to change tonight, but a man can always dream.

The people of Nevergal are having fun tonight, but as they're not going to come to me I'll walk a few meters to meet them. I find a stool, the circle of friends opens to make space for the stranger and this stranger makes himself at home. The chatter bounces between fast Italian and very good English. As I drink beer that nobody seems to be paying for, I discover that Nevegal is a ski resort, skiing in the winter months and climbing throughout the summer. We've arrived between seasons and the locals are enjoying their free time before the crowds return again in the summer. Everybody here is in some way involved in the business of tourism, yet they don't appear to be rivals. They're strangers to me, but they all speak very good English and are happy to talk about their lives.

Each of them was raised in the area around Nevegal, attended local schools and then graduated into their respective family businesses; this ski lodge, another local hotel, the equipment hire store, the supermarket and the local gas station. All of their businesses involve the sale of various goods and services to tourists, and those businesses have historically provided their families with a basic source of income. However, with unbridled enthusiasm they tell me that ever since Italy had adopted the Euro as its currency, their lives have become an awful lot easier.

Business is good, tourist numbers are rising, European development grants are plentiful and the banks that used to ignore them are now eager to support their flourishing businesses. As an Englishman living in England, I have a certain natural immunity to Europe and the Euro. They seem to be distant things that provide certain English newspapers with fantastical headlines, but beyond that they're really something of a mystery to me. Of course I know 'what' they are, it's what they actually 'do' that I struggle to fully understand. So, despite my overwhelming ignorance, we raise our glasses to the Euro and then to Brussels. 'Cheers'.

This morning I woke to a wonderful view of the Dolomites and shared coffee with a German cyclist by the name of Thomas. He'd arrived late last night and possibly due to my snoring, had pitched his tiny micro-tent at the opposite end of the large field. Now we share tales of our respective travels and Thomas shares with me the fact that just a hundred meters from the chalet is a beautifully paved road that would have brought us directly to this site. That's good news for my journey out of here, but I'm actually quite pleased that I hadn't found that road yesterday evening. The ride across the top of the mountain had been a great experience and the memory of the old pot-bellied villager napping in his filthy white vest is a memory that I'll cherish for a very long time.

Thomas tells me that his cycle tours are an annual event, always travelling alone and always transporting his trusty bicycle by train to the starting point of his journey. Aside from a tent, sleeping bag and spare clothing, he's carrying next to nothing on his bicycle and simply picks up everything that he needs by interacting with strangers that he meets along the way. Thomas insists that the most important thing that he carries with him is his curiosity and I can't help but admire his spirit and determination. I'd like to tie his bicycle behind the Tiger and bring him along with me, but that's not possible. Thomas has a new mission for today. He's heard on the local grapevine, namely the local Pizza Restaurant that he'd visited yesterday evening, that the comely receptionist from the lodge is inclined to provide favours to passing strangers. He wanders off towards the showers with a bar of soap, a change of Lycra and a definite skip in his step. I'm rather doubtful about the accuracy of the information that he's received, but he's a confident guy and I certainly can't blame him for trying. 'Good luck Thomas'.

Thomas the cyclist had been right about one thing. Nevegal does have a road and I'm buggered if I know how I missed it yesterday. What's even more mystifying is the fact that I still can't find it on the map, but it's definitely here because we're riding on it. We've dropped down from the heights of Nevegal to the shores of a mirror flat lake with magnificent views of the snow capped Dolomite's to the east. According to the signposts, this road heading towards Vittorio Veneto is called Route 51, but it seems to be known locally as the 'Death Road'. It's quite an emotive name and the small shrines placed at many of the beautiful curves attest to the accuracy of its name.

We pass a small motorcycle dealership emotively named 'Death Road Motorcycles' and pull into the first fuel station that we see. Towering a hundred meters above us is a magnificent flyover, an aerial carriageway the likes of which I've never before seen. It seems to exit from the side of a towering mountain and runs winding and slim for as far as my eyes can see. About its tiny footprints on the valley floor, there's no graffiti, no lingering stench of stale urine and absolutely no abandoned furniture or discarded shopping carts. This is an Italian flyover and bears absolutely no resemblance to any of its British counterparts. It's a beautiful sight, but I have absolutely no idea how to get onto it or even where it would take me. It's a supermodel of a road, a curving body held high above the valley on legs of pipe cleaner slenderness. I'd love to ride on that magnificent elevated road but the garage owner's English is worse than my Italian and no matter what questions I ask, the response is never anything more informative than a toothless smile. Unable to find a way onto it, I content myself with the view and the hope that one day, all flyovers might be built that way.

As we continue to head east, Italy is becoming visibly poorer and the roads more congested. It's not that there's any more traffic, it's just that there seems to be far less tarmac for the vehicles to enjoy. The landscape has become flatter, less involving and everything appears to have been built along the side of the road. Nothing exists behind those buildings and there are no areas of countryside between them. It feels like we're riding through the longest and narrowest town in the world and I'm already missing Germany, Switzerland, Austria and the Alps, but at least I'm enjoying the warmer air down here at sea level. Everything seems to be slightly more East than West, and even the toilets have changed. Gone are the thrones that we Englishmen tend to favour and in their place, foot printed basins that employ little in the way of posterior support. We're still in Italy, but it's clear that we're rapidly closing in on the Balkans.

We're approaching our last port of call in Italy, the coastal resort of Trieste. As we drop down towards the Adriatic Sea, the aerial view of the city is quite beautiful. It's a crescent of white buildings nestling on the narrow plateau between the chalky grey hills and the deep blue of the sea. It's the first time that we've seen the sea since leaving the ferry back in Calais and I'm getting a distinct 'Summer Holiday' kind of feeling. I have a sudden urge to knot a handkerchief, roll up my trousers and start complaining about foreign food. But, before I can afford to start coming over all British, I've got to survive the journey down to the promenade. The traffic reminds me of London and after the gentle road manners that we've enjoyed for the past week, it comes as a quite a shock to my system.

As I refuse to jump a red traffic light, an Alfa Romeo deliberately tries to mount the rear of the Tiger. I turn around and glare at the aggressor, and he responds by nudging me forwards again. What a bastard. He's waving a hand and telling me to go. The junction is clear but traffic fines are probably expensive in Italy and I'm not crossing a red light for anybody. Screw Alfa Man, he can travel at my pace for a while. The lights change and I'm in no particular hurry. Clunk into first gear, gently out with the clutch and slowly on my way. Deep breath and count to ten.

Aside from the traffic chaos, Trieste is a beautiful place. Sandwiched on a sliver of land between Slovenia to the east and the Adriatic Sea to the west, it reminds me of a budget French Riviera and even the crazy traffic has its visual attractions. Everybody who isn't driving an expensive car in a murderous manner, rides a scooter wearing what I can only assume to be the very height of Italian fashion. Girls with long flowing hair and oversized sunglasses, draw to a halt and place delicate stiletto heels onto the hot and dusty tarmac for stability. Everybody here has style, mountains of style, and they clearly spend an awful lot of time on their presentation. Seeing them in such numbers just makes me feel so bloody English. A weekend spent on New Bond Street with an unlimited line of credit and a Personal Shopper and I'd still look pretty much the same as I do now. I'm just not Italian and never will be.

We're camping a few miles north of Trieste, a small village that seems not to have a name. Close to our camp I've found a great little pastry shop where I buy delicious marmalade croissants and the elderly girls giggle and refer to me as the crazy English biker. We try to talk, but mostly they just seem to laugh and I'm sure that their jokes are usually about me. One thing that they do tell me is that I should be careful in Croatia. Apparently it's a nation of robbers and bandits. At least I think that's what they're trying to tell me and I assure them that I'll be constantly on my guard and will refuse to talk with strangers.

It's an interesting village and across the road from where we're camping is a well stocked supermarket where the display of produce owes little to convention. Everything in there is arranged in the most chaotic manner making it almost impossible to find anything that you might actually want to buy. On the first visit I mistakenly bought pizza yeast thinking that it was butter. But, I still enjoy going there and the printing on the top of their till receipts always makes me smile: 'Gonad Supermarket - Happy Shopping'.

In many ways I'll be sorry to leave Italy, but the £20 per day budget can survive no longer in these stylish and expensive parts. While in Italy it would have been great to visit Rome, Florence, Venice and Vicenza, and had this been 'Rich' and not 'Poor' Circulation, then I'm sure that I would have undertaken the comprehensive grand-tour. But it's not and I haven't, so I'll try not to whine about it too much. We need to quickly move onwards into more reasonably priced areas and this means that we're about to leave Western Europe behind us. So far, the only challenges that we've faced have been wholly of our own making and the journey itself has been easy. The Balkans is uncharted territory for both of us and I suspect that this is where the real travelling is about to begin.

Chapter 11:
Croatia

Trieste stands right on the border with Slovenia. In fact, if it was any closer then it would no longer be in Italy. Still riding around what I assume to be the edge of the town, slightly lost, I turn away from the main road and look for a suitable place to stop and consult my map, and accidentally find myself facing the border post. Good guesswork. Italy waves us farewell and Slovenia asks us to halt. For the first time in ten different border crossings, passports are shown. But it's just a formality, no visa is required and within seconds we're riding into Slovenia. An hour later, and we're riding out of Slovenia into Croatia. I had absolutely no idea that Slovenia was so small, or at least so narrow at its Adriatic end. We saw nothing of the country and aside from one cup of coffee, coffee that was memorable for all of the wrong reasons, I have absolutely nothing of substance to report about Slovenia.

I know that Croatia is slightly longer than Slovenia, so hopefully I'll be investing a little more time here. We arrive at the town of Rijeka, which appears to be a slightly less fragrant version of Trieste and is probably all the better for it. I sit in the main square of the resort and update my Blog using public wireless Internet. In Italy, Internet access had been securely guarded and relatively expensive. Italian cyber-cafes had insisted that I surrendered my passport before internet access could be granted, but here in Croatia things are very different indeed. On arriving in Rijeka, I'd asked at the tourist information office about internet access and the girl had looked back at me with a puzzled expression. 'This is Croatia Sir, Internet access is everywhere, and it's free'. She'd been right. I'd booted up my laptop and found five free and unsecured full strength connections. Welcome to the Balkans. Welcome to the twenty-first century.

I pick up the A8 heading south towards Split and after just a few short miles, I'm falling head over heels in love with Croatia. The people have been friendly, open and approachable, but riding south along the coastal road towards Split, I'm struck by the natural beauty of their country. To be honest, all that I can see are mountains to my left and the sea to my right, but I'm struggling to understand why every motorcyclist in the world isn't already waxing lyrical about this place. Ten meters to my left are the sheer cliffs of what I think are the Dinaric Alps rising up to meet a clear blue sky, and two meters to my right, beyond not the most substantial of safety barriers, is a sheer drop down to what I know for certain is the Adriatic Sea.

The road has been constructed using the line of least possible resistance. It clings to the face of the cliff and follows all of the natural contours. The tarmac is new and beautifully smooth, the road twists and turns, rises and falls. There is traffic on the road, mostly Dacia 1310 cars which are modern Romanian reproductions of the never beautiful Renault 12, but you never wait long for a clear opportunity to pass them. This road running south down the Dalmatian Coast is in short, the most perfect road that I've ever ridden, and in almost a million miles of riding, the list that it tops is reasonably comprehensive. We're not riding particularly fast, but this road doesn't demand speed. All it asks is that you take your time and enjoy the spectacle created when man works in harmony with nature.

To end our fist day in Croatia, we camp at the very edge of the Adriatic Sea and watch a huge orange sun sink gently into its deep black waters. I cook pasta on the stove and chill bottles of local beer in the sea. The beauty of this place needs no conversation to improve it, so we eat and drink in relaxing but still slightly awkward silence.

Barring a couple of inland adventures across the mountains, where we see clear evidence of the most recent Balkan conflicts, with every one of its many kilometres the perfection of the coastline continues to thrill and inspire me. Some maps show this road as the A8, others as the E65, but if you should ever venture to these parts, and I strongly advise that you do, just find the Adriatic Coast and stick to it. By car, motorcycle or bicycle, you won't be disappointed.

A few kilometres south of Split, I pull off the main road and head down into what appears to be a campsite. The place seems to be called Solana and perches on precarious terraces between the road and the Adriatic. It is definitely a campsite, but nobody's manning the office. I ask a sandal wearing camper what our options are and he happily tells me to pitch my tent wherever my heart desires. And that's exactly what I do. A hundred meters down steep stone and sand paths, I find a flat spot of land large enough for two well spaced tents and declare it our home for the evening. Were camping on a solid rock base covered in sharp little stones, and it's a steep one hundred meter climb to the nearest bar, but it's absolutely perfect.

Ten hours in the saddle and a constant one hundred unsheltered degrees of heat have taken their toll on my aging body. I'm hot, I'm dusty and I must stink to high heaven. I take off my leather riding boots, wish myself luck, and jump from the cliff into the Adriatic below. Wow, what a buzz, what a wakeup call. The water that had looked so inviting from above is absolutely bloody freezing. I'm an Englishman and I'm used to paddling in the North Sea, so by comparison this should feel like a lovely warm bath, but it doesn't. My tee shirt fills with air, thankfully. I've never tried swimming fully clothed before and it's amazing how heavy denim jeans, cotton tee shirts and woollen socks become in water. The inflated tee shirt gives me buoyancy and I thrash around until I acclimatize and the water temperature becomes bearable. I feel awake, alive and free. I seem to be the only person swimming here and maybe others have been put off by the coldness of the water. Then I realise that there's only a rock face in front of me. No steps, no beach, no landing point. How the fuck do I climb out again?

Having finally extracted myself from the refreshing water with only minor cuts and bruises to hands, body and feet, I sit in the large bar at the top of the cliff tucking into grilled fish and quaffing freezing cold beer. I engage in conversation with a ruddy faced Dutch couple who are travelling in a camper van. They're fun people. They've just driven up the coast from Albania, which they'd loved, and before that from Kosovo, which they'd hated. Apparently I must go to Albania, but before that I must meet Zaltan, the owner of both camping ground and bar. They pour me a glass of the deep red wine that they're drinking. It's local, made here on site at Solana but there's no label to tell me what's in it. It's heavy and it's strong. No wonder they look so ruddy faced, less than half a bottle consumed and they're already hammered. Maybe it's not their first bottle, or maybe it really is as strong and heavy as it tastes.

I'm told that tomorrow we must attend Zaltan's special annual Fish Party, the only event in Croatia that can't possibly be missed. With a wink, The Dutch people tell me that they attend the Fish Party every year and wouldn't miss it for the world. He smiles at his wife and then waves a hand slowly around the room: 'All of our friends come here every year for the Fish Party'.

A strong arm is around my neck, almost preventing me from breathing. I'm meeting Zaltan for the very first time. He introduces himself in broken English, welcoming me to his Solana campground and bar. He's as drunk as a lord and I get the distinct impression that most of his life is spent in that state. Thankfully Zaltan is a happy kind of drunk. In fact, all of the people in the bar seem happy. Mostly couples, different ages, different nationalities, but all happy, hammered and mingling together. More local wine arrives, unpaid for and unordered. My life story is told and I'm soon holding Zaltan's mobile telephone to my ear and listening to one of the sweetest voices that I've ever heard. The voice conjures up the image of a dusky maiden, black glistening hair, dark eyes and a frame that would make any clothes look expensive. The voice belongs to Ivana. She's a journalist on a newspaper with a name that I can't even begin to pronounce, and we'll meet tomorrow for an interview in Split. I hand the telephone back to Zaltan and he has one special favour to ask of me. Following tomorrow's interview in Split, I must make sure that Ivana comes back with me to the Fish Party. I promise to do my best.

After clearing up the breakfast dishes, I wait for instructions about the meeting with Ivana. Zaltan's daughter Mary hands me her telephone and tells me that Ivana will call me shortly. She smiles and tells me that if her boyfriend should call first, under no circumstances should I answer it, because her boyfriend is the jealous sort and isn't invited to tonight's Fish Party. I'm not sure if she's joking, and how the hell will I know if it's Mary's jealous boyfriend or Ivana who's calling? After a few minutes of nervous waiting, Mary's telephone rings. Thankfully it's Ivana calling and not Mr Jealous.

Following the directions I'd been given, we arrive at the Riva in Split. It's a vast expanse of perfect white marble stretching between the old city walls and the harbour. It's brand new and luxurious, café society where a tall skinny latte probably won't break the bank. The Riva wouldn't look out of place in Italy, but here in Split it stands out like a wart on an otherwise perfectly formed ancient anatomy. I've no idea what stood here before they built The Riva, but I'm sure that it would've had far more character than this. It's stark and flat, painful on the eye and devoid of all character. Somewhere along this featureless meadow of marble, we should find a large and imposing piece of modern sculpture, 'The Silver Apple'. Apparently everybody in Split knows where it is and we'll meet Ivana in its shadow at noon. The only problem is, we can't find it anywhere on The Riva and the people that we ask for help have never even heard of it.

I wander down a side street into the cool shadows of the beautiful old city and see a bookshop. I like bookshops, they're always a good place to find an English speaker when you need one. I ask about 'The Silver Apple' and the book-seller looks slightly perplexed. I explain about the arrangements for our rendezvous and from my pocket produce a slip of crumpled paper that should contain Ivana's telephone number. The book-seller disappears into the rear of the shop and returns a few minutes later with good news and a smile. We're to wait by the monument in the centre of the square and Ivana will join us in just a few minutes.

We sit waiting on the ledge of a small monument, a bronze statue of the great poet Marko Marulic of Split, a man whose works I've never read, a great poet who embarrassingly I've never heard of. We wait, sweating, melting and squirming beneath the burning sun in our protective but inappropriate leather riding gear. From the shadows across the square, a slender figure walks through a narrow arch. She's dressed in black and wearing the most enormous pair of sunglasses. She seems to be coming towards us. It can't possibly be Ivana. Seldom do voices and visions match so perfectly, at least they never do in my world. The sunglasses are removed and a smile breaks across her face, a beautiful face, a face that has grown men turning weak at the knees and stronger in other areas.

Hands are shaken and mouths are eventually closed. We willingly follow Ivana Dujmovic through the narrow streets like two kids chasing the promise of ice cream and candy. After too short a walk, we arrive at a small open air cafe at the edge of the Doge's Palace. We drink water and coffee, we talk in depth about Poor Circulation, we talk at length about Split and strangely talk briefly about Dante's Inferno. I have no idea if Dante's fourteenth century epic has any relevance to Split or Croatia, but I pretend that I'm more familiar with the work than I really am and hope to hell that she doesn't move onto Homer, or Marko Marulic of Split.

Two hours have passed, possibly even three, and when Ivana intelligently declines our invitation to join tonight's Fish Party, I somehow manage to squash my desire to kidnap her. We end our meeting back on the Riva where we pose for photographs with the Tigers and draw a small crowd of interested onlookers. They're mostly men and it's obviously Ivana that they're interested in, but we still appreciate them coming to shake our hands and say hello. Eventually, and very regretfully, we say goodbye to Ivana and promise to look at the article in tomorrow's newspaper: Slobodna Dalmacija. Along with every other warm blooded male on The Riva, we watch as Ivana walks away into the distance.

We arrive fashionably late at the Solana Campground and the Fish Party is already in full swing. Zaltan is busy making sure that everybody is getting nicely acquainted and appropriately drunk, seemingly at his expense. We join a long table of tourists from different parts of Europe and are made to feel extremely welcome.

We fill ourselves with locally caught grilled fish and assorted seafood, washing it down with some of the most unusual wine that I've ever tasted. It's not disgusting, just strangely unpleasant. It tastes like semi-fortified vinegar, it warms your throat like whiskey and our new friends here seem to love it. As the fiddles begin to play, the people rise to dance and in order to save myself from a premature death, I switch to drinking beer.

My hand is grabbed by a woman who I don't know and I dance for the first time in years. A quick glance tells me that everybody's dancing and nobody's looking at me, so I just relax and try to go with the Croatian flow. The music changes, my unnamed partner is suddenly in the arms of another man and I find myself in the company of Zaltan's daughter, Mary.

The music has a similar tempo, but this dance is very different. Close quarters, bumping and grinding. It's not something that any hot blooded male could possibly call unpleasant, but I try to keep a polite amount of space between our bodies. Mary's having none of it and 'polite' clearly doesn't interest her tonight. It's not just that I fear an assault by her more than capable father or jealous boyfriend, but I do worry that she'll soon notice the growing interest in my trouser department. I'm a man, it happens, what can I say?

After several more dances with ever changing partners, and a substantial quantity of beer, I'm standing in the corner laughing and joking with a young German couple. We're talking about nothing in particular but they're great value and amazing fun to be around. They seem like a hon-

Poor Circulation

eymoon couple and when they disappear for what I suspect is going to be a personal liaison beneath the star filled night sky, I'm not in the least bit surprised.

What does surprise me is that a few minutes later on an urgent mission to empty my bursting bladder, I meet the same couple in the semi darkness of the gentleman's lavatory. Not being the bashful type and with a large quantity of beer to expel, I proceed to piss and talk with them at the same time. Unfortunately, the natural process of pissing is interrupted when a second pair of hands decides to assist me. Thankfully those hands belong to her and not him, but I don't remember inviting either of them to help me.

I protest and that seems to stop her. She releases her grip, but only for as long as it takes for her giggling husband to lift her dress up over her head. Thankfully that's all he's removed, but clearly that's all she'd ever been wearing. I'm not a prude and I'm certainly not sober, but I didn't sign up for this kind of action tonight. While she enthusiastically tries to prevent me from returning my pecker to my pants, I manage to step backwards, make good my escape, and seek refuge in the relative safety of the party.

I find Adam sitting with a group of people back at the long table, but before I can explain what's just happened in the toilets, Mr and Mrs Swinger are settling down opposite us. She flops down onto her husband's lap, flirtatiously smiling at everybody. Her flimsy dress is now inappropriately high and drawing the attention of the lady sitting next to her. Clearly that lady doesn't think that it's inappropriate at all, quite the contrary in fact, and she's inviting her own partner to enjoy a shared and intimate experience. I look around and apart from Adam and I, it seems that everybody's well on the way to getting amazingly intimate with everybody else. It's time to leave, time for bed, my bed, alone.

Sneaking away from a campsite at dawn isn't our usual habit, but somewhere on the Solana campground were some happy swinging people that neither of us had any desire to bump into again. We'd crept away and returned to the beautiful road that swept us down towards Dubrovnik.

Sitting in the very south of Croatia, Dubrovnik is a UNESCO World Heritage Site and a city that Mom and Dad had adored. It had broken their hearts to see its beautiful ancient walls and buildings being destroyed by artillery shells in the siege of 1991. For me, and I suspect for many others, Dubrovnik had been the 'Poster Girl' of the Yugoslav Wars, the sight that made us all sit up and take notice of what was happening all across the Balkans. Following the break-up of Yugoslavia, Croatia had declared independence but the then Serb leader Slobodan Milosevic, in coalition with Montenegrin leader Momir Bulatvoc, had already mapped out their own plans for a Greater Serbia, and that vision had unfortunately included the ancient town of Dubrovnik. From October of 1991, the Serb-Montenegrin forces had shelled the city and news footage of the destruction had flooded across the world. A world that had all but ignored the on-going human cost of the year long conflict, was now appalled by the destruction of property.

The Yugoslav wars that continued up until 1995, cost the lives of at least one hundred and fifty thousand people, but the destruction of Dubrovnik and a tiny bridge in Mostar, will be the lingering images for many. Within the album that we'd discovered at the bottom of Mom's wardrobe, more space had been devoted to Dubrovnik than to any other place, and hopefully I'm about to discover why.

To enter Dubrovnik from the north, you cross a stunning modern metal bridge from which you can see most of the town. The town seems to have been built around water, the Adriatic Sea its channels and many inlets, and every piece of open ground has been developed. Small buildings tightly packed together with terracotta roofs and white walls that stand baking in the early afternoon sun.

Within minutes of entering the town, we find a convenient campsite where we meet a fellow traveller from Washington State in the USA. David's travelling around the Balkans for a month, perhaps a little longer, and Adam immediately takes to him. It's the first person that Adam's really interacted with since Mark and Lee returned to England, so I stand back and let the two of them talk.

David has a parcel of land close to Port Angeles just to the west of Seattle. He uses my map of the USA to show Adam some interesting routes that he might like to take down from Canada and across through the National Parks towards the East Coast of America. He explains the logistics and confirms just how easy it is to travel by motorcycle across North America, the good places to visit and the bad places to avoid. David invites us to come and stay with him when we arrive in America and gives us his address and telephone number. He's a really nice guy and has arrived at exactly the right time for both of us. He seems to have lightened Adam's mood and brought him out from beneath the dark cloud that seems to have followed him from Germany. The mood is visibly brighter, everybody's smiling, laughing and joking, and I feel that Dubrovnik will be good for all of us.

Dubrovnik Harbour in Croatia

We take the bus into town and begin to explore. The old town is busy, tourists from every nation take pictures of every physical thing and the bustle of Dubrovnik's narrow streets only adds to its beauty. I'm a tourist with a knapsack on my back and sunscreen on my lily white legs. It feels good to be off the motorcycles for a change. The bike tends to draw attention but walking here, I'm anonymous and enjoying the solitude within the crowds.

Mom had wanted to return to Dubrovnik after Dad's death, possibly to see for herself the scale of the destruction, but she hadn't. Perhaps the lingering evidence of violence and the fact that she would be returning here alone would have been too upsetting for her. I really don't know, but today I really feel that they've returned here together. I'd thought about coming here alone, leaving Adam to spend more time with David, but I think that Mom would have encouraged forgiveness. So we're here together, exploring in the old town of Dubrovnik.

I escape the throngs of tourists and climb steps towards what looks to be a summit. From here, I get a perfect view of the harbour and fortress below. Small boats rock on the deep blue water, large tour ships skirt past the fortress with passengers lining the decks and waving. The old walled city sits partially out into the Adriatic Sea and its narrow streets seem to have avoided the side of commercialism that blights so many similar places around the world. Combine the amazing buildings and streets with the natural hospitality of the Croatian people and you have an almost perfect blend of culture and history. In the cool shadows of the high thick walls there's no sign of the all too recent conflict. The buildings, walls and bridges have been seamlessly repaired and I think that Mom and Dad would approve of the restoration.

Perhaps there are still strong feelings of resentment between the previously warring factions here, but it's not something that I've really noticed. Of course, the good people of Croatia have warned me about the people in Montenegro and Albania, just as the people back in Italy had warned me about the Croats, but all things considered, take away the official borders and I'm finding that people are pretty much the same. Everybody wants exactly the same things in life, it's probably just that some people want a little more of everything than others. I'm sure that if we all became a little better at sharing and less inclined to fighting, then there'd be enough of everything for everybody and we'd all just smile and get along quite nicely together.

Perhaps this is a time for forgiveness, and this might be the right place to offer it. Dubrovnik is beautiful and the memory of the recent violence probably helps to put everything else into perspective. I'm pleased that I came here today with Adam and with the Special Package in my backpack, and tomorrow could be the start of an entirely new journey, another new beginning.

Chapter 12:
Montenegro

Apart from Slovenia where we didn't really meet any people, the folks in every single country that we've travelled through have been fine, and here in Montenegro I expect nothing at all to change.

We're heading south through Montenegro towards Albania, another country that we've been advised to avoid, and we'll only be here for a day. Come to think of it, the only people who've actually recommended a visit to Albania were the swinging Dutch couple back at the Solana campground. Your view of a country probably depends largely upon your own personal experience and expectations, and the Dutch couple's expectations may have been very different from our own. But, as we're heading in that general direction then it would be rude of us not to call in and find out for ourselves.

Montenegro only received its independence from Serbia in 2006 and is a recent addition to the European Union's waiting list, but strangely, Montenegro already has the Euro as its official currency.

My first impression of Montenegro, whose name means 'Black Mountain', is that every building and road here is in the process of being constructed or renovated. I'd always thought that European Union money arrived after membership had been established, so maybe this money is coming from somewhere else. I really don't know, but they must be spending billions of Euros rebuilding their road network, but unlike in Northern Europe, the roads here don't seem to close while the work is in progress. You just find the best path that you can, work your way carefully around the construction crews and try to avoid the substantial debris of the building process. Gently on the throttle, eyes open and hope for the best. It can be a little scary when oncoming traffic is doing exactly the same thing as you, but everybody is in exactly the same boat, avoiding the same obstacles and therefore aware of exactly the same dangers. Nobody plays stupid here and everybody seems to survive. In short, it appears to be a fantastic solution to the universal problem of traffic management during construction work. Give the people some personal responsibility and they'll more than likely use it wisely. What a concept!

Montenegro feels a little like Croatia on a shoestring. Everything that you could possibly need is physically here, and you seem to get an awful lot more of it for your money, it's just a little less polished and in the case of the road system, a little less finished. We get held up by a rock slide that's blocking the road ahead and filter to the front of the queue. We're immediately surrounded by the people we've been warned to avoid, and I talk with them as I always do.

Nobody here has ever seen a modern Triumph motorcycle and they're intrigued. They think that I've written 'Triumph' on my fuel tank for nostalgic reasons and that the bike beneath the grime is actually a Honda. Despite their doubts about my Tiger being a Triumph, they seem genuinely interested in what we're doing and there's not an ounce of jealousy or envy. We share drinks, take pictures and have pictures taken of ourselves and the Tigers. They ask about our experiences in Croatia and we give them the carefully edited reports. There's much laughter and conversation that I don't understand, but I get the distinct impression that they're amazed that we made it out of Croatia alive.

In the distance we hear three shrill blows of a whistle. Conversations end mid-sentence and the people scurry back to their vehicles. The barriers are removed and we ride on deeper into Montenegro, physically unharmed and with absolutely nothing missing from our motorcycles.

At the town of Kotor I have to stop. Kotor is a town that demands the eyes attention. It seemed to appear out of nowhere, an ancient walled town snuggling into a rock face and overhung by menacing limestone cliffs. Dubrovnik had been beautiful, but its ancient buildings had in the most part been set aside for the pleasure of the tourist. Kotor is aesthetically similar but atmospherically worlds apart. The buildings here are still homes, houses where people live and go about their daily lives and there are no tourist buses anywhere to be seen. In fact, it feels like we have the entire walled town and its people to ourselves.

It's a place that draws you in and up every narrow steep lane, acts of daily living are happening all around us. Cooking, eating and chattering. Rows of laundry hang out to dry on lines draped between buildings and elderly locals idly carry baskets of groceries between buildings. There are no young people here, only young kids and their grandparents, and it feels just like a town lost in time. Dubrovnik had been a beautiful attraction, but Kotor is an attractive community. The two towns share a lot of similarities but it's their differences that fascinate me the most. I can understand why Dubrovnik is what it is, but I actually prefer the more relaxed and honest atmosphere here in Kotor. You can't buy a skinny latte here but you can get a mug of normal coffee, and I love Kotor for that, but I suspect that it won't last forever.

When you have accessible beauty like this, it's impossible to keep it hidden for too long. Things will inevitably change here and the massive reconstruction programs suggest that those changes will come relatively quickly. In my selfish eyes such changes are not always improvements, but I'm not trying to scrape a living here and have to accept that progress will be inevitable. I'm just grateful to have experienced Kotor and its surrounds now, before the masses descend and overwhelm its natural and easygoing beauty.

With Kotor behind us, we stop at yet another barrier that's blocking the road ahead. This time they seem to be blasting into a cliff and the explosions are rocking the ground beneath our feet. I've never been anywhere remotely close to an earthquake, but having these relatively small shocks shaking the ground and mountains around me places earthquakes firmly on my growing list of things to be avoided. Things are moving that in my world simply shouldn't move; the ground, the buildings, the rocks. The tremors aren't huge, but for somebody more accustomed to the kindness of British geology, it's surprisingly disconcerting.

While I'm wondering how to take photographs of ground tremors, a group of motorcycles arrive behind us, an eclectic assortment of old and new, large and not so large models. It's a motorcycle club and they're proud to introduce themselves as the 'Montenegro Pirates'. They're heading south on the same road and appoint themselves as our official escorts. They seem to know the place where we'll need to start heading inland towards Albania and they'll point it out to us when we get there. Apparently, it's not a route that's signposted and without their help we'll more than likely miss the turning. Clearly my reputation for map reading and Adam's GPS challenges are already well known in these parts. Although Zaltan had warned us to avoid both Bandits and Pirates in Montenegro, we accept their offer and for the first time since the departure of Mark and Lee, we ride forwards as part of a larger group.

The journey south is both fast and slow. Down the long straight stretches of new tarmac, the Montenegro Pirates open their throttles and release the horses. They race ahead and at the first sight of a bend, there's an explosion on brake-lights and they paddle around it in slow single file. The first time this happens, I think that something's gone wrong with the leading motorcycle, but then it happens again and again and again. It feels strange, but I'm judging their actions with a British mentality. I was raised in a world where Health & Safety plays an ever increasing role in life and where roads are not opened until they're completely finished. Here on the outer edges of what Ted Simon calls 'The Unfinished World', you have literally no idea what's waiting to greet you around the next bend. It's often just another stretch of beautifully new and smooth tarmac, but sometimes, and it only needs to be once, it'll be something slightly more dangerous; an ending of the road, a large pile of gravel, a stationary JCB. It's a lesson learnt the easy way and I make a mental note to slow down and follow the local flow before my cockiness gets me into trouble.

After several minor detours and stoppages, we draw to a halt between the towns of Sukobin and Muriqan. This is the place where Adam and I need to head inland towards Albania. There's no signpost on the road and we honestly wouldn't have found it without the help of our guides. Looking out along the path that Adam and I must travel, I'm tempted to ride further south with our new friends. The tarmac seems to end here, the road to Albania looks rough, rougher than anything that we've ridden so far, and I have no idea what we'll find at the end of it.

Chapter 13:
Albania

The road approaching Albania is narrow and dusty, more sand than tarmac and we arrive cautiously at the small ramshackle border post. We've left Montenegro without formality, I didn't even stop, but on the Albanian side a well armed cordon of poorly dressed guards is waiting to greet us. We've seen guns on this journey before, but these weapons seem different. They're worn more casually, more menacing, and perhaps more likely to be used. That's really just my imagination working overtime, but I do feel inclined towards politeness. I smile broadly, present my passport and the administrative process begins.

An American United Nations official is already encountering difficulties. He's mistakenly taken his Russian girlfriend into Montenegro for a day of shopping. The shopping may not have been a mistake, but the act of leaving Albania has invalidated his girlfriend's single entry Albanian visa. She's now barred from re-entering Albania and neither of them is happy. They're shouting, swearing, sweating in the heat and banging on the desk of every official in the vicinity. Technically speaking they've 'screwed-up', and shouting obscenities probably won't encourage the border guards to go out of their way in order to help them, but they don't seem to see that.

The situation worries me, not because the Russian girl might not be allowed to re-enter Albania with her boyfriend, but because I'm not sure if I'll need my own visa to enter Albania. I should have checked Albania's visa requirements before leaving England, but I didn't. I don't believe I need a visa to enter Albania, another privilege of being accidentally British, but I suspect that I'm about to find out.

Next to me, a young Albanian guy and his heavily pregnant wife have just arrived from London. They're driving a car wearing British license plates, an E Class Mercedes Benz. It's a car that apparently belongs to his English friend in London. He lacks the correct papers to officially import the car into Albania, temporarily or permanently, and he's settling down for what he tells me will be a very long wait. I hope their wait isn't too long, because his wife looks like she could give birth at any moment, but they seem to be less worried about it than I am.

He sits down next to me to smoke a cigarette. His English is excellent and he tells me a joke. It's about an Albanian Tourist Board advertisement that's posted on a billboard in Berlin: 'Come visit Albania ... Your Mercedes is already here'. He thinks it's the funniest joke in the world, and says that it's the reason why it'll take a great deal of time, and probably a little grease, to get his friends paperless vehicle into Albania. I really don't understand it, and I'm not sure if it's a joke that's supposed to be funny for Germans, or for Albanians. I don't ask for an explanation.

To be honest, I actually know very little about Albania. I remember hearing somewhere that the poet Lord Byron came here many years ago and got royally buggered in the court of Ali Pasha, voluntarily I suspect, and that Albania once had a king called Zog. Aside from that, I hope that I don't need a visa to enter and I do know that the Albanian currency is the Lek, of which I have absolutely none.

A guard fumbles with my name, 'Goffry Tomas', and I resist the urge to shout 'Present'. He says nothing at all about a visa, but he does ask me for an entry tax payment of 10 Euros. He leaves me in no doubt that it's an informal sort of taxation that will later be shared with the other members of his team. He's got a gun, so I don't mind paying, and if it ensures entry into what's already looking to be the most lawless of nations yet visited, then it should prove to be money well spent. I hand over the crisp ten Euro note and encourage Adam to do the same. I fear that hesitation will only lead to a sudden increase in the level of local taxes. Ask no questions, smile politely, call him 'Sir', pay the price and move onwards into Albania.

Apart from the border guard who withdrew 10 Euros from each of our wallets, there were no official money changers at the border. I have some Euros, British Pounds and US Dollars, but absolutely none of the local currency, the Lek. I don't even know what the exchange rate would be. In Croatia most businesses accepted both the local Kuna and the Euro, so I hope that here in Albania it will be the same.

We're on a road that doesn't appear on my map, nor on Adam's GPS, but the compass tells me that we're heading 'East' and that'll work for me. The young guy at the border had told me that this area of Albania was slightly off the beaten track for tourists, and that what we'd see along our route might possibly shock us. As he'd finished his cigarette he'd helpfully added that the roads here would be 'absolutely shit'. Well, the roads here do seem to be in need of much repair, but unlike in Montenegro, there's absolutely no sign of construction work here. In fact, there's very little sign of anything except rubbish. Garbage, waste, detritus, mostly discarded plastic piled high and scattered wide along the side of the road. It smacks of neglect, a lack of pride, an absence of infrastructure and it stinks to high heaven. Much of it seems to be smouldering, not quite on fire but with enough combustion to give off a constant curtain of grey smoke that fills the air. There's an acrid stench of rotting life that accosts the back of my throat and makes stopping anywhere an unpleasant experience.

We try to ride beyond it, but the further we go the longer the line of garbage stretches. It's landfill without the 'fill' and a major blot on a landscape that might otherwise be amazingly beautiful. Perhaps I'm being unkind. We may well have arrived in Albania during industrial action by its Refuse Collectors, but I suspect not. Sadly, this seems to be the standard state of play in this particular part of the country.

We reach the edge of a town that should be called Shkoder. It's certainly marked on my map, but with no sign at the side of the road to either welcome or inform us, I'll just have to assume that this is it. The dusty streets are lined with the same discarded rubbish that we'd seen throughout the countryside. It's piled high and loose between every house and forms an almost unbroken barrier between the road and the buildings. Albania is clearly one of the poorest countries in Europe, but this appears to be poverty on a scale that I really hadn't expected. People are sitting on doorsteps, almost exclusively women and children, idling away their time chatting and sewing. Gangs of older kids are playing amongst the garbage, mostly bare foot and wearing little more than filthy rags.

The sound of the Tigers draws attention and we become a distraction to their play. The older kids are rushing at our bikes, touching, grabbing, waving open palms and asking for money. More of them are arriving by the second, scrambling across the garbage barrier to get a closer look at the new attraction in their town. It all started in a seemingly friendly manner, but as the chasing group swells, it becomes alarmingly claustrophobic. We try to push on, to outrun them, but it's impossible. It's obvious that reluctant superbikes wearing road tyres on sand are no match for enthusiastic kids in bare feet. There are just too many stationary cars and manmade obstacles along an already difficult road and each time we have to slow down, the growing crowd of kids is upon us. The number and average age of the crowd increases, and the earlier smiling requests for money have transformed into demands with menace.

We arrive at a narrow bridge and have no alternative but to stop. The crowd is all around us, tugging at pockets and pulling at the luggage. I kick away a pair of hands that are trying to lift my cooking stove out of its carrier, and another pair that are trying to disconnect my tankbag. I try to fend off all of the thieving little fingers, but there are just too many of them for me to deal with. Another minute stationary and I fear that I'll be left sitting naked on the skeleton of the Tiger.

I violently rev the Tiger's engine, but the kids are immune to its harmless growl. The bridge in front of us is narrow, constructed from wood but with too few fixings to be stable. A line of traffic is coming from the opposite side of the river. Cars, old model Mercedes wearing faded paint and the scars of too many lost battles. It's a single file route and we're trapped on the wrong side of the river with our growing crowd of determined little borrowers. Screw it.

Fear has a strange way of justifying inappropriate actions, but I'd rather take my chances with the oncoming traffic than with the kids. I twist open the throttle, stand on the footpegs and spin the Tiger up onto the first planks of the rickety wooden bridge. Fishermen of all ages stand along the side of the bridge, their lines and hooks dangling over the edge into the filthy water below. As I simultaneously hit the horn and the throttle, the startled fishermen squeeze into the barrier for safety. The oncoming Mercedes make as much room as they possibly can, but that still leaves little room to spare. I know that people are screaming and cursing at me, exactly as I'd be doing if I were them, but unfortunately there's really no alternative.

I check that Adam's still following me, and thankfully he is, but the crowd of equipment hungry kids is still hot on his tail. They're only kids, unarmed teenagers, and I feel like a coward for running away like this, but for the first time on this journey I'm feeling physically threatened and scared. Welcome to Albania, where in the space of a few short miles, touring has morphed into travelling.

I'm heading for the town of Puke. I've no idea what we might find when we get there, but with such an amazingly evocative name it would be rude of us not to find out. It's getting dark and the prospect of finding a safe place to camp isn't looking good. Official camping? I suspect not in this part of Albania.

'England, England, England, I Love London'. I see the motorcycle in the gloom, a Yamaha XT600 that's been heavily pared down and modified. Apart from its obvious lack of lights, something else seems to be missing from its frame. The rider's waving at me. He's shouting, but we're travelling in opposing directions along a road lined with shit and even if I wanted to, there's really nowhere for me to stop.

Checking in my mirrors to see if the other motorcycle has stopped, or is turning around to follow me, I notice something else that's missing, Adam. Avoiding what appears to be the rotting remains of a cow at the edge of the road, I pull into a makeshift turn-out and take a look over my shoulder. Adam has vanished. Please God not now, and certainly not here.

We've been in Albania for less than three hours and already experienced more challenges than we've encountered on the journey that's brought us here. It's travelling, it's what I set out to do, but the contrast between Montenegro and the wilds of Albania is far starker than I could ever have imagined. I think for a moment. 'Engine', the thing missing from the Yamaha was its engine. The crazy guy who loved London was riding a motorcycle without an engine. I spin the Tiger around in the dirt and race back along the path.

Finally, I see Adam riding towards me with a strange silhouette in front of him. It's a motorcycle of some description. A little closer and they enter the beam of my own headlight. It's the small motorcycle without lights, the bike belonging to the anglophile, the motorcycle without a motor. 'I'm Jack, will you join me for a nice cup of tea?'

Over cups of tea in a surprisingly well appointed cafe somewhere in the centre of Shkoder, we discover that as a refugee, Jack had lived in London for almost five years. Now, he's back in his native Albania and has recently finished building a new family home on the outskirts of Shkoder. He's a small lean man with eyes that appear to have been designed for a much larger frame. Lean men such as Jack are generally people with an abundance of energy, and Jack's a man who simply can't stand still. His arms are directly linked to his tongue and every enthusiastic sentence becomes a comedic aerobic exercise. He's a man with enthusiasm for life and I instinctively like him. Jack's house is close, we're invited to come and eat with his family and we can pitch our tents in his vegetable garden. He has dogs at his house, they'll protect the Tigers and we'll be safe there. His words imply that we're definitely not safe where we are now. A quick glance in any direction and it's clear to see that he might have a point. We might have escaped the youthful crowds on the other side of the river, but the many glances that we're receiving here seem to be slightly more menacing than welcoming. Jack's made us a very good offer, very timely, decision made.

Along rutted dust tracks, through abandoned factories and along railway lines, we follow Jack towards his home. It's dark and there are no street lights anywhere. His crazy bike, which I now see has a replacement engine from a diminutive Honda C70, has no lights. We try to light the road ahead for him, but that means trying to anticipate Jack's next movement. His riding style isn't making things easy for us and his irregular arm signals are far more 'cool' than 'informative'. Without warning, he darts left and our fully loaded Tigers have to turn on the same radius in order to prevent this madman from running into us, or into a deep ditch, and killing himself before he's served us dinner.

The lanes are now in total darkness, evidence of other people has long since disappeared and the old factory units on either side of the road are thinning out. On a relatively straight stretch of track, I reach down into the pouch containing my emergency petrol can. I pull out an eighteen inch heavy steel wrench and slip it down the side of my left boot. I'll admit to being scared. I've no idea where our new friend is taking us, but if it turns out to be a bad place, then I want to be ready. I've no idea what I'll do if bad people are waiting to greet us, but eighteen inches of cold steel makes me feel a little less naked and a little more comfortable.

Across more railway lines, we pass beneath the legs of pylons that seem to carry little more than the hopes of future electricity and then finally, we arrive at a house. It's a large house, lights shine from every window and the front door is open. A dog barks, a group of people come out onto the veranda and their beaming smiles are caught in our headlights. Jack is off his bike and talking animatedly to what I assume is his family on the veranda. As innocently as possible, I slip the wrench back into its pouch on the Tiger. I feel guilty for ever doubting our new friend's intentions and switch off the Tiger's engine.

Jack's family are warm and welcoming. We eat in their best room, share food that they can probably ill afford to give us and they refuse to take any money in return. We drink 'raki' that Jack makes illegally in one of his many outbuildings. We eat salad from their greenhouse and cheese made by Jack's wife using milk from her small herd of goats. We drink homemade wine that reminds me of the Fish Party back in Croatia and then finish of this feast with a giant bowl of goulash.

By the time the goulash is served we're already full, but it's impossible to turn down such amazing hospitality. Their attention to us is fantastic. It's dark and we're all absolutely hammered, so Jack doesn't want us to start pitching our tents in the garden. Instead, we're shown to a bedroom where we're invited to sleep for the night. It's probably Jack's own bedroom and heaven only knows where he and his good wife are going to sleep. Albania is the poorest country that we've visited so far, and Shkoder is possibly one of its poorest towns, but the generosity that we've been shown here this evening exceeds everything that we've experienced so far. Before starting out on this journey, experienced travellers had told me that the people with the least of anything to give, would give the most, and it seems that they'd been absolutely right.

In the morning we're invited to inspect Jack's motorcycle and it turns out to be a marvel of improvised engineering. If we thought that our budgets were small, and at times our actions inventive, then looking at Jack's bike puts all of our own challenges into perfect perspective. It's a minor miracle that it actually works at all. Proudly he shows us his mature vegetable garden and the developing vineyard. He decants six litres of his homemade 'raki' for us to carry with us on our travels and his ever smiling wife prepares breakfast in their modern kitchen. Jack lives with his wife, his teenage son, his sister who's recently separated from her violent husband, and his delightful niece who this morning dressed in traditional Albanian costume and posed for pictures in front of the Tigers.

Jack consults my map and scratches his chin. He looks some more and then scratches his head. He looks away and shakes his head. 'The road to Puke is bad, very bad, especially for a motorcycle and you'll find too many bandits. You're not safe going to Puke'. Jack looks genuinely concerned for our welfare. It's important to him that we leave Albania with only the best possible memories and he fears that seeing any more of his country will destroy that prospect completely. Normally we encounter people warning us about the people in the next country, but here Jack warns us about his own people, and that can't be a good thing. He points to my map and suggests that we should take a ferry from Koman, a town up in the mountains above Shkoder. The ferry, he claims, will take us directly into Kosovo and will be much faster and safer than taking the road.

Over breakfast, Jack explains that this region of Albania has an amazingly high unemployment rate, no government to speak of and that crime in this area is a very serious business. I ask him about the garbage that litters the streets and countryside and Jack tries to explain. It didn't used to be that way, but since the fall of Communism, Albanian's, along with everybody else, have developed a taste for the convenient commodities enjoyed in the West. Their food now comes pre-packaged, but away from the capital city and coastal resorts, nobody has thought about what to do with the subsequent waste. There are no litter bins, and even if there were then there'd be no local infrastructure to empty them or properly dispose of the waste. It angers Jack to see his once beautiful countryside drowning in garbage, and I have to agree with him. I tell him the joke from the border crossing, about the German's coming to Albania to visit their Mercedes cars. He laughs, and tells me that it's just a joke. Most of the old Mercedes are apparently here quite legally and it's only the newer models that are stolen. He doesn't explain further, but I get the distinct impression that Jack is no stranger to the shady world of illegal vehicle importation.

I don't push him on the subject but I'm still confused by his claim that we can sail seamlessly into Kosovo. I look back at the map and I still can't figure out how we can get from Koman to Kosovo on a ferry. I can see the body of water, which I think is called Lake Koman, but it simply doesn't stretch that far. But hell, it's the only plan that we've got and Jack's clearly the local expert and should at least know where the borders of his own country are drawn. We pack the bikes, say farewell to his wonderful family and follow Jack back along the track that we'd travelled last night. I have to say that in daylight it looks an awful lot less menacing and I feel like a coward for being so afraid of the shadows last night.

Jack leads us back through his town of Shkoder and clearly takes the non-direct route. To everybody we see, he waves and announces that we're old friends visiting him from England. He obviously has many friends to impress and it seems to take forever to clear the town, but eventually the road begins to rise and we head up into the mountains. The smell of rotting garbage slowly disappears and as we rise further, the air becomes crystal clear and fresh. The contrast is really quite startling. We're riding on admittedly very rough roads, but away from the ravages of humans, the countryside up here is stunningly beautiful.

Ahead of me, Jack's bike starts wobbling slightly more than it normally does, and then starts wobbling even more. And then he falls off. He isn't drunk, he's got a puncture. I offer to fix if for him but he says that were running short of time. We have to meet the ferry at Koman by 11:00am. The ferry waits for no one, not even his honoured guests from England. Jack's hands then demonstrate the speed and ease with which the ferry will whisk us into Kosovo. 'Go now my friends. Go Go Go'. He gives us verbal directions and we set off towards the town of Koman and the promise of a seamless journey into Kosovo.

After a few miles, the tarmac becomes rough and patchy, but at least it's still a road. We stop to consult the map and find ourselves in the middle of a very blank area of Albania. I compare the map to Adam's Garmin GPS unit and see the not so comforting sight of a small motorcycle on an otherwise totally blank screen. If there were any words to accompany the icon of the motorcycle then I'm sure they'd read 'Beware, for there be monsters here'. The compass tends to suggest that the left fork is the route to be taken, and we press on in hope. As we continue to climb, the road becomes progressively worse. The pot holes are deep, in many places deeper than the wheel spindles of the Tigers. There's more sand than tarmac and then finally there's absolutely no tarmac at all. It's just a menacing three meter wide path of deep dust and stones. To one side of us is an unguarded drop of several hundred feet down into the ravine below, and to the other side a steep rock wall. At every bend there are memorials to remember those whose journeys along this road were never completed. Hopefully we'll not be adding to their numbers today, but this is without doubt the scariest road that I've ever ridden.

It's a road that's often blind and always narrow, streams flow across it and occasionally large commercial vehicles charge murderously in our direction. They don't slow down or stop, they just charge on no matter what's ahead of them. If lucky, you can run the motorcycle into the gutter and lean hard against the rock face to let them pass. If you're unlucky and get caught on the wrong side of the single track, you just get as close to the edge as you dare, close your eyes and hope for the best. Nothing has actually hit us yet, but nothing has passed us with more than a few centimetres to spare. Added to the traffic, the Tigers aren't reacting well to the loose surface and I'm beginning to think that Triumph had been right, these are simply street bikes wearing adventure frocks. Reducing the air pressure in the tyres seems to dramatically improve the traction, but I fear that the thing that really needs to improve is our riding ability. We really ought to have had more off-road practice before leaving England, but there's a very long list of things that we really ought to have done. Riding and sliding this way is scary shit for both of us, and the sooner we reach the ferry, the better.

The town of Koman finally arrives and seems to consist of three small cafés and two even smaller houses. In one of the cafes I enquire about the Ferry to Kosovo and I'm waved onwards, higher up into the mountains. We head on, climbing until we see only a hole in the rock face in front of us. It's not quite a tunnel and not quite a cave. I nervously enter. The floor, walls and ceiling are all of the same sandy colour and texture making navigation difficult. I keep riding into the darkness fuelled only by the knowledge that retracing the route to this point would be even more suicidal. Something appears in the headlight and I skid to a dusty halt. Ahead of me in the dusty gloom, my eyes focus on a reclining cow. It appears to be sleeping, but I'm not sure if cows actually sleep. Whatever it's state of consciousness, it certainly isn't scared of Tigers and it's not going to move out of my path. I edge my way between the napping bovine and the tunnel wall, and continue onwards slightly more carefully than before. Eventually, a light appears. I keep riding towards it and after a few more metres ride out onto a large concrete jetty that's baking in sunshine. This is the ferry terminal from Koman to Kosovo and the next stage of our journey is about to begin.

A small Albanian man wearing a broad smile and cheap suit approaches us. He's too slick for his own good and slightly too friendly for my liking. He carries a briefcase and a calculator and therefore is probably of the breed known as 'Fixers'. He happily confirms that the 11:00am Ferry departed at 10:00am. For once we've arrived on time, only to find that 'on time' is actually an hour too late. We're doubly unlucky because he also tells us that the next ferry isn't until 3:30pm, 'Inshallah'. We form a huddle and make two important executive decisions. Firstly, we're not going back down the road recently travelled and secondly, Mr Fixer's palm will remain ungreased. Living on motorcycles makes unplanned breaks like this more bearable. We carry everything that we need with us on the Tigers. So, I do what any other Englishmen would do beneath the

Jack and his family at their home on the outskirts of Shkoder

baking sun on a concrete jetty in the back-end of Albania. I strike up the petrol stove and make tea.

Finally, at a little after five in the evening, the ancient ferry chugs slowly towards our temporary home, the dock. With the appearance of the antiquated vessel, the vehicles that have arrived to join us start their engines in earnest and prepare to board. The vessel is still at least half a kilometre away from us and is yet to unload its current cargo, but already they jostle to board it first. We're English and so coolly wait our turn. We don't rush at the best of times and in this sort of heat, we try to avoid rushing absolutely anywhere for anything.

As the vehicles try to reverse off the ferry onto the dock, one of the ferry's platforms isn't working. We have our passports thoroughly inspected by a uniformed official and pay 10 Euros for the privilege of leaving Albania. Last to board the ferry, we wedge the Tigers between cars and the ferry casts-off, destination Kosovo and the promise of beautiful tarmac roads. We head to the top deck of the vessel and watch as the mountains slip silently passed us providing amazing view after amazing view. These mountains are unspoilt by man and are truly spectacular. Along the side of the ravines we can see the alternate to the ferry, the road that Jack had warned us about. He was right, it looks far worse than anything we've experienced so far. Beneath my breath, I thank him once again.

The one hour sailing has taken almost three and we've arrived here in Kosovo as the sun begins to set. Entering Kosovo had been relatively easy. They hadn't checked any documents for the Tigers and the compulsory insurance premium that I'd expected to pay hadn't even been mentioned. A uniformed official had simply inspected our passports, taken 10 Euros from each of us for temporary import duty for the motorcycles and waved us through into Kosovo.

We're now heading for the city of Prizren, but it's already getting dark and I'm not sure if we'll make it that far tonight. I'd expected to start making good progress in Kosovo, but the promise of beautiful tarmac seems to have been a false one. Twenty kilometres away from the ferry terminal and we're still riding on a rough sandy track. In fact, the road looks and feels very 'Albanian'.

Another few kilometres and we arrive at a 'T' junction with a road sign. The road sign confuses me, so I consult the map with my flashlight. I'm still confused, so I cross check the map with Adam's GPS unit, but there's still no clarity. I light a cigarette and ponder the evidence. After several deep inhalations, it dawns on me why the roads are so bad, and why the customs formalities had seemed so relaxed and informal. We're still at least fifty miles inside bloody Albania.

We're not happy about the 20 Euros that we've each just needlessly paid in order to leave Albania and enter Kosovo. It's almost a full day's budget for each of us, but I can also see the funny side of it. We've just been royally buggered by bogus border officials at a place where no border had existed. We fell for their scam, hook line and sinker. But what an absolutely brilliantly executed scam it had been. It's a new memory to savour for life and something else to tell the grandchildren. Onwards to Kosovo and don't spare the Tigers.

Chapter 14:
Kosovo

It's dark, darker than any night I can remember. There's no moon and not a single star to be seen in the stormy black sky above. We haven't seen street lighting since leaving Montenegro, there's no distinguishable horizon and the only lights are those of our Tigers. We plough blindly onwards but the sand and gravel track is so deeply rutted that the motorcycles just pick their own paths. We should stop and make camp, it's the safest thing to do, but there's not a single patch of non-vertical ground that isn't already a part of this makeshift road. We're caught between steep cliff walls and sheer drops into canyons, just as we had been on our way towards Lake Koman this morning. All we can do is to keep moving forwards and hope. We'll keep riding until we find either a town, or the dawn, whichever comes first.

Just as I'm losing all hope of ever seeing civilization again, it happens. Without warning or reason, a black line across the rough sandy track marks the beginning of tarmac. We're probably no more than ten kilometres from the border with Kosovo and the sandy track has suddenly transformed.

We're riding on a brand new, beautifully smooth, four-lane highway with long sweeping curves, gentle crests and a visible border between the road and the shoulder. There are no road markings, and most of the associated road furniture is still to be fitted, but the tarmac, that gorgeous black carpet beneath my tyres, feels like heaven. Behind us, a major storm is brewing. We can hear the booming claps of thunder and wild cracks of lightening that every few seconds light up the landscape around us. It's chasing us towards the border, running us out of Albania and we're only too happy to be racing ahead of it.

We pass through small hamlets that straddle the road and with each spectacular crack of lightening, signs of the recent conflict become visible. Every building has a traumatic tale to tell; pock marked, burned out, derelict. Every now and again, as the road sweeps to the left or to the right, my high beam picks out an abandoned military position; the long barrel of a not long silent gun, the cratered concrete shell of an old bunker and the menacing slits of a machine gun emplacement. To the accompaniment of thunder and lightning, it feels like we've entered an active war zone, a three dimensional computer game where we've become the hunted. I'm sure that we're still in Albania, but once again I'm both geographically and historically confused. I didn't think Albania had been a part of the Yugoslav and Kosovo wars, but clearly the evidence here suggests that they were. Eager to keep well ahead of the storm, I pick up the pace and try to enjoy the surreal experience.

With Adam following at a relatively safe distance behind me, I tip left into a long sweeping bend. A sign flashes past me, the only sign that I've seen on this road: 'Tunnel 50m'. As the Tiger clips the third apex of the long sweeping bend, what I find is not a tunnel but an electricity pylon, a menacing steel construction smack-bang in the centre of my lane. No time to brake. Left or right? I choose left, and put all of my faith in Triumph engineering.

The Tiger responds instantly and a foot-peg bites hard into the tarmac. Something at the rear of the bike clips the pylon's leg, the motorcycle bucks violently and instantly changes direction. The handle bars swing furiously between left and right locks. Thirty years of riding motorcycles on the road and it's my first experience of a full-on 'tank slapper'. I'd like to say that I used a lifetime of experience to bring the Tiger back under control, but that would be a lie. Aside from clenching my ass cheeks, I did absolutely nothing to help the situation. The Tiger did everything and despite my best efforts to kill both of us, it somehow managed to save the day. It was certainly a rich experience, an event that lasted for no more than two or three seconds, but it's an experience that I've absolutely no desire to repeat. Lesson learnt. If I get wet I'll dry out, but if I get killed then the journey's pretty much over, so I remind myself to slow the fuck down and to start enjoying the view.

With my heart rate returning somewhere close to normal, we arrive at the genuine exit point from Albania. It rewards us with an assortment of uncomfortably uniformed guards who seem intent on saluting me. After a few uncomfortable but humorous minutes of snapping heels and saluting hands, I realise why it's happening.

I'm wearing my Gore-Tex waterproofs, army surplus and very military in style. I've got a mosquito bite on the top my right ear and every time I start raising my hand to scratch it, they salute me. I feel a little bit silly and decide to live with the burning itch for a while. But then they spoil my mood by asking me to part with more money: 'Exit Tax, 2 Euros please'.

Looking on the bright side, the official tax seems to be a lot lower than the unofficial variety. Aside from local taxation and a few Euros for the ferry, we've spent absolutely no money in Albania. Come to think of it, we also spent nothing in Montenegro, Slovenia, Bosnia and Liechtenstein. Admittedly, we did pass through those fine countries at quite a brisk pace, but five countries with no money spent feels like a very strange kind of achievement. I know that it isn't very helpful for the local economies, but their loss is certainly our gain and my budget is actually holding up quite well.

'Welcome to Kosovo Mr Thomas, I hope you have a wonderful stay and please ask if you need any assistance'. On this side of the border the guard's uniforms appear to fit properly, and their guns, instead of being casually slung into waistbands and belts, have proper leather holsters. To me, that makes them a lot less menacing, but it still encourages politeness. Sadly, we need to purchase transit insurance for the motorcycles, but the border guard who speaks perfect classroom English, helps with the translation. The minimum insurance is for thirty days and costs us 20 Euros each. It's expensive, but it's compulsory, so there's absolutely no point dwelling on it.

My new best friend then kindly informs me that Manchester United have just clinched the English Premiership, Boris Johnson is the newly elected Mayor of London and the Champions League final between Manchester United and Chelsea will be shown live on television here in Kosovo. It's been a pleasant but slightly expensive welcome into Kosovo, but we're tired, it's dark, and the storm is still chasing us. We need to find a place to rest for the night.

Time spent at the border crossing has allowed the storm to gain on us. We arrive in the town of Prizren and as we fill up with fuel, the rain begins to pour. The young lad who fills up my Tiger appears to be an apprentice fixer, smiley and chatty in equal measures. The fuel is thankfully cheap, so I tip him 2 Euros for his service and ask him if there's anywhere reasonably cheap where we can rest our weary bones for the night. Without providing me with an answer, he just vanishes into the service station. That's gratitude for you.

I go in search of coffee and find some of the finest yet served. Physically Kosovo seems to be a world apart from Albania, but I believe that Kosovo isn't even a properly recognised country. Just before we'd set out from England, I can remember reading somewhere that Kosovo had declared independence from Serbia, but I don't think its status as an independent country has as yet been confirmed. As far as I know, Serbia still claims the region of Kosovo as its own and the United Nations Mission in Kosovo are here to keep the peace. At least I hope they keep the peace, because I certainly don't do wars.

As I sit beside the Tiger contemplating the political fabric of Kosovo and draining the last dregs of delicious coffee, a large new Mercedes with black paint and matching windows, draws to a halt in front of me. With a hiss of anticipation, the front window lowers and a shadowy figure requests in relatively good English, that we follow him. Before leaving Albania, Jack had warned me to be wary of such people in Kosovo. But, ignoring Jack's advice, I leave the heavy steel wrench in its holder and once again put my trust in the kindness of strangers.

Through dark back streets, the Mercedes races ahead. Across slippery wet cobbles, between small shops and cafes that are closed and in darkness, we follow the mysterious car at an uncomfortable speed. I've no idea where we're going, I don't know who this person is, but I'm far too tired and hungry to do anything but follow him. Finally, the car draws to a screeching halt at a well lit shabby chic hotel in what I assume is the centre of town. The driver emerges and introduces himself as the owner of the filling station where we'd just filled up with gas. With him in the car is his entire workforce, including the young lad who'd accepted my generous tip. In response to my request to find reasonably priced accommodation, they've closed the filling station early and escorted us here to a hotel that we would never have found by ourselves.

The hotel comes as a welcome relief from squatting and camping. Between all too frequent power cuts, we steal electricity for our various gadgets and borrow free sachets of everything from the service trolley in the corridor. I'd promised not to stay in hotels and twice I've broken that rule, but thankfully this hotel is cheap. Mr Mercedes had entered before us and cut an exclusive deal with the duty manager. They'd raised a quizzical eyebrow when we'd asked for only one room, but I hadn't taken time to explain that the arrangement was purely for financial reasons. They arranged secure underground parking for the Tigers and even turned a security camera onto them for additional protection.

The short ride to reach the entrance for the secure parking had been interesting. It'd been executed during one of the many power cuts and maybe the darkness had helped to disguise the fact that we probably broke every motoring law in Kosovo. With Adam following, I'd taken us the wrong way along the busy one-way High Street, turned left against a 'No Entry' sign and completed the last hundred metres riding through pavement cafes. It was the only way that I could see of getting there, it was either that or a journey of chance around an unknown and confusing one-way traffic system in darkness. Besides, I'm a despatch rider and it's good to keep in practice.

This morning, slightly later than planned but a little earlier than could be considered lazy, we're heading out of Prizren beneath clear blue skies. The roads leading south out of town are busy with traffic. There are police and United Nations military vehicles everywhere. Something flies through my open jacket and into the top of my tee shirt. I don't check my mirrors or indicate, I don't look for a convenient place to pull over, I just jump onto the kerb and kick down the stand on the pavement.

Within seconds, I'm off the Tiger and ripping off my clothes. Adam, several stationary policemen and half of the UN force in Kosovo, look on in wonderment. 'Bitch!' It's stung me six times and the large white welts are already surrounded by growing red blotches. The dreaded burning black fly has found me. I've no idea what these little bastards are called, but they look like black wasps and contact with any part of their bodies seems to replicate the sting of a bee. The policemen are laughing and pointing fingers. I feel like a wimp, embarrassed at being defeated by a fly, so I quickly replace my clothes and act like this is just the normal behaviour of any Englishman in the sun. We ride on.

By daylight, the severity of the recent conflict here in Kosovo becomes clear and every building seems to have a traumatic story to tell. I believe that Kosovo and Serbia were both part of the Former Republic of Yugoslavia, but in late 1998 they came to blows in a dispute over territory. Kosovo had demanded its independence and Serbian leader Slobodan Milosevic had taken exception to their request. The ensuing conflict had been ruthless and bloody, and the United Nations had eventually come down on the side of Kosovo and implemented air strikes against Milosevic's superior Serb forces.

The action by NATO forces had stopped Milosevic in his tracks, prevented further bloodshed and introduced an entirely new phrase to the English language; 'Humanitarian War'. In the West we'd been told that Milosevic was a bad sort, and our sympathies had fallen firmly with the outgunned and outnumbered freedom fighters of the Kosovo Liberation Army. 'Freedom Fighter' is an emotive term, but up until a few weeks before NATO's military intervention, the United States, United Kingdom and United Nations had all had a slightly different official classification for the Kosovo Liberation Army: The KLA were officially classified as an 'Islamic Terrorist Organisation', which suggests that the difference between a 'Freedom Fighter' and a 'Terrorist' is determined only by a politician's fancy. I'm not saying that the NATO intervention in Kosovo wasn't justified, and it probably saved an awful lot of lives, but when an external force settles an internal fight with additional violence, the original fight never reaches a natural conclusion and the peace that follows is probably a false one.

I guess the outcome of those political and military actions are what we have now, but exactly what we do have now in Kosovo, I honestly couldn't say. The people here seem friendly, happy and welcoming, getting along with their lives and doing everything that they need to do in order to get by. However, I've got the underlying feeling that I'm travelling through a powder keg that could ignite at any moment. Left to their own devices, I'm sure that Serbs, Bosniaks, Croats, Kosovo's and Albanian's could probably get along quite nicely together, but I honestly fear that at some point in the future, politician's and the media will insist on playing with their matches again.

I'd like to understand the truth behind what really happened here, and what's happening now, but because of the way that history and current events are documented, maybe the real truth will never be found. History as we know it, tends to be written by people with a vested interest in what it tells us. As Winston Churchill famously said 'History will be kind to me, for I intend to write it'. I hate not knowing the answers to questions, but as I travel, I seem to be finding far more questions than answers, and that's maybe why I'm travelling.

By lunchtime, we reach the Macedonian border and we're each charged the princely sum of 50 Euros for temporary motorcycle insurance. We'll be in Macedonia for less than four hours and the cost hurts like hell. But insurance isn't optional in these parts and the 'European Insurance Policies' that we'd purchased back in England are useless out here. We pay the price, and entre.

I know very little about Macedonia and during the planning stage it was never much more than a country that I'd pass through in order to reach Greece. I know that The Republic of Macedonia is land-locked and that the local currency is the Denar, but that's only because I changed some money at the border crossing. I didn't know what to expect from our short time in this country, but I was about to find out, accidentally of course. Sometimes the best experiences are the accidental ones. When you go with the flow, you often find unusual riches that you could never have imagined.

In Macedonia there exists a motorway unlike any other in the world. It runs from Skopje, heading south towards the border with Greece. It begins like any other major road, passing through towns where congestion and pollution constantly remind me of home. The road is blighted by endless road works and maniac drivers. You then approach a toll gate where you pay 40 Denar (fifty pence) for access. An alternative 'Free' road runs south and I can only assume that the locals all take that option. This Motorway, designated the numbers '1' and '75', is almost free of traffic. So release the Tigers and let the fun begin.

Just south of the toll gate, the north and south carriageways part company and skirt around opposite sides of a range of hills that I really can't name. The three wide lanes of tarmac are quite bumpy in parts, but are more than usable. But for the absence of countdown markers at each bend, and the abundance of speed limit signs, you'd swear that you were on a racing circuit. Actually, this motorway reminds me very much of the Nuerburg Ring in Germany, but at just 40 Denar a go, it's a hell of a lot cheaper to enjoy.

Most motorways are relatively straight, they tend to carve the easiest possible line from point to point, but here the planners have chosen to follow the contours of the hillside, every single gorgeously beautiful fast flowing one of them. Reading this account of the journey might give you the impression that we're constantly racing our bikes, but that's not really true. With just £20 for daily expenses, including fuel, we have no alternative but to nurse the motorcycles. We try to conserve fuel, tyres and other consumables, and that means taking our time and riding well within the limits of the Tigers. On the other hand, we're not just here to enjoy the places that we visit, or the people we befriend along the way. We're here to enjoy the journey and if we'd wanted to potter along in traffic at 20mph all day, then we'd be travelling by campervan.

We chose to ride motorcycles, because motorcycles are what we love. So, when an amazing road appears and the way ahead is clear, the riding becomes slightly more spirited. These are roads that we'll never ride again, so we try to make them as memorable as possible, but hopefully memorable for all of the right reasons.

This motorway is one of those amazing roads, not quite a contender for 'World's Best Road', but it's certainly on top of the 'B-list'. Our carriageway is probably twenty-five metres wide and the road ahead is clear. We pick up the pace and start having fun. We're nowhere near the limits of the bikes capabilities, we're relaxed, we're smiling, and we take it in turns to lead. The curves are varied, some tighter than others, some amazingly long and cambered, but all can be taken at relatively high speeds.

The few cars that we do meet are travelling at much lower speeds, they hug the centre lane and we tend to pass them without ceremony. In the far distance, I see a small white car vanishing over a crest and ignore it for the moment. Around huge outcrops of rock, the road becomes a series of blind and fast switchback turns. We each take different lines, crossing in the centre and it puts me in mind of a television advertisement from many years ago: Fiat Strada's performing an amazing synchronised ballet on a banked racing circuit to the music from Figaro. We're obviously not quite as graceful, but the Tigers seem to be the ideal motorcycles for this kind of riding.

The peaks of the rocks are getting lower and the road opens up in front of us. We accelerate and pass the white Lada riding line-a-stern. At such close quarters, the markings on the sides of the Lada are clearly visible: 'POLICE'.

Stop or run? I can sense Mom looking to Dad for guidance, but he's just shrugging his shoulders. He'd always told me that I should never run away from anybody or anything, but I'm not sure if 'Anyone' would include angry Macedonian traffic cops. The police car's a Lada, and we're only a few miles north of the Greek border. But, will he have the ability to radio ahead to his colleagues? What do Macedonian prisons look like from the inside?

My speedometer was showing '120' when we passed him, but was that in kilometres or miles? I fear that it might have been miles per hour. I ignore the flashing blue light that's growing smaller in my mirrors and run for the border with Greece and the freedom of deserted beaches. Poor Circulation, chasing heaven and raising hell.

Chapter 15:
Greece

Entering Greece from Macedonia was simplicity itself. We'd arrived at the border with nothing in pursuit, shown our passports and ridden innocently through. It's early evening, but it's hotter than hell and the Greek traffic is suffocating. It feels familiar, like London in a heat wave, so we head for the nearest stretch of coast where we hope to find a beach where we'll rest our aching bones. We've got time on our side and the next few days can be dedicated to idleness. Recharge the batteries, drink retsina and eat fish until the calendar dictates that we once again start heading east.

We ride on, following the compass towards the nearest coastline and as night falls, arrive at a town called Retikas. It's not a town that appears on my map, but that matters little. The ground is flat, the taverna's open and the Retsina's cold. The grilled sardines arrive and the night is made complete with Greek coverage of the Eurovision Song Contest. At home in England we tend to mock this annual event, but in these parts it's a contest that they seem to take rather seriously. Every other customer is glued to the television, clapping along with songs and confidently predicting the results.

I meet the local vendor of religion, a giant of a man with a welcoming smile and red flowing beard. We talk for an hour and Father Michael tells me that he loves England and beer. I take that as a not too subtle hint and order him a litre of ice cold lager. He speaks good English, but only when he chooses to. He's warm and friendly and laughs at the end of every sentence. He notices the image of Buddha that hangs around my neck and raises an eyebrow. I tell him that I'm not a Buddhist, but an atheist, and he just chuckles to himself. He tells me that he has one wife and five beautiful children and that surprises me. I'd always thought that priests weren't allowed to marry, but apparently they can, because there are many different kinds of priest. I'm not certain what kind Father Michael is, but he's certainly the kind that I like.

Of course, Father Michael wasn't always a priest and he tells me of the past. His best years, years spent in a hamlet called Komotini where he'd helped people to escape into Greece from the then communist state of Bulgaria. He'd clearly enjoyed those days of positive human trafficking, but now he fears for Greece. He laughs and tells me that now the opportunities for young Greeks lay in the opposite direction, for Greece is not what it was and Bulgaria is the new land of opportunity.

Then, he escorts me outside and from the rear seat of his car, collects a small case containing what I suspect are the tools of his priestly trade. In a language that I assume to be Latin, he blesses both motorcycles and offers a special prayer to ensure that the Special Package arrives safely at its destination. With the ceremony completed, Father Michael wishes me a goodnight and drives away. Official priest or not, he's shared an hour of his fascinating life with me and I'm grateful for his generosity.

This morning, I wake in my tent to glorious sunshine and the sound of the sea. We're camping only meters from the waves, at the side of another taverna where the owner has kindly allowed us to pitch our tents without charge. Today we plan to ride into Bulgaria and then return to Greece before heading towards Istanbul. My map shows a small road heading north from the town of Komotini towards the border where we can cross into Bulgaria. It's the place Father Michael had mentioned and somewhere that I really want to see for myself.

Using the compass and a little blind faith, we start riding north along roads that have never seen tarmac and remind me very much of Albania. The signs for the small villages are all in Greek and don't seem to correspond to any of the names on my map. That doesn't really matter because if we keep riding north, then eventually we must reach the border with Bulgaria.

At a small village high in the hills, we stop to drink water and I ask in the local grocery store for directions. They don't seem to understand my request, so I'm ushered to the office of the local mayor where they do understand. It's clearly explained that although we are close to the border with Bulgaria, there is no way of crossing the border from here. The mayor then explains that while there's no 'official' crossing point into Bulgaria, there might be a path that's known only to the locals. Unfortunately, as the Mayor, he couldn't possibly assist in my illegal entry into Bulgaria. Then, with a mischievous glint in his eyes, he slips me a small scrap of paper upon which he's been doodling.

Outside in the sunshine I take a closer look at it. It's a sketch map upon which he's marked the route to the border, the landmarks that we should look for and the military posts that I guess we should probably avoid. What a lovely Mayor, he certainly gets my vote.

We slowly climb higher into the hills, avoiding donkeys, snakes and tortoise at every bend. The road becomes increasingly difficult but the Tigers perform well. When Triumph Tigers roll off the production line at Hinckley in Leicestershire, they wear 'Michelin Anakee' tyres. These tyres are classified as 'Dual Sport', but they certainly prefer tarmac to sand. On tarmac they're perfect, and on sand they're suspect, but we're hoping for longevity and must learn to live with their shortcomings on roads such as these.

Slipping and sliding on sand demands serious concentration, and while trying to remain upright we accidentally ride straight passed a military post that the mayor had advised us to avoid. I can hear Mom telling me to be careful, but thankfully the bored soldiers just seem to look at us with a hint of suspicion before returning to their task of sleeping. We turn east along an even rougher track following the line drawn on the roughly sketched map. After six or seven kilometres, we finally see it, the border between Greece and Bulgaria.

Amid a tangle of rusting razor wire, there are white skeins and posts that mark the border between the two nations. We've found the unofficial crossing point into Bulgaria, possibly the same crossing point that Father Michael had used many years earlier. I carefully draw back some loose razor wire and we informally enter our twentieth country of the journey, Bulgaria.

Ten years ago, we might have been shot on sight for doing this, and maybe today it's still a serious criminal offence. But what the hell, there are probably already arrest warrants issued against us in Macedonia, so we might as well add Greece and Bulgaria to that list. I just hope that Interpol have bigger fish to fry.

It would be easy to stay much longer in Greece, but we've only got eight days until we're due to enter Russia and at our current rate of progress, it will take every one of those days to reach the border. We've been riding east all day and stopping to look at anything and everything of interest. It's hot. In fact for Englishmen it's uncomfortably hot and we find ourselves constantly drawn back towards the coast in search of the refreshing cool breeze from the Aegean. I somehow manage to miss the large town of Lagos and find ourselves in a small marina called Fanari.

Fanari's a small town that's had an awful lot of recent investment. Much money has been spent on new public parks, promenades, trendy cafes, small nightclubs and bars, but the place is almost deserted. Fanari seems to have everything it needs, but people. At a deserted café, we eat kebabs sliced from a suspiciously large skewer of meat. They're delicious, but I do worry about eating precooked meats in quiet restaurants like this. I ask the solitary waiter if there's anywhere that we can possibly pitch our tents for a night. I'm hoping that he'll say 'Right here Sir', but sadly he doesn't. Instead, he studies the map and points to a place just a little further east. 'Fanari Camping Ground', we'll find camping there.

A few miles beyond the strangely quiet marina, we stop beneath a huge blue and white sign. 'E.O.T. Camping Fanari'. At the main entrance there's a small office and a security kiosk, but the barriers into the campground are closed and secured with giant padlocks and great lengths of chain. Looking through the grimy office window, I can see that in the past this place has been highly recommended. Rosettes for quality and service adorn the office walls, but the annual sequence of awards seems to end abruptly. 'Campsite of The Year 2004', and nothing thereafter.

The monkey that lives on my shoulder is talking, then shouting, and then screaming at the top of his voice. Curiosity overcomes me and I scramble over the barriers. Adam follows and what we find inside is really rather spooky. It's a site of some fifty acres that contains five hundred or so touring and static caravans. Each caravan is neatly positioned in a small walled enclave with its own once beautiful private garden. The caravans are all empty of people, but filled with the evidence of inhabitation.

The people have gone, but they've clearly left this place in a great hurry. Partially eaten petrified meals sit on tables, sinks are full of dirty crockery and fridges hold the rotten remains of fresh produce that was never eaten. Every single caravan, large and small, expensive and economy, has been abandoned. The overgrowth around the site suggests that the place has been untouched for at least two or three summers. But why was it abandoned in such a hurry? At the opposite side of the campsite, we find an abandoned shop, a restaurant, a cafe and a long empty swimming pool. Vandals have destroyed everything and left their spray painted tags on every flat surface. Beyond the crumbling wall is a private beach, a few hundred metres of pristine sand with strong high fencing at either end.

We take photographs and video before realising that the sun is beginning to set and back down in the beautifully shaded site, the paths are now in total darkness. 'Rather Spooky' has now become downright 'Bloody Scary'. I start hearing noises that aren't really there and see shadows that really ought not to move. We know roughly how to get back to the Tigers, but we must tread carefully to avoid tripping in undergrowth that's now overtaken the gravel paths. Treading carefully lasts for all of a few seconds, and then we start running. I run like I haven't run in a very long time and after we vault back over the entrance gates, we break into uncontrolled laughter.

Yes, we're laughing now, but I don't mind telling you that I was honestly scared in that place. I'd love to know the story behind the abandonment of E.O.T. Camping Fanari, but I'm really not keen on exploring any more, even in daylight. Thankfully the Tigers are exactly where we'd left them, unmolested by ghosts and able to transport us away from one of the scariest places that I've ever had the pleasure, or misfortune, to visit.

Other than my meeting with the priest, the short and illicit adventure into Bulgaria and a rather spooky tour around the abandoned campsite, Greece has been something of a disappointment. I'm not sure what I'd expected, but it seems that the people here are perhaps a little bit shy. When we stop, the people observe us from a safe distance and they don't approach us unless we approach them first. Maybe it's a cultural thing, but I'm actually beginning to miss the poking fingers and personal questions that were openly asked in the Balkans. Perhaps Asia will be different. Roll on Turkey.

Chapter 16:
Gallipoli, Turkey

Entering Turkey couldn't be easier. I pay 3 Euros for a one month motorcycle insurance certificate, 10 Euros for a three month tourist visa and 7 Euros for 200 'Cont' cigarettes. There are no additional taxes, official or unofficial, no palms to be greased or open pockets to be filled. It's all just very polite and efficient. I pay the money, the visa is stamped into my passport and I ride on through into Turkey.

Despite the best efforts of various British governments to tarnish our reputation around the world, being British still affords me certain privileges. The availability of 'Visa on Arrival' is one of them. My British nationality has absolutely nothing to do with who I am, or what choices I've made in my life, it's simply a happy accident of birth. But, it makes travelling an awful lot easier than it otherwise might be, and for that benefit alone, I will count my blessings.

Safely across the border, we pull into the first petrol station. I don't have any Turkish Lire, but thankfully they happily accept my Euros. We've got an awful lot of Turkish miles to cover and I've just discovered that Turkish petrol isn't just expensive, it's bloody expensive. At first, I'd thought that the young pump attendant had ripped me off by converting my Euros in favour of himself or his boss. But he hadn't been trying to cheat me. The fuel works out at just over £6 per gallon and that's 20% higher than it had been back in London. Because of this, our ride across Turkey might now become a rather slow and economical one.

After entering Turkey, I'd always intended to ride east and spend a few days exploring the amazing city of Istanbul. I've been there before, back in the days when I was an awful lot younger and slightly richer, and I'd absolutely loved the experience. It's a place that Mom and Dad had considered visiting shortly before Dad had been diagnosed with prostate cancer back in 1997. Istanbul wasn't one of Mom's 'Official Wishes', but it would be nice to take them there now.

Unfortunately, Adam doesn't feel confident enough to ride into the city. I have to agree that the eclectic vibrancy of Istanbul, the things that make it such an exciting city to visit, also make it amazingly chaotic. Istanbul is fun, vibrant and wild, and if you're going to officially cross from Europe into Asia, then Istanbul is probably the most memorable place to do it, but there are alternatives. Mom clearly wanted to go there, Dad too, but I feel that Mom's also encouraging me to compromise. The alternative route would take us down onto the Gallipoli Peninsula and then across The Dardanelles from Europe into Asia. I'm slightly disappointed that we won't be riding into Istanbul, but I'm also excited by the prospect of seeing Gallipoli. I've never been there and I'd like to see for myself the places where so many lives were needlessly lost in the Great War.

After a short ride to the Turkish town of Kesan, we turn south and arrive in the port of Gallipoli on the Dardanelles. I find a Cash Machine that thankfully gives me the option of conducting my transaction in English, but strangely, it will only give me Euros. Turkey isn't a member of the European Union, and because of certain political and human rights issues it might be some time before full membership is achieved, but the cash machine won't give me any Turkish Lire. I don't mind using Euros here, but when all of the prices are advertised in Lire, doing the mental currency conversions could be tiresome.

Thankfully at the third bank, I find a Cash Machine that does allow me to withdraw Lire and I find out that I'm not quite as wealthy as I'd hoped. It would be nice to have a wallet full of notes with the number '1000' written large in the corners. Let's face it, that's never going to happen for me when I'm dealing in Euros, Pounds or US Dollars, but I'd hope that it might happen here in Turkey. However, at just 1.8 Lire for every 1 Euro, the Turkish Lire bares no similarity to Italy's former currency. It seems that at least until I reach Russia, I'm destined to remain poor.

Back at the bikes, I meet a young man from Hackney who's returned to

Turkey in order to complete his National Service. He seems quite relaxed about the idea and he's certainly not missing East London. He wishes us luck for the journey and as he wanders away he's replaced by three young kids who are also fluent in the essentials of English. 'Beckham', 'Ronaldo', 'Rooney', 'Chelsea', 'Man U'. They pose for photos and will only leave me alone after they've eaten all of my biscuits and relieved me of three Poor Circulation badges and a copy of The Riders Digest magazine containing the story of the journey. We've been in Turkey for less than a day and we've thankfully returned to interacting with really friendly people. It's great, everybody wants to talk and kill time with us. We're probably less than a hundred miles from the border with Greece, but the people here seem to be much more approachable.

We check on the times for tomorrows ferry crossings to Lapeski on the opposite side of the Dardanelles. They seem to run at thirty minute intervals throughout the day and the total cost will be just 6 Lire. That's £4 for two motorcycles and two riders and it's an absolute bargain. With our exit route from the peninsula booked and paid for, we head out to explore the area.

South of Gallipoli, I turn west at Kilye Cove and head for the war memorials at the centre of the peninsula. It's Sunday, it's early afternoon and the tourist coaches are moving thousands of people on the narrow and melting road system. We visit Johnston's Jolly, Lone Pine and Quinn's Post Memorials where the mood is sombre and reflective. It's mostly soldiers from Australia and New Zealand who're buried here, yet their graves and memorials are still immaculately maintained. Gallipoli is often seen as just a joint Australian and New Zealand campaign, but the number of British casualties was actually far higher than the combined losses of the other allied forces. At the memorials we visit, if you ignore the burning midday sun, then you could easily think that you were back in Ypres or Flanders. Without knowing anything about the history, in places like this you can simply feel that at some time in the recent past, a catastrophic event has taken place.

The Gallipoli campaign began in 1915 as an attempt by allied forces to capture Istanbul and secure the supply route into Russia. Under the direction of Winston Churchill, the Royal Navy had attempted to destroy the defences on the Gallipoli peninsula with a massive artillery bombardment but had suffered heavy losses and withdrawn to safer waters before their mission had been completed. In April 1915, divisions of the Australian and New Zealand Army Corps (ANZAC) had landed on the beaches of Gallipoli, but due to the failure of the Royal Navy's bombardment, the Turk's had been well prepared for the expected invasion.

The unsuccessful campaign lasted for almost eleven months and during that time more than one hundred and thirty thousand lives had been lost. Following the end of World War I, the Dardanelles Commission reported that the Gallipoli Campaign had been badly planned, poorly researched and that the British Government had exasperated the situation with its procrastination and incompetence. I can't imagine ever seeing the words 'Successful' and 'War' in the same sentence, unless of course it was a 'Successful War on Famine', but brave and innocent people losing their lives because of poor planning, poor research and government incompetence seems frighteningly familiar. Clearly, some lessons are never learned.

Higher up in the hills, hundreds of families gather together at noon and pray at the Turkish Memorials. Following the Muslim midday worship, the 'duhr' prayers, they sit down on large blankets and together enjoy their food and drink. In stark contrast to the ANZAC memorials which are beautiful but sombre, the Turkish memorials seem to feel more like an area for reflective celebration of the young people who gave their lives here. They're not celebrating war or victory, but they seem to remember the lost lives in a way that we would find difficult to accept in Northern France or Belgium. It's actually very refreshing to experience this at first hand and we could probably all learn some lessons here. I leave the Turkish memorials with a better understanding of what happened here in Gallipoli. But, unlike my previous visits to Ypres, I'm not heavy with regret but filled with confidence that if the people of the world can continue to view such pointless destruction in the same way, then there's a greater chance that such conflicts will never be repeated. 'Inshallah'.

We've found a deserted camping ground close to the small hamlet of Kum on the southern tip of the peninsula. The tents are pitched as close to the sea as possible and I'm sitting looking at the motorcycles. In fact, we're both sitting down and looking at them. I should unpack the stove and start cooking dinner, but I honestly can't be bothered to do it. Today's been hot, probably the hottest day of the journey so far, and it feels as if all of my energy has been sapped away with my sweat. I'm not complaining, because seeing the ages of the fallen young soldiers back at the memorials has reminded me of just how lucky we are. At certain times, despite my many claims to the contrary, both of us have probably felt that what we're doing is in some way a 'Hardship', but today's experience has hammered everything into perspective. Tonight we'll eat dinner at a restaurant attached to the campsite and raise a few cold glasses of beer to the memory of the fallen from both sides, and say a temporary farewell to Europe. I can almost hear Dad shouting at me from the Tiger: 'You don't know you're born son'.

Dinner was great, an 'All You Could Eat' buffet with somebody else cooking the food and washing the dishes for a change. It was good to relax for an evening and wasn't as expensive as I'd feared. I'm now sitting on the empty beach with a pack of cold beer, the Special Package and my diary. I'm watching the sky turn a deep shade of orange as the sun finally sets. It's beautiful here and the only sound is that of the waves breaking on the beach at my feet and a few hungry ducks that have gathered a few metres behind me. The bottom of the sun touches the sea and I'm sure that I can see the still waters boiling all around it. It begins to sink deeper and the sky beyond the huge orange orb turns to inky blackness as it waits for the moon. Watching the sheer brilliance of this sunset, I can easily understand why certain ancient societies thought that the sun actually fell into the sea each evening, and rose from it again in the morning. It's one of the most inspiring sunsets that I've ever seen in my life and I've exhausted the memory card in my camera taking photographs of it.

I've switched on my mobile phone and once again on this journey, I've got full signal strength in the absolute middle of nowhere. I've sent a text message to my daughter Hannah back in England. I'm missing her laughter and friendship, but I expect to receive nothing more than a very limited literary response from her. She's a teenager so it'll probably be 'OK', which now seems to have been shortened to just 'K', but at least her regular emails offer a little more substance. Perhaps she thinks that Vodafone charge by the letter, or perhaps she's just as I said, a 'Teenager'.

I wake to the sound of the Muezzin calling the faithful to dawn prayers from an unseen minaret. I don't understand all of the words, but it's a sound that I love to hear. It reminds me that I'm travelling and it's an exciting start to another new day. Adam's head appears from his tent, but his initial opinion differs wildly from my own: 'What a fucking racket'. I laugh. I don't think Adam's having a 'dig' at Islam, it's just something that he's never heard before and the timing and volume have clearly taken him by surprise. As we pack up the tents and prepare to leave Europe behind us, I try to explain the five daily prayers of the faith, and that the Muez-

The Lone Pine Memorial at Gallipoli

zin calling is just like the peeling of church bells at home, only different.

On the ferry from Gallipoli to Lapeski, I meet my new best friend, Osman. Using sheets of paper upon which he's written various random phrases, he practices his English with me. While we talk and joke together, Osman holds tightly onto my knee or onto my hand, sometimes he holds onto both, but he never holds onto neither. His English is very good and in return for spending time with him, I get the opportunity to practice my amazingly rusty Arabic. He should really be teaching me the basics of Turkish, but Osman insists that as I already speak a smattering of Arabic, then refreshing that will be far more productive than trying to learn Turkish from scratch. I give Osman a Poor Circulation badge and it's as if I've just handed him a priceless diamond. He's almost in tears and can't stop thanking and hugging me.

The ferry crossing has taken just thirty minutes, but passing the time with Osman has made it feel more like five. As we prepare to ride our motorcycles away from the ferry into the town of Lapeski, Adam asks me about my physical interactions with Osman. He's probably worried about a sudden change in my sexuality, but I can only smile and tell him: 'Welcome to Asia'.

Chapter 17:
Turkey

On the Asian side of the Dardanelles, we ride north hugging the coast, and for no other reason than the attractiveness of its name, I turn away from the busy main road and head into the town of Biga. I stop at what looks to be a large international bank at the side of the road and withdraw some money from one of its many Cash Machines. As my confirmation receipt appears from the ATM, I hear an unfamiliar voice behind us. I turn around and see a cool young guy standing next to a Yamaha Virago motorcycle. He's wearing wrap-around shades and no crash helmet. 'Follow me, we will drink tea together'.

We follow the Yamaha around the corner and enter a cobbled street with a large sign stating 'Pedestrians Only', which we ignore. We park the Tigers on the pavement next to a rather strange looking chopper, the likes of which I've never seen before. Our new friend on the Yamaha introduces himself as Tevfik, and tells us that he owns the Converse Store here in this shopping street in Biga. His long-haired leather wearing friend Ayhan sells handmade ethnic jewellery from the stall behind us and passes the slower periods of the day entertaining pedestrians with rock ballads on his acoustic guitar. Ayhan turns out to be the owner of the unusual chopper, an aging motorcycle that I really quite like, but that Tevfik seems to mock. We sit together and drink hot sweet tea served in small shot glasses, delicious and refreshing.

Into the street comes a familiar looking motorcycle, a bright yellow Suzuki GS500 with two people aboard. I've already seen that motorcycle today, twice in fact. We're introduced to the new arrivals, rider Volkan and his passenger Ozgur. Together like long lost friends, the six of us sit in the centre of the shopping street talking about England, Turkey and motorcycles. Hot refreshing tea keeps arriving out of nowhere, glass after refreshing glass. Occasionally the tea is accompanied by rounds of beautifully toasted panini with tomato, cheese and salami, but we have absolutely no idea who's ordering or paying for any of it.

Tevfik then brings out a cura, a lute like instrument and accompanies Ayhan on his acoustic guitar. They give us a rendition of Turkish folk songs followed by Bob Dylan. It's by far the best improvised busking session that I've ever had the good fortune to attend. These guys are not just amazingly hospitable strangers, they're also mighty fine musicians.

Ozgur explains that he owns a fish & chip shop in Devon and is back in his native Turkey for a short holiday before the summer season begins again in England. He and Volkan were on their way to meet friends in Istanbul when they'd first seen us pass them on the road out of Lapeski. They'd turned around and chased us on and off for the last hour, hoping to catch up with us and guide us here to this very spot. Fate? Destiny? Chance? Call it what you will, they hadn't managed to catch us but we're here now and enjoying their company.

It seems to have been decided that soon we should all start riding north, up along the coast towards the sea of Marmaras where we'll find beachside camping for the night. From there, Volkan and Ozgur will head off to Istanbul, but before we start riding north Volcan must first oil his motorcycle chain at the auto souk. I've worked in the Middle East and I know what an 'Auto Souk' is, but for the life of me I can't understand why we need to go there in order to oil a motorcycle chain. I offer to do the job for him, here and now in the street, but Tevfik insist that we should all ride to the auto souks together.

While Volkan oils the chain on his Suzuki, Tevfik takes me to one side and quietly tells me that he has 'Secrets'. Apparently they're secrets that only I can be shown, but I must promise not to tell another living soul about them. I love mysteries, and I have absolutely no idea what these particular secrets will involve, so of course I agree to go with him. Leaving the others behind, I nervously ride pillion on Tevfik's wobbling Yamaha.

We cruise around the auto souks and at every small industrial unit, his friends come to the entrances to wave and shout greetings. It's clear that Tevfik is an important and popular fellow in these parts, and he isn't afraid to show it. Having ridden passed every building in the district, we finally arrive at a small workshop where I'm introduced to an old but distinguished looking gentleman. He's quite short and lean, with wispy white hair that's a stranger to grooming. He wears classic blue overalls with the confidence of a man who knows how to use them. Tevfik warns me that I can speak openly with the old man, but under no circumstances should I touch him, unless of course he invites me to do so. I'm confused, but once again I blindly agree. We smile, and seemingly comfortable with my ability to maintain the secrets that are about to be revealed, the old man invites me to follow him into his workshop. The three secrets are to be revealed to me in turn, and as Tevfik explains, each will be a little more amazing than the one that went before.

The first of these secrets is being guarded by a snappy little dog. It's tethered on a short rope and trying hard to bite at my ankles. Whatever the first secret is, it's certainly being very well protected. In fact, it turns out not to be guarding the secret at all. The snappy little dog is the secret. It's not a dog, it's a jackal. I'm not entirely sure why this should be such an amazing secret, but then again, I'm not too familiar with guard dog etiquette in this part of the world.

For the second secret to be revealed, I'm escorted to the rear of the old man's workshop and taken to what I suspect to be the enclosed maintenance pit, the sunken trench that's generally used to inspect and repair the undersides of vehicles. An oil covered metal trap door is lifted and I'm invited to look down into the pit, but all I can see is darkness. Then, a switch is thrown and light comes up from the bottom. It's not an inspection pit at all. I'm looking at an amazing natural formation of rocks, an underwater cave that's teaming with fish of all varieties and what I assume to be the king of the natural aquarium, a giant grey moray eel that must be two or three metres in length. I'm stunned, this is totally surreal. In a grimy old garage in the auto souks of Biga, beneath an unremarkable floor, the likes of which you would see in any other garage anywhere in the world, I'm staring down into a natural aquarium that wouldn't look out of place in Disneyland. I have no idea why it's here, where the fish came from or even why it's such a closely guarded secret, but I'm grateful that they've shown it to me.

I've made a promise to Tevfik, a promise that I won't reveal the first two secrets until at least a year after the date upon which they were first revealed to me. Once again, I've no idea why he's made that request, but I've agreed to it anyway.

But that still leaves the third, and in Tevfik's eyes, the most amazing of all three secrets. I think that I've already seen the third secret. It's not something that's hidden, or even disguised, but it's probably something that would only be of interest to a motorcycle enthusiast. I'd noticed it when we'd first arrived here. I'd wanted to take a closer look at it, but the old man had noticed my interest and quickly drawn me away and introduced me to his jackal. As the trapdoor is closed and the lights to the underground aquarium extinguished, Tevfik asks me if I know what the third secret might be?

I tell him yes, it's a motorcycle. It's a small part of motorcycling history, and I've certainly seen one or two of them before, but it's not something that I'd ever expected to see hanging high from an iron rafter in the auto souks of Biga. It's a beautiful thing, styled by an Italian with a pencil rather than a bean-counter with a mouse and built in Germany where they know a thing or two about engineering. Black curving bodywork and glistening chrome, it's not simply an amazing motorcycle but an icon of design from an era when form was ultimately superior to function. Tevfik is in the process of purchasing the motorcycle from its owner, the old man of the souk. I'd like to know the price that Tevfik's being asked to pay, but I feel that it would be rude of me to ask. The old man is smiling and nodding, and I suspect that he's well aware of its true value. Tevfik's friends know nothing of this pending deal, or even of the motorcycles existence, but Tevfik knows that on the day that he rides before them on this beautiful 1930's motorcycle, he will indeed be the coolest dude in Biga.

Given more time, I would love to inspect the motorcycle more closely, but sadly there is no more time and we must leave. The old man embraces me and kisses both of my cheeks. He's party to the deal that I've made with Tevfik and happy for me to reveal the first two secrets a year from now, but the beautiful motorcycle must remain a secret until the deal is finalised and Tevfik has made his grand entrance.*

Volkan and Ozgur decide that it's time for us to follow them to the town of Erdek where we can swim in the sea and then camp for tonight on the beach. They claim that Erdek is on their way to Istanbul, though I

In early 2011, close to his home in Biga, Tevfik lost his life in a motorcycle accident. Tevfik never completed his deal with the 'Old Man of the Souk' and to the best of my knowledge, the motorcycle remains in his possession. For Tevfik's generosity, friendship and trust, I will forever be grateful. Ride in peace my friend.

Poor Circulation

suspect that it isn't, so they'll escort us there and help us to find a suitable place to camp before heading off to meet their friends. We say goodbye to Ayhan and Tevfik and follow the yellow Suzuki out of Biga at remarkably high speeds.

Erdek is some 70 miles from Biga, but it takes very little time to get there. The water is the warmest of the journey so far and we swim and talk in the shallows for an hour or more. A local boy is enlisted to guard our motorcycles while the owners of the Albatross Cafe Bar provide us with free beer and tea.

Unexpectedly, Ayhan arrives to join us on his unusual chopper. He'd found a small notebook that I'd accidentally left behind me in Biga, and he'd thought that it might be important to me. He's brought it seventy miles on his old two-stroke chopper and I'm amazingly touched. To celebrate Ayhan's arrival, Ozgur insists on taking us all out to dinner in the centre of town and Adam and I are not allowed to pay for anything.

After dinner, Ayhan gives free guitar lessons to a local girl while we head away with Volkan and Ozgur to find a suitable camping ground. We head along the coast road until the sun begins to set and Volkan stops for the fourth prayers of the day. With all of us being strangers to this area, we request assistance from two local brothers who are probably in their late sixties. Within seconds of meeting them, I'm heading east as a pillion on a rather swift but unsettlingly unstable little scooter. Above a small beach we pull to the side of the narrow road and inspect a potential campsite down by the water's edge.

Two men appear to be camping here already and a heated discussion takes place. One of the campers is holding a rather lethal looking snake that's just been killed by his dog. He smiles and shows me it's menacing fangs. I get the distinct impression that he's trying to scare me away from wanting to camp here on their beach. Despite my aversion to snakes of any variety, the beach looks ideal. The two men, who also turn out to be brothers, seem to live here on a permanent basis. They've created a little hamlet with an arrangement of tents, a small snake catching dog and a slightly larger fishing boat. It's a veritable home from home and after the heated discussion ends, the rider of the scooter raises an eyebrow to me 'Quais Sidiqu?' – 'Good my friend?' I raise a thumb in response and struggle with my Arabic: 'Kula quais al humdilila' – which I think means: 'This will do nicely'.

Arrangements for the nights camping have been made. I invite Ozgur and Volkan to share our tents for the night, it's the very least that I can do in response to their amazing hospitality, but sadly they must ride on. It's already 9pm and they'd hoped to be in Istanbul shortly after noon. They're already nine hours late and have several hours of hard riding ahead of them, so sadly they must leave now. As we watch them ride off into the night, Ishmail, the elder of the beach brothers, invites us to join them for 'chai' on the sand by the water's edge.

We're drinking more hot sweet tea with two strangers, Ishmail and Kalam, and listening to a dolphin chuckle and vent just a few metres from the shoreline. Kalam smiles and passes me a smouldering hand rolled cigarette that gives off a very familiar aroma. I take a deep draw, cough and the cares of the world start drifting away. We're from very different worlds but for one night at least, our lives have crossed and we share this beautiful beach together.

After a hard days riding from the Marmaras Sea, we finally reach the Black Sea. We'll follow the coastline of the Black Sea towards the north eastern port of Trabzon, from where we'll sail across to Sochi in Russia. I'd originally planned to ride up through Georgia into Russia, but it appears that since leaving England, Georgia has fallen out with Russia and all hell is being unleashed. I hate watching wars on television, and seeing the aftermath of them in the Balkans and Gallipoli is about as close as I ever want to come to one. So unfortunately, a visit to Georgia will have to wait until more peaceful times exist.

Today has been blisteringly hot and I search for another camping ground as close to the Black Sea as possible. I ask several people for help but they just keep sending us to places where we find small motels and lodges, but nowhere suitable to pitch our tents. It seems that they don't understand the European concept of 'Camping'. There are flat pieces of land that would be suitable, but when we're this close to the sea it seems a shame not to enjoy it. The beach would be my preferred option, but unfortunately the narrow sliver of land between road and beach is either already developed, or currently under construction. It appears that the once secret Black Sea coastline has been discovered by the money makers and is in the process of being exploited.

After several hopeful opportunities have been cruelly dashed, I ride back down the road and talk with the security guard at what appears to be the most exclusive housing complex on the seafront. I smile and ask if he'll allow us access to his fine beach for a spot of overnight camping. He seems uncertain, but I'm not sure if he's uncertain about camping or about me. Eventually he succumbs to my English charms and after being bribed with the most handsome gift of a Poor Circulation pin badge, he allows us to pass through his immaculate iron gates.

Once safely past the barrier, we come across an almost perfect set of sand dunes. Unfortunately, we're both a little inept at riding on sand and it's impossible to get the Tigers through the steep dunes and onto the beautiful beach beyond. As we're scouting for an alternative entry to the beach, I meet Ali. He and his father both have houses on this luxurious complex and he invites us to park the motorcycles at his home. From there, we can enjoy free and unrestricted access to the beach and all of their homely facilities.

An hour later, the tents are pitched just above the Black Sea and we're enjoying strawberries dipped in honey on Ali's beautifully appointed veranda. Ali turns out to be none other than Ankara's Chief of Police, England's equivalent to the Commissioner of the Met. Together with Ali's retired father and their respective wives, we fill our bellies with gorgeous food and make every effort to exhaust his seemingly endless supply of ice cold beer. As we all tuck into fresh strawberries dipped in honey, I find it impossible to stop laughing. After every mouthful, the wives announce that the strawberries are 'Bollocks' I have no idea what 'Bollocks' actually means in Turkish, but once again Poor Circulation has landed on its very fortunate feet.

As the sun sets, I sit alone on the beach updating my diary and drinking a final ice cold beer. In the past four nights we've camped on four different beaches, at the edge of four different seas, straddling two different continents. Tonight there probably won't be any dolphins to entertain me, and the sun certainly won't sink into the Black Sea, but life really can't get much better than this.

We're closing in on the port city of Trabzon, but not quite as quickly as I'd expected. The road is longer than I'd ever imagined and it's impossible not to keep stopping and interacting with Turkey's amazing people, especially those people who wear uniforms. This afternoon, we'd been travelling along a stretch of dual carriageway, inland from the coast and seriously dull. We weren't really speeding, just keeping pace with the local traffic, but I'll admit that we were travelling in the fast lane.

I'd had no idea that Turkey had two different speed limits, one for motorcars and one that's slightly lower for motorcycles, but we'd probably been exceeding both of them. We'd failed to notice the first police car, but the second was impossible to avoid because it had blocked the road ahead of us. At the shoulder of the road, voices were raised, police officers not ours, and documents were checked, ours not theirs. Nobody mentioned an actual speed, but we'd exceeded the lower speed limit by 50kph and the size of the fine was made quite clear, almost 200 Euros each.

It was time to talk and smile. Bring out the camera and pose for photographs, lots of photographs, make the police officers the centre of attention, important people on our journey. Offer them a copy of The Riders Digest magazine, an article about Poor Circulation, show them the photographs of our motorcycles and scribble a signature. Ask for the spelling of the officer's names, time to spread the great news about Turkey, time to make them famous. I promised to publish their pictures in the next issue of the magazine and we were waved on our way with nothing more serious than a verbal warning and a smile.

Our ride along Turkey's Black Sea coastline has been something of a revelation. Before starting this journey, this had been nothing more than another line that I'd drawn on the map, a route that would take me towards Georgia and Russia. Each day, the views from the coast road have filled my mind with dreams of building a house on the cliffs above the beach, or in the shelter of the perfectly formed coves that appear around every bend on this magnificent winding road.

The people are remarkably friendly and each day has been broken into segments where we've met new people and share bread and chai by the side of the sea, usually at their expense. Nobody hurries here, except on the roads which can be manic at times, but turn down into a cove and you'll usually find a small café on the water's edge, surrounded by an arch of red roses and enjoy the most refreshing glasses of chai that you can possibly imagine.

The experiences in Turkey have been sufficient enough to warrant their own individual book and are too great in number and richness to mention in depth. There was the rural baker and his elderly father who without a word of English between them, plied us with freshly baked bread, chai and conversation for two hours beneath a ramshackle shelter in the absolute middle of nowhere. A night spent sheltering from a significant thunderstorm on long tables beneath the canopy of a closed café on the seafront. The 3:00am visit from the cafés owner, who rather than lambasting us for soiling his premises, opened the café and provided us with free food and drink until dawn, and of course, the attitude of Turkey's friendly police officers.

Forget package tours to Greece and Spain, everybody should get a motorcycle and head down to Turkey's Black Sea coast. The road isn't quite as stunning as that running down the side of the Adriatic in Croatia, and the fuel is certainly far more expensive, but it's still relatively unspoilt here and the people are the most generous that you could ever wish to meet. It seems that once again on this journey the people who have the very least of anything, give the most of everything and ask for absolutely nothing in return. And for that, we are both truly thankful.

Chapter 18:
Georgia

'Police check will be at ten, maybe eleven ... or maybe a little later'. I love clarity. The ticket agent seems unsure of the precise time, but I get the feeling that 'precise' isn't a word normally associated with this overnight ferry service from Trabzon to Sochi. We should really be crossing the land border into Georgia, but as Georgia and Russia are currently exchanging insults and bullets, we've decided to take the easier route out of Turkey, the ferry.

'Then you must meet customs ... maybe at three ... or possibly five'. I ask why payment for the ferry crossing has to be made in US Dollars and not the local Turkish Lire, but the agent doesn't answer. I know that we're probably being hit for payments that we could probably avoid, but we're already a couple of days behind schedule and this 'Agent' seems to be our only hope of an early entry into Russia. I ask for an official receipt, perhaps hoping that this will somehow reduce the price, but I'm met with smiling silence. It seems that when you have a monopoly on the only means of exit from a port, and the alternative overland route is closed because of war, you charge whatever your market can afford and then manipulate the currency conversion rates. Sadly for us, that manipulation doesn't seem to be working in our favour.

The agent's place of business is a small and anonymous looking office located at the entrance to the port, the kind of place where many people come and go but little ever seems to happen. We wait, and then we wait some more. I get the distinct impression that they've forgotten about us. But, just as I'm about to remind everybody that we're still patiently waiting, there's a little action to relieve the boredom. The agent asks us to take our passports out onto the street where we find an immigration official who looks an awful lot like Captain Jean-Luc Picard.

He's sitting high in a comfortable chair having his shoes shined by a kid who seems to have no shoes of his own. The agent nods towards him and we offer our passports to the man with the shiniest shoes in Trabzon. He doesn't seem at all interested and the agent breaks into animated chatter. A heated debate takes place between the two men. It's fast and furious. In Western Europe we'd consider it to be an argument, but here I think they just refer to it as commerce. After a minute of raised voices and waved arms, they seem to reach some form of uneasy agreement. The officer pulls a rubber stamp from his uniform pocket and our two passports are duly stamped, 'Exit Turkey'. I suspect that standing here on this street, we're still officially inside Turkey, but now according to our passports we've already left. I've no idea what's just happened, but something is probably slightly better than nothing.

Another man arrives at the office, he might be a colleague of our agent but we really don't know. It's a hundred degrees in the shade and he's wearing large sunglasses and a heavy black leather jacket over an open necked shirt. He's trying for 'Gangster' but the effect is more 'Porn Star'. With the flash of a gold front tooth, he beckons us to follow him to an unknown destination. He's impatient, a man in a hurry, snapping his heavily ringed fingers. I look to the agent for guidance but he's suddenly decided that he speaks neither English nor Arabic, so we just follow this stranger towards the bonded area of the port.

Once inside the port, we follow in his shadow from office to office, but nothing of substance ever seems to happen. After an hour of pointless wandering and conversation, the stranger tells us that we can now ride our motorcycles onto the dock for our rendezvous with our ferry, the 'Princess Victoria'. We haven't seen any documents change hands, and the fixer's conversations with port officials had all seemed quite social in nature, so we're really not sure what's happened.

Earlier in the day we'd been informed that gaining permission to bring our motorcycles into the port would be a complicated administrative process, a process that would no doubt justify the high price being charged by our agent. Seeing what's just happened, which was absolutely nothing, it's probably something that we could easily have done ourselves. Another lesson learnt after the fact, and next time I'll just try to do it all myself.

On the far reaches of the dock, we meet our ferry, the Princess Victoria. From markings on the side of the vessel, it's clear to see that it was once registered in Algeria but is now sailing under the flag of Cambodia. I know nothing about the nuances of ship registration, but I'm sure that its change of national status had nothing to do with an increase in safety standards. P&O Ferries this is not. We sit on the dock, hiding in the limited shade offered by the Tigers and watch as crates of oranges and tomatoes are loaded onto the ancient rusting vessel.

An hour passes, and then a second. Every time we think that our turn has come to board the Princess Victoria, another lorry arrives and unloads its perishable produce. Finally, when there's no more than a metre of free space remaining in the rear of the vessel, we're waved forward. When we'd first arrived on the dock, the prospect of riding up the steep steel ramp into the vessel hadn't bothered me. Now, several loads of oranges and tomatoes later, the vessel sits a lot lower in the water and the entrance looks even more challenging. The steel ramp is slippery, seriously downhill and covered in the juice of dropped and splattered cargo. There's no control, just a downward slide straight into the boxes of tomatoes at the bottom of the steel ramp. I ram hard into the cartons splattering tomato juice everywhere, but nobody seems to mind, so I don't either. With Adam safely onboard, we park the Tigers at a jaunty angle leaving just enough room for the door to close behind them. Perfect planning or a happy accident? We'll probably never know. This is a car ferry but aside from an aging forklift truck, the Tigers are the only other vehicles on board. So what do others know that we don't?

After nine hours of pointless waiting and bureaucracy, on board the ferry we meet a group of twenty Iranian tourists. They're a happy troupe of doctors and their partners from Tehran taking their first trip into Russia. Their questions about our journey and experiences are endless and the feeling of warmth and friendship is unmistakeable. We drink tea, share their food and pose for endless photographs. They ask why we didn't choose to travel through Iran and I try to explain the costs and technical difficulties that kept Iran out of my plans. They seem to understand and apologise as if it was their personal fault, which of course it isn't, but it makes me feel guilty anyway. I get the impression that they're slightly embarrassed by the way their country is seen by the West, so I tell them that my decision not to visit Iran had nothing to do with Mahmud Ahmadinejad.

I don't know why I said it, and I certainly wish I hadn't. I've absolutely no idea what these people think of their President, but he's their President and what do I really understand about him or his policies? Probably only what the BBC wants me to understand, so I put away my shovel and stop digging the hole. It's too late to visit Iran on this journey, but I promise to visit them at a future date and I know that my welcome will be warm.

Aside from a lack of vehicles, the Princess Victoria also seems to be rather short on souls. Apart from Adam and myself, the twenty Iranian tourists, a Georgian chess champion and six long-legged heavily perfumed Russian girls, everybody else onboard is an integral part of the crew. Twenty nine passengers rattling around on a ferry designed to carry hundreds makes it feel like something of a 'Ghost Ship'. There's space for everybody, but each group seems to find its own little enclave far away from the next.

The painted Russian lovelies have annexed the front of the boat, the Iranian tourists the rear, and I find Giya in the middle. Giya Balkvadze introduces himself as the five times national chess champion of Georgia, master of twenty languages and eight martial arts. He's currently travelling back to Moscow where he lives with his family and he's not shy about his many achievements. Just in case I might forget some of them, he kindly writes them all down in the back of my journal. We're sitting in the bar, but it appears that the bar hasn't been open at anytime in this millennium. In fact, the Princess Victoria is lacking in all guest services, with the possible exception of one. I haven't had an opportunity to spend any time with the Russian girls yet, but I suspect that I couldn't afford much of their time anyway. That's just a guess, but probably not such a wild one.

I play a game of chess with Giya, which he of course wins, then a second and a third. It's really no contest and as he begins to take on members of the crew, I wander away in search of floatation devices and life boats. The Black Sea is calm, but the Princess Victoria is creaking along like my knees on a winter's morning. I'm not really worried, but maybe it's best to be cautious.

Last night in the coffin sized cabin, Adam had snored the night away in the bottom bunk, but for me on the top, sleep simply hadn't come. I'd wandered around the vessel and darkness hadn't really improved the

Princess Victoria's appearance, or my feeling of wellbeing. Eventually I'd found the deserted first class lounge with its huge leatherette chairs and killed the time until dawn updating my journal. Dawn arrived at around 5am and I'd looked through a porthole and seen that we were sitting outside of a large port, which I assumed to be Sochi.

At last, Russia was in sight and I felt that the real adventure was about to begin. For reasons that were never explained, we sat bobbing outside of Sochi until 8am before two pilot boats had arrived to escort us into harbour. It was a frustrating wait, Russia was so close but still untouchable. But, now we've docked and I've set foot on Russian territory for the very first time. It feels good, exciting and scary in equal parts.

Giya had kindly assisted us with the Russian immigration forms and before waving goodbye, he'd handed me $100 to donate to our charities and sufficient Russian Roubles to cover two nights in a Sochi hotel. Everyday I'm amazed by the generosity of strangers and the fact that people everywhere seem to have such a welcoming attitude towards the people of other nations. If only the politicians and media who represent these good people could adopt similar attitudes, then perhaps we'd all get along quite nicely together.

Our personal entry into Russia was really quite painless. We'd waited in a short line and handed over our passports and immigration cards when asked to do so. And that was it, welcome to Russia. The problem now is that although Adam and I are officially in Russia, the Tigers aren't. They're still sitting on the Princess Victoria and we must successfully complete a number of administrative procedures before we're reunited. The first procedure is to obtain motorcycle insurance for our time in Russia. Thankfully the insurance agent has an office here in the port and speaks relatively good English. However, when it comes to telling me why he'll only provide insurance policies for a maximum of fourteen days, and not the ninety days that we require, he seems lost for an answer. He tells me that this is Russia and it's just how things happen here. I'm not worried about it, maybe it's similar to the 'Cover Note' system back home in England; good for fourteen days before being superseded by the 'Official Policy Document'. Whatever it is, it costs around a thousand Russian Roubles and the documents that we've signed should allow the bikes to be released from the ferry.

We then try to complete a pair of temporary import forms for the Tigers. Unfortunately, the forms are all in Russian but we do our best to complete them correctly. The forms are cross referenced to the Tiger ownership documents and our own personal ninety day Russian visas, and once finished we hand them to the solitary customs officer and wait.

It's hot here, blisteringly hot and it's difficult to imagine that Sochi will be hosting the Winter Olympics in 2014. I know that it's now early summer, 4th of June 2008, but I can only guess that Sochi must be home to some very tall mountains that I can't yet see. I didn't expect to be visiting Sochi, so I really didn't do any research, but you could probably say the same thing about most of the places that I had planned to visit. One thing I do know is that throughout this journey we seem to have spent most of our waiting time on concrete docks beneath the burning sun with nowhere to hide. Sochi's no different in that respect, but here we don't even have the Tigers to provide shade. We're not allowed to touch them, at least not before the customs officer has checked them against the documents and allowed them to be removed from the Princess Victoria. Sadly, the customs officer in question has vanished. We're totally in the dark and haven't got a clue about what's supposed to be happening. Communication doesn't seem to be a strong point around here. He took our documents without a word, or a smile, and aside from his physical movement the only other sign of life had come from his frown. He hadn't looked happy and judging from his odour, perhaps he'd been trying to find cheer in a bottle of vodka. Whatever his problem is, I fear that it's also going to become our problem. He holds the keys to our gateway into Russia and I'm not sure which buttons to press in order to get them opened.

An arm wraps around my shoulder, a giant Russian bear hug. It's George, Captain of the Princess Victoria. 'Geoffrey my friend, Russian vodka I love, Russian food I love, Russian girls I love the most, but Russian laws are shit. Welcome to Russia comrade'. Just like us, Captain George has been waiting patiently for customs clearance, probably waiting for the very same customs officer. But it appears that Captain George is tired of waiting, and with a roll of US Dollars in his hand, suggests that he understands the system a little better than we do. He wanders away towards the office where the customs officer was last seen, but Adam and I can only sit and wait.

We lack George's command of Russian and access to US Dollars, but Captain George has promised to help us if he possibly can. After a few minutes, Captain George comes out of the office with the customs officer close on his heels. Neither of them looks happy, but I'm not sure if that's bad news for George, or for us, or possibly for everybody. As they pass our position on the dock nothing is said, and I'm worried that out of sight is out of mind, so I stand up and follow in their shadows.

Poor Circulation

At the Princess Victoria, the customs officer pokes the topbox on my Tiger, and then pokes it again. It seems as if he's looking for a response, but this kind of Tiger doesn't bite back, it's domesticated. I've no idea what he wants and he doesn't seem keen to explain, so I take the keys from my pocket and offer them to him. He doesn't take them, but he stabs another finger at the topbox. I reluctantly open it, raise the lid and thankfully he just nods his head. That seems to satisfy his curiosity. He doesn't want to look inside or even to check the Tiger's identification numbers, he just seems content that the hinges work on the luggage. Seemingly satisfied that neither Tiger represents a threat to the future wellbeing of Russia, he waves his arm in a mysterious way. I don't know what his gesture really means, but Captain George wants our Tigers away from his perishing tomatoes and that's good enough for me.

We park the Tigers on the dock, close to the exit gates, and then we wait again. Another hour passes before the now unsteady customs officer reappears and again starts stabbing an inquisitive finger at my topbox. What's so fascinating about my bloody topbox? I really don't care, so I just open it and hope that it makes him happy. Satisfied that the hinges still work, he nods his head and actually seems to smile. It gives me hope, hope that our bureaucratic interface is finally coming to an end, but unfortunately that feeling of hope is a false one. Still smiling, he pulls the two now crumpled temporary import forms out of his back pocket. He looks at them and then asks, 'Tomas?' I nod. He waves our forms in front of Adam's face, 'This is shit', and then throws them at him.

Another hour has passed. The English speaking insurance agent has helped us to find and complete new temporary import forms, but he can't see anything wrong with the originals. It's disconcerting but I'm not ready to give up yet. Armed with the new documents, I find the customs door closed, so I knock and walk in without waiting for an answer.

He's sitting at his desk, no sign of a bottle but the air smells sick with booze. I place the documents side by side in front of him, stand my ground and smile. I'm not going anywhere and I hope that he's getting the message. It feels like a stand-off, but he knows that he's in control and I can only hope that he's had enough fun for the day. It's uneasy, but it's productive. He lifts the top cover of a document pad and carefully tears off the top two pages. A pair of temporary import forms pre-completed for both of the Tigers. He'd probably filled them out hours ago, hopefully while he was still comparatively sober, but I'm way beyond the point of caring. I pick up the papers, no signatures required, and return to the Tigers.

A few minutes later, a man arrives with a very large key. It unlocks the gates leading out of the port but there's yet another obstacle to overcome. During the long hours spent sitting on the dock, a car has parked in front of the gates and prevents them from opening. It's not the customs officer's fault, but he's an easy man to blame. Welcome to Russia.

Chapter 19:
Russia, Sochi

Sochi gives us our first taste of Russia, and it's probably a very good appetizer. We've left Asia and re-entered Europe and Sochi feels amazingly modern, vibrant and bright, totally not what I'd expected. I've got itchy feet and I want to start riding, but unfortunately due to some quirk of Russian bureaucracy, we have to remain here in Sochi for at least two nights. Apparently, at our port of entry we must register our Russian visas with the appropriate authorities. Having no idea which authority is appropriate or what procedures we must follow, the easiest option is to check-in at a large hotel and have their staff register them for us. Thankfully, Giya has provided us with enough money for two nights here and we've chosen the Hotel Moscow as our home.

The Hotel Moscow is an interesting place, and while Adam whines about the hotels stark facilities, I marvel at the wonderment of the place. It's what they call a 'Soviet Tourist Hotel', but what Adam prefers to call a 'Gulag'. He's paranoid that our small twin room is bugged and holds a finger to his lips whenever I mention the behaviour of the alcoholic customs officer back at the port. He might be joking, but with Adam, you never can tell. For me, this building is simply fantastic, a magnificent throwback to the days of communist rule containing all of the idiosyncrasies that I associate with it. In the bathroom, the toilet sits in the centre of the floor which means that the door can't be fully opened. I suspect that when it came to cutting the toilet drains into the hotels bathrooms, nobody bothered to tell the workman exactly where to cut them. The worker who later fitted the toilets probably hadn't asked any further questions and sited each ceramic stool directly above its designated hole, thus, rendering the bathroom doors almost unopenable. I know that I'm being unfairly critical of old communist labour practices, but I just find the whole concept agreeably charming. Anyway, it's only for two nights, Giya's kindly paid for the room and Adam will eventually get over it. As for me, aside from our experience with the uniformed asshole at the docks, I'm already falling in love with Russia.

By day and night, Sochi is stunningly beautiful. It's more cosmopolitan than I'd ever imagined and the girls here are unbelievably beautiful. They're everywhere, in very large numbers and often wearing very little in the way of clothing. I'd been told that the girls across Russia would be beautiful and that I'd probably fall in love many times, but this is ridiculous. The sheer density of twenty-something girls is unnatural, but it might be unique to this area. Sochi is a seaside resort, the Russian Riviera and maybe it attracts the beautiful girls along with the oligarch's summer money. Everybody here is beautiful, stunningly beautiful. It's like a city devoted to 'Club 18-30', where the dress code is designer bikinis for the girls and Speedo's finest budgie smugglers for the boys. To an outsider like me, it seems entirely unnatural, but I think I could probably get used to it.

After forty days on the road, city living also feels strange in other ways. Ice cream, grilled meats, pasta, chilled beer and vodka are available twenty-four hours a day without ever needing to strike-up the stove. It's easy living, but easy living is also expensive living and thankfully we're only here for two nights. Any longer and our budgets couldn't handle it.

I remember back to my college days in the early 1980's, a time when people who'd probably never visited the USSR claimed that you could pay for a holiday in Russia by filling your outbound suitcase with Levi 501's and selling them on the black market in Moscow. If those days had ever existed, then they're certainly gone now.

Following the deaths in quick succession of President's Brezhnev, Andropov and Chernenko, in 1985 Mikhail Gorbachev had come to power. First he'd introduced 'Perestroika' which had brought reform to government and then 'Glasnost' which had allowed for the freedom of speech. Gorbachev had opened the door for Yeltsin and Yeltsin had introduced the free market economy and the dream that all Russians would finally get to eat cake. Putin had followed Yeltsin as the President of a newly reformed and downsized Russia, added cream to Yeltsin's cake and topped it off with a beautiful cherry. Russia now has a free market economy where the people can legally buy their own Levis 501's, but seeing the majority of life that continues just a few meters beyond the glossy façade of Sochi's tourist district, I suspect that only a privileged few can afford them. Those lucky few can be seen living the high-life here in the tourist areas with their designer labels, super yachts and red Ferraris. The ostentatious display of wealth here is really quite amazing and I worry that the envy of those who can afford far fewer toys will at some point spill over into hostile resentment. The environment of freedom in today's Russia is to be applauded, but the remarkable economic about-turn might be difficult to swallow for the many who I suspect are missing out on its benefits. George Orwell told us that 'All animals are equal' and then added that 'Some animals are more equal than others', so maybe the relative distribution of wealth has always been this way in Russia. I've no idea, but maybe along the way I'll find out more.

Today I became best friends with the manager of the local motorcycle dealership, but it wasn't good news for us. I asked him about the availability of tyres that we need for the Tigers, and I gave him the sizes that we require. He checked his inventory then scratched his head and consulted a friend. His friend made a note of the tyre sizes but sadly came back to us empty handed. Next to be contacted was a specialist motorcycle tyre supplier but the answer was the same, 'Sorry, but no such tyres are available anywhere in Russia'. Bang had gone my earlier theory that everything was available in the new Russia, but maybe it's just the sizes that are a problem.

Back in Turkey, suitable tyres had been available, but I'd hesitated at the price and walked away from them. Opportunities always look much better when they're walking away from you and now, I dearly wish that I'd just bitten the financial bullet and made the purchase. Oh well, it's just another lesson learned on this long road of discovery and I'll take it firmly on my chin. I'm sure we'll find tyres in the next big cities, Rostov or Volgograd, and failing that we'll have two sets of replacements shipped out from London by CitySprint. It'll probably be expensive, but it's a long ride across Russia, we need the replacement tyres soon and our wallets will probably survive.

After three busy days and two restful nights in Sochi, it feels good to be loading my world back onto the Tiger again. As we tie the final straps and start the engines, a crowd gathers around us. Since leaving the docks, our motorcycles have been parked at the entrance to the hotel and attracting much attention. Thankfully it's been the 'good' kind of attention, interest rather than theft, and nothing at all has been stolen or even tampered with. I can hardly imagine what would have happened if they'd been parked outside of an inner-city hotel in England.

Now, the good people of Sochi are taking photographs and asking a thousand different questions. The maps on our panniers make it easier to explain our journey, but still they tell us that we're crazy for even attempting to ride across Russia. They tell us that it's a long way to the eastern coast with very bad roads and many dangers, but on asking my own question, none of them have ever made that journey before. We thank them for their advice and concern, but it's time to start finding out for ourselves if such a journey is possible or not. Others have made that journey before, lots of others, and under far more difficult circumstance, so of course we'll make it.

As we ride away from the centre of Sochi, I can clearly see the Princess Victoria still tied to the dock with its perishable cargo onboard. Captain George makes this voyage on a regular basis, so I assume that his paperwork is all in order, but three days beneath the burning sun can't be good news for his tomatoes. I can only imagine that either his roll of US Dollars was too small, or the attitude of the customs officer too big, but I know that he won't be a happy man. We escaped into Russia without paying any bribes, perhaps we were lucky, but it seems a shame that the 'Official Welcome' doesn't represent the obvious warmth of the Russian people.

We can't help Captain George, nor change the Russian system, but hopefully along the way we'll learn to make the most of everything and help others who follow to do the same. Goodbye Sochi, I'll remember you for all of the right reasons.

One thing that does worry me about riding across Russia, is navigation. Adam's announced that his GPS unit has no maps loaded into its memory but I've got the compass on the front of the Tiger, and I've got the paper map. It's a nice big map, but all of the place names on the signposts are written in the Cyrillic alphabet. Well they would be, because this is Russia and that's the alphabet that they favour around here. It takes a little getting used to, but maybe my dyslexia actually helps. It's more about recognising words rather than reading them, something that's probably second nature to me. So far, it seems to be working and despite heavy traffic, we're making good progress towards the city of Rostov.

I pull into a service station for fuel, and make three important discoveries. Firstly, the fuel here is called 'Benzene', and secondly, it's relatively cheap. It's the first cheap fuel that we've found, and as Russia will represent at least half of our road miles it's excellent news for the budgets. The third discovery is not quite so good. For the non Russian speaker, the process of filling the tank with reasonably priced benzene is fraught with challenges. It seems that we have to guess how much fuel each bike will need, deposit the appropriate amount of money with the girl sitting behind the iron bars of the kiosk, and then fill up the Tigers. If too little benzene has been requested, then the pump will stop somewhere short of a full tank. On the other hand, if too much has been requested, then our feet will be swimming in an ocean of wasted fuel. We've been warned that the fuel pumps will not automatically cut-off once the tank is full. That might not be true, but I really don't want to find out the expensive or explosive way. It's really something of an opera, but like everything else here in Russia, we'll get used to it eventually.

Along these major roads the traffic seems intent on racing, always in a hurry, always with blaring horns and always with little regard for regulations or safety. At every bend, aging trucks deposit long slicks of diesel fuel that are easy to spot but difficult to avoid. It's furious and confusing, but in a weird 'Welcome to Russia' sort of way, it's also quite enchanting. You just need to stay alert and keep your eyes peeled in every possible direction. Nobody's trying to kill us, we're all just trying to make progress along the same stretch of road and it's safer to keep to their pace than to ours.

At the town of Tuapse, I put my faith in the compass and turn inland following the road that should lead us towards Majkop. Despite my earlier confidence, the name on the signpost doesn't seem to make sense, but it also says 'P254', which is the road that we need to take.

We're climbing now, high into mountains that I assume will play host to the Winter Olympics. The road changes for the better, sweeping left and right hand bends and the congestion of the coastal road disappears behind us. As we rise still further, the surface begins to vary between rough tarmac and compacted sand. It's not the road surface that I'd hoped for this early into our journey across Russia, but it's really more 'Concentrating' than 'Difficult'. Then, eighteen miles along this road, and riding well below the legal speed limit, everything suddenly changes.

Chapter 20:
Russia, Apseronsk

Midway through a sweeping right-hand bend, two police officers are waving black and white batons in my general direction. I'm not sure what they're asking me to do: Stop or keep moving? Confused, I indicate left and pull across the road into the parking area alongside their car, switch off the engine and climb down from the Tiger. We've passed through two earlier police checkpoints, but this time I'm being summoned to join a casually uniformed officer in the discomfort of his car. The officer's command of English is zero, so that's an equal match for my Russian.

After a sequence of awkward outbursts and silences, rudimentary communication is established by drawing illustrations on an A4 sheet of paper. Firstly, he draws a curving road, a line down its centre and two arrows moving across the line at right angles. I particularly like his verbal interpretation of a speeding motorcycle; 'Vroom Vroom', but I really don't like what he's telling me. I think I'm being told that we've just committed the offence of 'Crossing the Solid White Line', and that our driving licences will be confiscated until we've paid an on-the-spot fine of 5,000 Russian Roubles (£110) each.

At first I think that the police officer's joking. He's all smiles and laughter, but I worry that his smiles are in anticipation of a good day, his good day at the expense of mine. I'm not sure how to react to him, so I just smile and try not to lose my temper. After several minutes of rising conversation and countless childlike additions to his initial sketch, I manage to convince him that there isn't a white line anywhere on the road, and therefore, we couldn't possibly have crossed it. Reluctantly he concedes to my point, but he doesn't seem pleased with the outcome.

There's a minute of painful silence, a minute that he puts to good use. He's tapping his wooden baton into his palm. Each new stroke is slightly more menacing than the last. He's trying to intimidate me and it's working rather well. I'm not going to say anything. If I open my mouth I'll probably tell him what I'm thinking, and that probably wouldn't be good for my freedom, so it's his move. The baton taping stops and the burley officer returns it to the holster on his well appointed leather belt. He opens his door and for the briefest of moments, I think that I've won my first interface with the Russian police. I turn to open my own door but a strong hand stops me. He wants me to wait, and I assume that he'll be back.

His absence gives me time to think, but I'm not happy with where my thoughts are taking me. The car is an aging blue Toyota Corolla, inconspicuous and without any police markings, or even a radio. The two officers are wearing uniforms, but there are no name tags or identification numbers. I'm seriously beginning to wonder if these guys are really police officers, or just a pair of local chancers. Either way, they're quite clearly here to enrich themselves but I'm not sure which alternative I prefer. Whether they're policeman or imposters, I rationalise that they probably aren't going to shoot a pair of unarmed tourists, because that would really screw-up their day. Sadly, my conclusion does little to quell my fear. Policemen or imposters, they're here to collect bribes, something that they probably do every day of their lives, and I'm just the naive virgin who's accidentally stumbled into their brothel of corruption. I don't have any answers, so I try to think about what Dad would do in a situation like this. I really don't know what Dad would actually do, but I do know that he wouldn't be terribly English about it.

Before my imagination has the opportunity to venture into even darker places, the officer clambers back into the roasting car, and smiles. A smile between strangers is usually a good sign, but here and now, I think not. He takes the original A4 drawing from the dashboard, crumples it into a ball and casually tosses it onto the rear seats. On a second sheet of paper, he draws a police car and two stick-motorcycles zooming off into the distance; 'Vroom Vroom'. The new offence is 'Failing to Stop', a very different offence, but one that apparently carries the same penalty as 'Crossing the Solid White Line', 5,000 Roubles each. If he wasn't so greedy, then he'd stand a chance of getting paid, but the price that he's asking is way beyond my financial and moral reach. He's a greedy arrogant ass-wipe of a man, but he's also extremely large and scares the shit out of me. I'm laughing, but not because I think it's funny, it's just my nervous reaction to this seemingly dangerous farce.

I start tapping on the window, pointing at my Tiger. It's clearly parked right alongside his car, a car that probably hasn't moved all day. 'Failing to Stop?' He understands what I'm telling him, but he really doesn't care. We both know that this is a game that he'll inevitably win, but we just don't know how long it will take to complete or the final value of his prize.

There's a little more silence, a Russian stand-off where neither of us speaks. He's returned to tapping the baton into his sweaty palm and I feel the need to move. I've finally worked out what Dad would do right now, he'd hit the bastard with whatever weapon he could find. The only weapons that I have are my firsts, fists that are only half the size of those belonging to the man sitting next to me, but touch isn't the only sense that can be assaulted.

Thanks to the invention of quick-release buckles, before he has time to stop me, my left boot is off and I'm working on the right. It's not pleasant for either of us, but that's the whole point of my action. It's my impro-vised non-violent defence. He raps my left knee with his baton and starts shouting in fast Russian. I haven't got a clue what he's saying, so I just start talking back at him in English at a similar speed. It's nonsense, but it's nonsense of the comforting kind.

He fiddles with his mobile phone, talks briefly to a mystery colleague and then passes the phone to me. His mystery colleague speaks relatively good English, but he's clearly not joining this conversation to assist me. He makes the situation clear, or at least confirms my original assumption. We're in Russia, and around here the law works a little differently. We can pay the fines and move on, or we can refuse to pay and spend a few days in a cell before moving backwards into Turkey. The choice is ours. After the call, he presses several more buttons on his phone and then hands it back to me. The screen shows two phrases written in Russian with what I assume to be the English translations below. I'm not entirely surprised when I read the words: 'Honey Pot' and 'Bribe'.

I've been in the car for an hour, but it feels more like a week. Outside, Adam looks on as the second officer opens my topbox and starts empty-ing its contents onto the ground. I've no idea what uniformed Russians find so interesting about my topbox, but as he picks out the Special Package and starts holding it up to the sunlight and poking it, I decide that it's time to start cutting my losses. One by one, I've retrieved most of my own documents from the dashboard and discreetly slipped them back into the pockets of my jacket. The officer still has my wallet, but that really doesn't worry me. It's my 'False Wallet', a wallet designed to satisfy pick-pockets and keep my real wallet safe. It contains out-of-date bank cards, money for the day ahead, a few US Dollars and my paper UK driving license. I'm not too worried about the license, it's actually just a very good colour photocopy designed to be surrendered in situations such as this.

What does concern me however, is that he's also holding some of Adam's documents and I'm not sure if they're the genuine articles or not. The car windows are open, front and rear. We're negotiating, and each time he's reduced his financial demand, I've made a small concession of my own. I'm now wearing both of my boots, but the atmosphere in the car is still far from pleasant. In the wallet I've got just over 2,000 Russian Roubles and a few low denomination US Dollars. Encouraged by the second officer's interest in the contents of my topbox, we seem to have reached an uneasy agreement. I'll keep 1,000 Russian Roubles for fuel and food, and they'll get to keep the remainder of the banknotes and return the wallet and Adam's documents to me. He's not particularly happy with the deal, but that still makes him an awful lot happier than me.

I'd been determined to try and avoid fuelling corruption on the roads here in Russia, but I've fallen on the first day of riding here. It's probably cost less than it might have done, but I really don't know if I've learned anything that'll help me to avoid similar situations in the future. I'll move the Special Package away from my topbox and replenish my false wallet, but if I end up sitting in another sweaty police car, real or fake, then I'll probably still just shit my pants and surrender.

Due to our unexpected delay, and the added density of traffic, we're behind schedule and there's no hope of us reaching Rostov this evening. The sun's already kissing the horizon and I don't relish the thought of riding too far in the dark around here. We're in a town called Apseronsk where I see a large Honda Fireblade parked at a roadside cafe. It's the first big Japanese motorcycle that I've seen on the road here and as a fellow biker, hopefully its owner will be able to help us. According to my photocopied pages of a Berlitz guide, in the Russian language 'Packalet' means tent and 'Cyamping' means camping.

A little earlier in the evening I'd tried using these two Russian words with a family driving along our road. They'd nodded their understanding and escorted us towards a suitable camping ground, a camping ground that turned out to be a hotel. In their defence, the sign pointing towards the hotel did show the icon for a tent, and when I'd asked at reception for 'cyamping', they'd smiled and offered me the key for a room, so I'd returned their smiles and moved on.

I've now found the owner of the Fireblade and his name is Jirair. He speaks relatively good English and has agreed to escort us to a suitable site for the night, but sadly it won't be camping. Apparently 'camping' as we know it in Europe doesn't really happen here in western Russia, and Jirair finds it difficult to understand why we'd want to sleep in tents when perfectly acceptable rooms are available. He has a point, and after our first day on the road here in Russia a bed would certainly be welcome.

Happily, we weary travellers follow our new best friend to a large private house in the next town. I go inside and talk with the owner of the house, Jirair's best friend, and negotiate the price of a room for one night. The cost will be 500 Roubles, which is a shade more than £10 and seems to be more than reasonable. I'm shown upstairs to a private apartment that comes complete with a sauna, hot tub, full sized snooker table and the most amazing power-shower that I've ever seen. It's not the camp ground that I'd been searching for, but with secure parking for the Tigers, it's absolutely perfect.

Back downstairs, I tell Adam that we've found our beds for the night and we guide the Tigers into their new secure compound. Despite paying the earlier bribe and the added cost of this room, a quick calculation tells me that I'm still keeping within my budget of £20 per day. Today hasn't been the best day of the journey so far, but it's certainly not the worst.

Chapter 21:
Russia, Rostov

It's been only our second full day of riding in Russia and it's the second day that's been hijacked by corrupt police officers. I'd hoped that yesterday's legal interface had been an isolated incident, but it seems that the many warnings about police corruption across Western Russia have substance. This morning had started badly. I'd opened my wallet and realised that the $100 note given to our charities by Giya on the ferry to Sochi, had been missing. It was missing from the wallet but I'd known exactly where it had gone, it was in the trouser pocket of a policeman.

Yesterday when he'd emptied my wallet in his car, I'd forgotten that Giya's donation had been in there, so he'd ended the day a hundred dollars richer than I'd thought. There was nothing at all that I could do about it, so we'd left the comfortable room in Apseronsk at around eight this morning and by nine, Adam was sitting in a police car.

I'd like to cry foul play, but confused by too many road signs Adam had turned left and ridden the wrong way down a dual carriageway. Thankfully, he'd realised his mistake quickly and turned around, but so had the police officer who'd being sitting at the junction watching him. It cost an hour of time and another 1,000 Russian Roubles, but it was another lesson learned. Apparently breaking the rules in Russia is no more expensive than following them.

Forty miles deeper into Russia and it's my turn to feel the warm breath of the law. It's not yet eleven in the morning, but the officer at the police checkpoint insists that I'm driving under the influence of alcohol. I haven't had time to turn off the bike or remove my helmet, but he's repeatedly stabbing a thumb into his neck, a gesture that in this part of the world means drinking. I can only shake my head in disbelief and follow his directions.

I'm escorted to a mobile police office where several other officers with nothing better to do are invited to test my breath. They all agree that I'm hammered, and they're all absolutely wrong. Yesterday I hadn't been confident that the two men had been genuine police officers, but this group certainly are, and that knowledge gives me slightly more confidence. I've got eighty-five days remaining on my Russian visa, so I figure that they're in a bigger hurry than I am. They're not going to shoot me, and if they arrest me they'll get a mountain of paperwork and absolutely none of my money, so I decide to sit down, take off my boots and play the waiting game.

It takes an hour of inactivity to convince them that I haven't been drinking, or more importantly that I'm not going to enrich them with Roubles, but eventually they grow bored and wave me on my way. Yesterday I'd been frightened by people like this, but today they just make me extremely angry. Before leaving home I'd been warned that this problem would be more prevalent in Western Russia, not necessarily because the police here are more corrupt, but because they can see from our passports that we're recent arrivals in Russia, less experienced in their ways and therefore more vulnerable to their demands. I hope that as we travel east the number of legal interfaces will diminish, but at the moment it's not looking too promising.

As the hours and miles follow, the trumped up charges keep mounting; speeding, crossing another solid white line, another count of speeding and driving under the influence of alcohol again. At every police checkpoint the charge is different, but the intention is always the same. They're trying to lighten my wallet and it's really pissing me off. So far in Russia, every civilian that I've met has been amazingly warm and welcoming, but aside from one solitary girl who'd helped us at Sochi immigration, every other person in a uniform has been a complete and utter asshole. But it's just what it is, a seemingly unavoidable part of the Russian experiences and I'm determined not to let it ruin my time here. I'm the guest in Russia and I've come here to learn, not to preach. I'm a very lucky man because if I wasn't here I'd be at work in London, and I know which of those options I prefer. There's absolutely no contest, so I'll take a deep breath, get over it, and get on with it.

Today, we've covered almost a hundred and fifty miles, but it's taken us thirteen hours to ride them. We've finally arrived on the outskirts of Rostov, the city that we'd hoped to reach last night, but there's no sign of anywhere to camp. As I stand at the side of the road feeling slightly lost and gazing at the map for answers, two scooters pull to a halt in front of me. Aboard the scooters are five young guys on their way home from a day of swimming at a nearby lake. A few miles back down the road, they'd noticed our unusual motorcycles travelling towards their city and had decided to give chase and offer us their assistance. The fact that five people aboard two tiny scooters have been able to catch up to us on the road speaks volumes about our rate of progress.

They introduce themselves as 'The Rostov Scooter Boys' and their first task is to take us to an international ATM where I replenish my supply of Roubles. Next on the agenda is a campsite for the night. Norik, their spokesman and unofficial leader, tells us that camping isn't possible in this area, but he doesn't bother to explain why. It seems that we'll be staying in another hotel tonight, and the Rostov Scooter Boys know exactly where we'll find one.

It's dark when we arrive at the hotel and I'm so tired that I don't even bother to look up at the sign, so I have absolutely no idea what it's called. However, it looks worryingly opulent and definitely the best hotel that we'll have stayed in so far. I gently voice my fear about its effect on our budgets but Norik tells me not to worry. His English is excellent, he's a bright kid and seems to understand the concept of Poor Circulation. Without another word, he vanishes into the reception area and returns a minute later with a huge smile and good news.

I've no idea what the standard room-rate would be for this hotel, but for Adam and me a twin room tonight will be 500 Roubles each (£10). Norik and his friends want to show us their city, but we're simply too tired and too hungry to go touring tonight. It's clear to see that they're disappointed but there's only enough energy left in our tanks for the activities of eating and sleeping. I thank the boys for their help, give them each a Poor Circulation pin badge and wave them on their way.

Consumed by tiredness, we take the lazy option and order dinner at a pavement cafe just a few yards from the hotel. It's a beautifully warm and still evening and as the second round of cold beers arrive, I do my best to lift Adam's spirits. He's been quiet all day but tonight he looks totally drained and exhausted. I try and encourage him to talk about what he sees as the challenges that face us, but he's hesitant to respond. I know that he's finding our dealings with corrupt officials quite difficult to accept, but this is new territory for both of us. I try to convince him that as the Russian miles pass, we'll learn how to deal with them more effectively, but tonight I don't think Adam's in the mood for convincing, only worrying and sleeping.

Dressed in our filthy leather jeans and tee shirts at this rather trendy pavement cafe, we must look totally out of place, but sitting not five metres away from us are two flirtatious girls who clearly want to talk. Adam's not at all interested in conversing with them, in fact he's so tired that I doubt he's even noticed them smiling at us. Before leaving Turkey, I'd promised Adam's parents that I'd see him safely across Russia, but I'd promised them absolutely nothing about keeping myself safe. Adam retires to the room, but I decide to linger for a little while longer. 'Good evening girls'.

This morning in the hotel car park, I found a pair of familiar looking scooters. Norik and his friends had come down to the hotel in order to guide us onto the correct road out of Rostov. We're heading for the city of Satchy and then onwards to Volgograd. Just two days ago I'd estimated how long each stage of the journey would take us, but those estimates have now been thrown away. Each part of the journey will take as long as it takes and each night we'll arrive exactly where we arrive. No strict timetable and no daily mileage targets, we'll just go with the Russian flow and bend with the changing experience.

We talk with Norik and his friends, exchange email addresses and promise to keep in touch. They're teenagers, but their presence seems to offer safety. I'm apprehensive about the road ahead and having a group of friendly Russian guides would be fantastic, but we're riding around the world and tomorrow they'll have to go back to school. Of course they love motorcycles and want to travel, that's why they'd chased us down last night, and there's absolutely no doubt in my mind that their day will come.

With our farewells complete, we follow them along busy roads towards the airport and then wave a final farewell as we ride north onto the M4. If the future of Russia rests in the hands of young people like Norik, Shasha, Tima, John G. and John M., then I'm confident that that future will be a very bright one.

Chapter 22:
Russia, Volgograd

I stop at the side of the road to take photographs of a military statue. It's a really nice statue but if the truth be told, I don't need much of an excuse to stop riding these days. Russia's an awful lot hotter than I'd imagined it would be and the endless congested roads sap away my energy like a sponge. It's our forty-eighth day on the road, our thirty-eighth day since leaving England and I think Russia is the twenty-second country. We're a couple of days behind schedule, but that doesn't mean that we're travelling too slowly. On the contrary, we're really travelling too quickly and run the risk of missing out on too many great experiences.

Leaving Rostov yesterday morning I'd reached the conclusion that it wasn't our time-keeping that was wrong, but the schedule. I'd planned the initial route from the comfort of a computer stool in England, and had simply marked crosses at places of interest and joined them together with the straightest possible lines. I'd never even considered that there might be interesting places and people waiting to greet us in between those crosses. At this new and relaxed pace, if those interesting places and people do exist, then we're certain to bump into most of them.

The interesting statue shows three Russian tanks racing into a cloudless sky. I assume that the tanks are T-34's manufactured here at the Volgograd Tractor Factory, or as it was better known in it's day, the 'Stalingrad Tank Factory'. It was the tank that probably saved Russia during the bloodiest battle in the history of warfare, the Battle of Stalingrad, 1942-43. It was a battle where more than two million people lost their lives. I'd like to claim that I'd done some research on this subject, but sadly my knowledge owes everything to Hollywood and nothing to the Encyclopaedia Britannica.

Far away in the distance, standing majestically high above the city of Volgograd, is the unmistakable statue of Mother Russia. Baking in the midday sun, her flowing robes are dazzling in the light, her head held proudly high and her sword pointing directly towards the sky. We're still several miles west of the city, but even at this great distance I can see that she's one very impressive lady. So captivating is the sight, that I didn't even notice the approaching police officer.

With my best Sunday smile and outstretched hand, I greet him with my latest lucky word, 'Priviet', which I think means 'Hello' or 'Greetings' in Russian. It's a new tactic in my fight against corruption, a 'First Strike' policy that seems to catch them off-guard and hopefully avoids any financial unpleasantness.

He cautiously takes my hand and shakes it without stealing any of my fingers. I point to the Tiger and wave my camera: 'Photograph?' He obliges with an official looking pose and a limited smile. It breaks the ice and within a minute, he's sitting in the saddle, flicking various switches and verbally spelling out his email address. I've no idea if he thinks that I'm friendly or mad, or possibly both, but it's a tactic that seems to be working. Since leaving Rostov yesterday morning, we've passed unmolested through five different checkpoints and continued on our way with nothing but best wishes for the journey and photographs for our albums.

I'd intended to search for a hotel, but the statue of Mother Russia acts like a giant magnet. It draws us towards her and every kilometre closer increases her impressiveness.

Standing in the car park beneath her feet, she towers above us. The plaque tells me that to the tip of her sword she stands eighty-five meters tall and that the construction was completed in 1967. It also claims that she's the tallest structure in the world, but I think that it might be a very old or politically biased information plaque. The tallest structure in the world or not, she's certainly a mighty big girl.

A stocky little fellow by the name of Uri, a car park attendant with one missing finger and a host of random tattoos, volunteers to keep a careful eye on our motorcycles. Such a volunteer in England would have me riding away to a much safer place, but here I just graciously accept his offer.

For an hour, we walk around Mother Russia's base and visit the Eternal Flame that casts shadows across the names of the lives that were lost here almost sixty-five years ago. It's Sunday and the good people of Volgograd seem to have converged on the statue, every last one of them. It's beautiful here, but probably best appreciated when it's a little quieter and not quite so bloody hot. We'll leave her to the locals for today, we'll go and find a place to sleep and visit her again during the week when it's hopefully a little cooler and quieter.

Back in the car park, Uri is indeed keeping a watchful eye on our Tigers. With a wooden baton and a menacing expression, he's fending off a myriad of inquisitive teenage fingers. It's friendly interest from kids who seem genuinely interested in what we're doing without any hint of envy or jealousy. I answer their questions, allow them to play around on the Tiger and pose for photographs. It's the kind of attention that I enjoy, and once their thirst for information has been quenched, they simply exit from my life and go on their way. Uri introduces us to Tamara, an unofficial tour guide who speaks very good English, and so she should, because by day she's an English teacher at a school here in Volgograd.

I ask our new best friends about motorcycle shops here in the city, places where we might find replacement tyres for the Tigers. On a map that I've torn from a brochure advertising the Volgograd Motorcycle Show, which will sadly not take place until later next month, Uri and Tamara draw several crosses. They think they've identified the most promising locations for sourcing new tyres, and I think that I can probably find them. Uri then suggests that we should come and stay in an apartment belonging to one of his business associates, but Tamara takes me to one side and advises against accepting his offer. Tamara points to her arm referencing Uri's tattoos and then his missing finger. Tamara's actions leave me with the distinct impression that Uri's business associate might in fact be a 'Business Associate' in the Russian sense. We thank them both for their time and help, and prepare to leave the statue of Mother Russia behind us.

Adam's Tiger starts without a problem, but I press the button on my key fob and the alarm system refuses to disarm. I press it again and again, but still nothing happens. I take out my spare key and try once more, but still there's no response from the Tiger. Uri wanders up to me and smiles. He points to the red and white short-wave radio mast that towers above us and says something in Russian to Tamara. She looks towards me wearing a slightly worried expression. It seems that my alarm will not disarm because the radio waves here are too strong for the Tigers system. I'll need to move the Tiger at least two kilometres away from the radio mast before it will work.

Apparently it's a common problem here and Uri seems to earn a second income from helping car owners to overcome the problem. Unfortunately, the Tiger's system is a mystery to him, his attempts to overpower the short wave radio signals fail and I'm left with no alternative but to start pushing. Unfortunately for those around us, my inability to disarm the alarm system means that as I move the Tiger it assumes that it's been stolen and reacts exactly as it should. The sound is extremely loud and shrilling, shattering the tranquillity of this peaceful place of respect. I'm embarrassed and move away as quickly as I possibly can.

Thankfully, the statue sits at the top of a rather steep hill and once the Tiger's moving, I can jump aboard and freewheel down to the bottom. Eventually all good things must come to an end, and as the road begins to rise the Tiger slowly grinds to a halt. I look at the long rising road in front of me and I certainly don't relish the thought of pushing three hundred kilograms of dormant Tiger up it. I try pressing the key fob again, but not so much as a 'Beep'. The intense ringing of the Tiger's alarm is attracting attention and a local taxi driver walks over to investigate. He seems to think that I'll need to keep pushing for at least another kilometre, possibly even two, but he's willing to help me.

As he pulls a handy tow-rope from the trunk of his taxi, he tells me that he tows some vehicles to the heart of Volgograd before they're free from the interference of the short wave signal. It's not very comforting news for me, but it's clearly a nice little earner for him. In the absence of beer, I sit at the side of the road and light a cigarette. It's at least a hundred degrees in the shade, but there's no shade and very little breeze to comfort me. My leather jeans and boots are retaining the heat and every time I glance at the road ahead, it seems to look even steeper than before. Then, from somewhere in the far reaches of my mind, I see Top Gear presenter Jeremy Clarkson pointing a key fob into his ear, opening his mouth and disarming a car parked several hundred metres away from him. I'm not sure if my vision is a real memory or just my mind playing tricks on me, and my mouth certainly doesn't have the same dimensions as Jeremy Clarkson's, but it's worth a try.

I stand up, point the key fob into my ear, open my mouth and turn towards the Tiger. I press the button once. 'Beep Beep', the indicators blink twice and silence descends. I quickly turn the key in the ignition, disengage the clutch and press 'Start'. Miracle of miracles, it bloody well works. The Tiger growls into life. Jeremy Clarkson has saved my day, and that's a sentence that I never thought I'd write.

A few kilometres closer to the centre of Volgograd, I find the first cross that Uri had marked on our map. It turns out not to be a motorcycle dealership but a small marquee erected in the car park of a large shopping centre. Through the plastic windows of the tent I can see nine or ten Japanese motorcycles with price tags on the headlights. A sign on the entrance seems to tell me that it's closed on Sunday but will open again at ten tomorrow morning. It's still blisteringly hot, we're both exhausted and I decide that the best option is to leave a message here and then find the cheap hotel that Tamara had recommended. I hastily write a note explaining who we are and what we're looking for here in Volgograd. I attach a Poor Circulation pin badge and a copy of The Riders Digest magazine to the note and then slide it under the plastic door of the marquee. Then, we cross our fingers and head off in search of a bed for the night.

We've been told by Tamara that the Hotel Tourist on the north side of the city is a cheap and popular destination for European tourists. Trying to follow my inadequate map, I lead us through a complex of dull and dreary tenement blocks where the endless grey of concrete is broken only by the brightly coloured laundry hanging from the balconies. Dogs bark and snap at our ankles as we pass and the road turns from asphalt to stone, and then to sand. The map and compass tell me that I'm leading us in the right direction, but my instincts tell me that civilization's in the opposite direction. I can understand that in Russia the roads between cities might not be great, but in a city the size of Volgograd I hadn't expected quite such a rough ride. It's not pretty, but it suggests that Tamara's description of 'Cheap' might actually be true.

At the banks of the River Volga, I turn left and continue riding. The light is fading and as far as Volgograd is concerned, I feel that we're now definitely on the wrong side of the tracks. This area is not what I'd call posh, and it seems like an unusual place to have a hotel that's dedicated to tourists. In front of us is an abandoned factory of unknown purpose, and to the side of it I can see a sign, 'Hotel Tourist', but the sign fails to say 'Welcome'.

Inside, it appears that the Hotel Tourist is another relic of an age when authority liked to keep its visitors cosseted and cared for in an easily managed environment. It is in every way apart from its name, an exact replica of the Hotel Moscow that I'd enjoyed so much in Sochi. On entering the foyer it feels as if we were the first visitors to this once almost grand establishment since the fall of the Berlin wall. It's more shabby than chic but at just £12 per night for a twin room, the Hotel Tourist will be absolutely perfect.

A day or a week in Volgograd, we really don't know, so we pay for one night and I'm given a small slip of paper that I should take with me to the fourth floor. Arriving on the fourth floor, I hand the slip of paper to the 'Floor Manager' and she selects the appropriate room key from the drawer of her very neat desk. She then hands the room key to her 'Floor Assistant', who escorts us along the corridor to our room. It's a system that seems overly bureaucratic when checking into a hotel, but we soon find that it's a system that's repeated every time we leave the bloody room. The ladies guarding access to the room keys on each floor are affectionately known here in Russia as 'Floor Grannies' and if we're going to be staying in hotels, it's just another quirk that we'll probably get used to. Actually, it's really quite charming in a very Russian sort of way.

Mother Russia standing tall and proud above Volgograd

Chapter 23:
Russia, Volgograd

As I'd promised on the scribbled note of yesterday, we arrive at the motorcycle marquee in the car park of the shopping centre at around ten in the morning. A young man immediately gets busy on his mobile phone and chats for several minutes. With feigned interest, I inspect his collection of motorcycles but I seriously think that I've chosen the wrong 'cross' on our map.

Then, an aging but immaculate Honda CB1000 arrives at the marquee with an English speaking rider. We shake hands and he explains that they'd received our note when they'd arrived here this morning. On the note I'd written the size of tyres that we're seeking, but sadly he expects that such tyre sizes will not be available in Volgograd. He apologises as if the lack of tyres is his own fault, and then he too becomes busy on his mobile phone. I'm not sure what's happening. The English speaker who didn't give a name, has told me that he's sorry about not having the appropriate tyres, but I don't know if that means that we should go, or stay here while he explores other options. Adam's distanced himself from the activity, so uncertain about what's happening, I pop outside into no man's land for a smoke.

A Range Rover, rare in a city where the Lada is king, and seemingly fitted with every available extra including black-out security glass, screeches to a theatrical halt beside me. A man emerges from the car with tightly cropped hair and a large stocky frame. He introduces himself as Ruslan and shakes my hand firmly. He signals for me to wait, and then enters the marquee talking quickly in loud and forceful Russian. As Ruslan returns from the marquee, I summon Adam to join us and make polite introductions.

I've no idea who Ruslan is, but he invites us to ride with him in the Range Rover and he strikes me as the sort of chap who wouldn't take too kindly to a refusal. Within seconds of the doors locking, we're racing through the streets of Volgograd towards destinations unknown. We avoid traffic by using the pavements where pedestrians politely step out of our way. We bounce across building sites where workers scatter and as we emerge back onto the more usual carriageway, policemen run into the road and instead of stopping the distinctive Range Rover for reckless driving, they halt the oncoming traffic and politely wave us through. As we speed past them, the policemen nod to Ruslan and the heads of the other drivers in the stationary cars all seem to look enviously in our direction. I have no idea who Ruslan is, but it's not too difficult to see that here in Volgograd he's a person of influence who appears to not only enjoy immunity from the law, but also the cooperation of it. At first I'd thought that Ruslan was showing-off, trying to impress us with his driving skills, but his casualness seems to suggest that this style of driving is quite normal for him. In London I'm a despatch rider and I move around the city quite swiftly, but I have never travelled through any city, in any vehicle, quite as quickly as this.

At a large and empty workshop somewhere close to the main railway station, at what I assume to be Ruslan's desk, we're invited to use the Internet. Unfortunately the computer keyboard is switched to the Cyrillic script and I'm not sure how to change it back to English. I'd ask Ruslan, but he seems to be busy talking quietly in the corner of the workshop with two men wearing smart black suits and very shiny shoes. Semyon, a friend of Ruslan arrives at the workshop and introduces himself. He drives a black Mitsubishi with the same black-out security glass and clearly frequents the same barber and gymnasium as Ruslan. Semyon speaks more English than Ruslan and announces that they're best friends, and business associates. Semyon laughs as he announces that he and Ruslan are 'Volgograd Business Men' and declares that in Moscow they usually refer to Volgograd Businessmen as 'Gangsters'. I'm not certain which part of the statement is supposed to be the joke, but I feel that it's only polite to laugh along with him.

Semyon is a jovial guy, a perfect foil for Ruslan's seriousness and he quickly has the keyboard switched to English. He looks over my shoulder and sees the tyres that I'm looking at. He makes notes of the sizes and then gives me the nod to move on. After thirty minutes of browsing, Semyon has filled an A4 sheet of paper with scribbled notes. He looks at the page and smiles. 'Geoff my friend, I don't know if they have these tyres in Russia, but if anybody can find them, we can'.

Throughout this journey, many strangers have made many claims, but Semyon's claim I can believe. We've known each other for less than two hours, but I've already decided that the large 'CROSS' on my small map of Volgograd, had been drawn in exactly the right place. Poor Circulation has once again landed firmly on its fortunate feet.

With Ruslan's business meeting completed, we're whisked at speed down side roads towards an anonymous building that sells imported Taiwanese scooters and tyres. Amongst the racks of products, we find perfectly good tyres, but sadly they're not available in sizes that will fit our wheels. We head back to Ruslan's workshop where people constantly come and go. The dress code for this workshop certainly favours Armani suits above overalls. In this city of a million people, Ruslan and Semyon seem to know everybody, and everybody seems to know them. They live their lives constantly shouting at people or talking enthusiastically on their mobile phones. At the workshop, shadowy faces look suspiciously in our direction before turning towards darkened corners where they conduct their conversations in private. Doors are closed and voices are often hushed, business is taking place here 'Ruslan Style'.

It's now lunchtime and we're taken to another anonymous looking building. Behind the doors we find a dark yet inviting restaurant that's bustling with busy people. The restaurant is full of men wearing a combination of sharp business suits and official uniforms with lots of brass and braiding. A central table is selected for our enjoyment and the incumbent diners are politely moved away to another table in the far corner of the room. As they shuffle to their newly designated table, they glance towards Ruslan and politely smile. It's a strange kind of establishment that I suspect is a restaurant by day and a gentleman's club by night. It doesn't advertise that fact, but it has that unmistakeable feel about it.

Our new best friends buy us lunch and the food is absolutely delicious. They keep ordering from the extensive menu and we fill our faces with new and interesting dishes. This is a strange kind of 'Man's Land', a place where the men conduct business and the beautiful girls sitting at various tables appear to be little more than silent garnishing. Each time the door opens and daylight fills the room, heads turn towards the door. Smiles and nods are exchanged between diners and the people here all seem to know each other. Without pointing, Semyon starts to identify certain individuals within the room, but their names mean absolutely nothing to me. I point out that there are a lot of impressive uniforms in the room and Semyon whispers that we're very close to the former headquarters of the KGB and the new home of the FSB, the KGB's successors. I'm not sure what that information should mean to me, so I just smile and remind myself not to make direct eye contact with anybody beyond our own table.

After lunch, we're taken back to the workshop where Ruslan informs us that one of his contacts has found suitable tyres. That's great news, but unfortunately the tyres are in Moscow. Moscow I know is quite a distance from Volgograd, but apparently that's not going to be a problem. Ruslan has family and friends in Moscow and they'll be only too happy to help us. They'll collect the tyres in Moscow tomorrow, pay for them, and then place them on overnight transport to Volgograd. Ruslan will have the tyres collected from the railway terminal here in Volgograd and fit them to our Tigers on Wednesday. However, we must first find a bank before four o'clock, because Ruslan must transfer the money for the tyres to Moscow. In the speeding Range Rover, I ask Semyon why they can't just pay for the tyres with their credit cards and let us reimburse them with cash. Semyon holds a conspiratorial finger to his lips: 'No Credit Cards'.

Double parked on the busy street outside of the bank, Ruslan takes an envelope from his sports bag and walks towards the door. Semyon winks at me and reaches for Ruslan's bag. He unzips the top and opens it. It's not a small bag and it's stuffed with bundles of cash. I've no idea how much money is in that bag, but it's certainly more cash that I've ever seen in one place before. 'We do not like Credit Cards my friend, here in Russia, real business men prefer real Money'.

With the money transfer complete, Semyon takes us for a tour of the city while Ruslan conducts a little more business at the workshop. Ruslan had driven his Range Rover quickly, but that was nothing in comparison to Semyon. From the outside his black Mitsubishi saloon looks sleek and stylish, but otherwise quite conventional. However, the distinctive red Brembo brake callipers peeping through the overlarge wheel rims, the discreet cooling vents cut neatly into the bonnet and the unmistakable whir of a rather large turbocharger speak volumes about the cars hidden potential. We learn that Semyon once worked for the Government, the Russian equivalent of 'HM Customs and Excise', but now prefers being his own man. He drives with a casual confidence without ever stopping the conversation and we experience what must be the fastest ever tour of Volgograd. We learn a lot about their fascinating city and even more about their connections. Semyon's father is a senior official here in Volgograd and he confidently informs us that while we're here, we'll have no more problems with the police. It seems that both Semyon and Ruslan have family connections that are important in these parts, and here in Russia, important connections seem to mean everything.

As evening falls, we arrive at a traditional Cossack restaurant called 'Trolly Wally', where Ruslan is waiting for us. The staff and customers all seem to hush when we enter, deference is shown and our corner table is dealt with immediately. The food is endless and the iced vodka flows freely. A small group of suited Russian businessmen rock on their benches as small square glasses clink together in toasts and a group of traditional Cossack singers entertain their table. Like the earlier lunchtime restaurant, Trolly Wally probably isn't mentioned in any tourist guidebook, but it certainly should be. However, Semyon tells us that the Russian's like to keep the best things for themselves and once again, we're not allowed to pay for anything, and that includes the taxi that will return us to our hotel.

Halfway back to our hotel, Semyon climbs out of the taxi at his waterside home and stumbles away into the darkness: 'Rooney Rooney Rooney'. 'We love Man U. We love Man U. We love Man U.' It's been an amazing day where everything has fallen neatly into place, and tonight Semyon seems like the happiest person that I've ever had the good fortune to meet. Things are looking up, and even Adam's beginning to smile.

Chapter 24:
Russia, Volgograd

After enjoying the Hotel Tourist's complimentary comedy breakfast, I tell the receptionist that we'll be staying here for one more night. I expect her to smile and say 'Da', just as she had done yesterday when I'd extended our stay for one more night, but today things are different. She frowns and tells me 'Niyet'. In broken English she says that we can stay for one night, two nights, or we can stay for five nights, but a total of three or four nights isn't possible. Clearly she doesn't understand my request. I just want to extend our stay by one more night. But apparently she does understand my request, she understands perfectly, but she can't allow us to stay here for that particular length of time.

As confusion begins to overwhelm me, Ruslan walks into reception and saves the day. He talks for a few seconds with the now blushing receptionist and apparently, we can now stay here for as many nights as we choose. I choose one night and she takes my money. Ruslan shouldn't be here today, he hasn't read the part of the script where Adam and I go out exploring in Volgograd on our own. Apparently that's not going to happen, because today he plans to take us sailing on the Volga.

As we head towards the quay, it's clear to see that the good people of Volgograd are all out and about and dressed in their finest clothes. Ruslan tells us that this is a National Holiday in Russia and everybody in Volgograd will be heading towards the water where they like to make the most of the short summer season.

From the concrete dock we admire the boats cruising up and down this huge river and one boat seems to be travelling a little faster than all of the others. It's white and slick and leaves behind it a plume of water that's visible from a great distance. This particular boat is a little larger and fancier than all of the others, and it's heading for the quay where we're standing. Of course, this boat belongs to our friend Semyon. 'Priviet my English friends, please climb aboard the fastest boat on the Volga'. I suspect that fast boats and independent businessmen go hand in hand in these parts, and this boat certainly suits them.

We cruise the Volga at great speed and entertain bathers with wild plumes of spray and rock music blasting out from the boat's formidable music system. We pull alongside smaller vessels where bikini clad maidens stand and wave to us. They call to Semyon by name, and Semyon calls back. They want to join us, but Semyon tells them that this is strictly a day for the boys. Semyon seems to know everybody along this river, especially it would seem the tallest and most beautiful of the girls. It's a real shame that he doesn't want to share a small part of our day with any of them, but it's his boat and he's the boss. It's clear to see that Admiral Semyon and Captain Ruslan are in their absolute elements out here on the river, and this is definitely the only way to live in Volgograd.

This evening was spent with Ruslan, Semyon and their stunningly beautiful friend, Ulyana. Once again we were wined and dined at their expense before being taken for a night time tour of this beautiful city. In Volgograd the people are rightly proud of their city, at the centre of which stands a single tree and a couple of crumbling buildings. The tree and buildings are the only things that remained standing after the Battle of Stalingrad in 1942-1943 and are haunting reminders that two million people perished here during those fateful months of the Second World War.

We're taken to 'Pasha's House', the crumbling remains of a corner building where for an entire month in the winter of 1942, opposing forces had fought floor by floor to gain advantage. The line of the street in front of Pasha's House marks the perimeter of a thirty meter piece of ground stretching back towards the Volga. This tiny sliver of Stalingrad was the only piece of land that remained under Russian control, and at its centre stands the last remaining building. It's a redbrick steam mill with walls spotted with massive holes from exploding shells and millions of smaller holes from bullets. Everything else that was Stalingrad, and I mean absolutely everything else, has been rebuilt since that time.

By any other name, this city would have been abandoned by the Russian forces, retreating across the Volga to form a new defensive line on the other side of the river. But this city was Stalingrad. Whether through vanity or through a deep understanding of his people's spirit, Stalin had ordered that the city that bore his name should never fall into enemy hands, and it didn't. It was saved by his people, men women and children of all ages, the Heroes of Stalingrad. I've visited Coventry in England and Dresden in Germany, but the trauma suffered by those cities pales into insignificance when compared to the absolute destruction that occurred here.

Ulyana puts a gentle hand on my shoulder and introduces me to the elephant that's been lurking in the room ever since we arrived here. 'It's a shame that nobody learned any lessons from this', and she certainly has a point. She then asks why after the end of the Second World War, with its vast arsenal of nuclear weapons, had America and the West wanted to destroy Russia, and I turn the question back on her. Why had Russia wanted to obliterate the West? She laughs and points towards the busy road behind us: 'In the nineteen sixties, America put a man on the moon, and forty years later, we still build the Lada'. She's smiling, but she's also deadly serious. 'Do you really think we wanted to start an unwinnable war with America?'

I don't have much time for conspiracy theories. Without exception they all seem to be light on fact and heavy on innuendo. If they had more of the former and less of the later, then we wouldn't even call them 'Conspiracy Theories', just 'History'. I firmly believe that in 1968 man did walk on the moon and that nine years later Elvis left the building on a permanent basis, but Ulyana has just turned my forty-five years of world understanding right on its head. Were the threats from Russia genuine, or were we simply sold on the fear by our politicians and media in order to satisfy some hidden political agenda? Semyon's been listening to our conversation and jumps in with a practical view of his own: 'The Cold War was very good for Volgograd, because the tank factory was always busy'. Like Ulyana, Semyon's observation is served with a smile, but it feels like another rug of understanding has just been pulled from beneath my feet. Was the Cold War a collusion to create the Arms Race, and the Arms Race little more than a convenient solution to economic stagnation on both sides of the Iron Curtain? I've no idea, but suddenly my understanding of the world that I've lived in for forty-five years feels like nothing more than a lie.

Volgograd has opened my eyes in many different ways, and what I've discovered here has probably changed my way of looking at the world, and how this world is being reported. Our friends here in Volgograd have been amazing hosts and teachers. In my eye's they're the new Hero's of Stalingrad and I say 'Thank You' from the bottom of my heart.

Yesterday as we'd cruised on the Volga, the tyres had arrived from Moscow and Ruslan's mechanics had fitted them onto the Tigers. Last night we'd planned to bring both motorcycles back to the Hotel Tourist ready for an early start this morning, but Adam had forgotten to bring his keys to Ruslan's new workshop. Thankfully, we're in Volgograd where such minor details seem to be irrelevant. Ruslan decides that we'll stay for an extra day, and even better, an extra night at his expense. Such hospitality is difficult to refuse and we once again climb happily into the back of Ruslan's Range Rover.

We're taken on another whistle-stop tour of bars and restaurants with the beautiful Ulyana. Ulyana is intrigued by the story of Poor Circulation and as an interpreter for an oil company here in Volgograd, she speaks perfect English. Ulyana explains that at schools here in Russia, the kids learn to speak English by reciting the works of William Shakespeare in class. If that's the accepted method of teaching the English language here, then it's amazing that so many Russian's can actually speak any English at all.

Ulyana finds it difficult to understand why we don't really appreciate Shakespeare and Dickens, Wordsworth and Byron, because here in Russia they love and celebrate their great writers. She politely informs us that we should be ashamed of ourselves for ignoring them.

I silently wonder if the 'Great Russian Writers' that Ulyana refers to had appreciated their time in the gulags quite as much as their audience had appreciated the beautiful words that had sent them there. Thankfully, it was only a thought and not something that I said out loud, but I'm a little embarrassed that such a thought had even entered my head. Come to think of it, didn't some of our own distinguished writers, for various nefarious reasons, become familiar with the hospitality of our own prisons?

We end our last evening at a 'Bikers Bar' where we meet local riders with an assortment of motorcycles ranging from a tricked Suzuki Hyabusa to a chopped Ural of uncertain vintage. They're a happy group of friends, in fact they're absolutely no different to bikers anywhere else in the world. They ride motorcycles, drink beer and enjoy unhealthy food and laughter. It's raucous, it's fun and it's amazingly boozy. We drink beer and eat huge quantities of 'Shashlik'; skewered meats marinated in a spicy sauce and grilled on an open barbeque. It's absolutely delicious and a perfect accompaniment to the endless supply of ice cold beer.

The mosquitoes are also hungry tonight and they're feasting on my English blood, but they strangely leave everybody else's blood, including Adam's, alone. Ruslan vanishes for a few minutes and returns with two tubes of insect repellent which seems to work rather well. The bikers laugh as I start applying the lotion to my skinny English legs, but I really don't care. I can shoulder many discomforts, but mosquitoes certainly aren't one of them. Ulyana warns me I shouldn't fear the mosquito in Stalingrad*, but that I should fear the mosquito in Siberia, because they are very large indeed. She mimics a helicopter and we all laugh. A business associate of Ruslan's laughs along with us and then seemingly corrects Ulyana's earlier statement. Apparently I shouldn't worry too much about the mosquitoes in Siberia, because compared to the Siberian Mafia, the mosquito bites will seem painless. It's not the last sentence that I'll hear tonight, but it's probably the one that I'll remember the most.

Back at our beautifully quirky hotel, and already quite hammered, I drag Adam to the bar for a final nightcap. At the table next to us sit four new ladies of the night. They're as stunning as they are fragrant and they rock gently in unison to the music of Abba while smiling to all and sundry. Gentleman callers sit with them for a few minutes at a time. They purchase drinks for the girls and then move on to pastures new. In stark contrast to the drab interior decor of this never beautiful hotel, the atmosphere around the girls is bright and electric. The girls smile wistfully towards us and we of course smile back. We're just killing time and enjoying the cheap entertainment, but the girls have far more commercial motives for being here.

Shortly before midnight, on what will certainly be our last night in Volgograd, we bid goodnight to the girls and retire for the night with our virginities and wallets intact.

---

*Although 'Stalingrad' reverted to its original name 'Volgograd' in 1962, many residents still refer to it by the former name.

Chapter 25:
Russia, Ufa

At Ruslan's sparkling new workshop, a place where people do actually wear overalls and diligently work to repair motorcycles, we pose for photographs with the freshly shod Tigers. This is definitely our last morning in Volgograd, but it will be very difficult to leave these amazing friends behind us. Just before I pull on my helmet to ride away into the unknown, Ruslan takes me to one side and offers me some words of pleasing comfort. 'Don't worry about the Mafia in Siberia, you are our friends, and we have friends everywhere, so you will have no problems'. He smiles and gives me a giant hug. It's exactly what I'd wanted to hear, and having known Ruslan for just a few short days, I have absolutely no doubt that his statement is true.

We ride away feeling slightly tearful, waving our arms but without looking back over our shoulders. I'm sad to be leaving these people behind but I'm excited by what lies ahead of us. Farewell Volgograd, Ruslan, Semyon and Ulyana, I will miss you all.

It's down to nothing more than good fortune, but so far on this journey we've asked the right question of exactly the right person and at precisely the right time. The latest stranger to cross my path beckons his son to come and join our conversation. Thankfully his son speaks a little more English and I learn that his family own the petrol station where we've just completed another pantomime performance of filling our tanks with fuel. I'd asked about the availability of camping and for the first time since entering Russia, I seemed to have found people who actually understood that camping meant sleeping in a canvas tent. The son now tells me that camping is available and points to a large modern building with the word 'MOTEL' written large above its entrance. I try to explain that we have very little money and show him the tent that hasn't been used since leaving Turkey. The father scratches his head and points to an annex at the side of his motel. 'We understand your Camping, but why use your tents for camping when you can camp inside here for free?'

The annex room that they offer us is an old steel cargo container posing as an outbuilding, but it gives us everything that we could possibly need. We'll share the space with a cat, four tiny kittens and a serious collection of erotic art, but after the relative expense of city life in Volgograd, it's comes at exactly the right price. After cooking pasta on the stove and cleaning the dishes, I grab an ice cold beer and start working on the Tigers.

The new tyres give each bike an unusual combination of Metzeler on the rear and Pirelli on the front. Individually these are perfectly good tyres, but as a combination on the Tigers they're making slow riding on tarmac quite challenging. It's nothing too serious, it just feels a little bit strange and adjusting the tyre pressures throughout the day seemed to correct most of the problems. Adam's still not comfortable with the handling, so I transfer all of the remaining communal equipment onto my bike and hopefully the lighter load and increased space to move around on the motorcycle will help him.

An accidental benefit of the extra weight transferred onto my Tiger means that I can now actually touch the floor with both feet. That probably won't stop me from falling off, but at least I won't have quite so far to fall. After addressing the luggage issues, I remove and clean the brake callipers, adjust both of our final drive chains and check all of the nuts and bolts for tightness. The Triumphs have performed amazingly well, but today we've seen the first actual breakage. The chain guard on my Tiger has snapped just above the rear spindle, but it's thankfully very easy to fix using nothing more than a hot nail and a pair of cable ties.

As I busy myself melting new holes into the plastic chain guard, the family come from their Motel to investigate. They want to pose for photographs before the sun finally sets, but as I'm slightly busy and very oily, I ask Adam to come outside and satisfy their needs. Adam reluctantly obliges and they begin to snap away with their camera.

I'm watching them from the safety of the concrete beneath Adam's motorcycle and within seconds, I'm wetting myself with laughter. The Mother of the family is clearly trying to play match-maker between Adam and their Daughter; a plump and boisterous girl with a delightful smile and an absolutely filthy laugh. She arranges Adam and her Daughter in a pose and Adam is standing upright, stiff as a board. The Mother has arranged them with Adam's arm around her Daughters back and his hand resting directly on top of her right breast. Adam probably thinks that the positioning is an accident, but when the Mother invites him to 'Squeeze', all doubts vanish and his embarrassment is complete.

Adam laughs and refuses to oblige, but the Mother is insistent. She moves forward and demonstrates the action that she's looking for and seems disappointed when Adam continues to refuse. They change places and it's Mother's turn to pose. Skirt hitched high to show her pink thong, a knee raised to Adam's waist and a pout for the camera. Adam's encouraged to explore the ampleness of her posterior, but again he refuses. In his shoes, so would I, but rather than being offended by these activities, it seems that her husband is doing much of the encouraging.

My mind drifts back to the Fish Party in Croatia, and I decide that my life so far has been far too sheltered. Afterwards, Adam explains that while the physical experience wasn't altogether unpleasant, it was mentally one of the most challenging experiences in his life.

This morning Adam was the first to rise and shortly after six o'clock, we were on the road. I'd like to think that he'd found some enthusiasm to start riding so early in the day, but I think that this morning he'd found the road to be a more inviting prospect than the family.

We've accidentally bypassed the city of Saratov and we're heading towards the main M5 Motorway, a road that should take us to Samara, Ufa and then onwards into Siberia. The navigational plan is simple, but its execution is proving to be somewhat troublesome.

Twenty miles short of the M5, the road that we're riding along comes to an abrupt and unannounced end. A steel barrier menacingly wrapped in razor wire blocks our path. At the barrier are two well armed soldiers who seem to have run out of smiles. I consult the map but it's short of answers. Unless there's another road that's been recently constructed and not marked on my out of date map, then I can't see an easy way around this unscheduled dead end. With just a few common words between us, I talk with the soldiers and establish that we're exactly where we think we are on my map, but that this section of road just hasn't yet been built yet.

That's something of a problem, and although on certain days local traffic is sometimes allowed to use this unfinished stretch of road, today is unfortunately not one of those days. We can hear in the distance, and feel in the ground beneath our feet, the explosions of what they call a 'Live Military Exercise'. It seems that the military activity is taking place to the northeast of our position, and the direction that we want to take is directly north, but that's certainly not something that I'd stake my life on.

On the bonnet of their armoured vehicle, I spread out my map and show them exactly where we want to go. I move my pencil north and it connects directly with the M5 Motorway. They understand exactly what I want to do, but what they want me to do is something totally different. One of the soldiers takes his knife and traces a different line on my map, a line that moves back towards the West. I've never played this version of the game before, but I think that in a contest of 'Map-Pencil-Knife', 'Knife' always beats 'Pencil' and it looks like we'll have no alternative but to retrace our tracks.

We're then joined by a man who looks like an officer. Nobody salutes his arrival, but his shirt collar is heavy with buttons and brass. He looks at the map and talks for a minute with the two soldiers. It's another of those conversations that sounds like an argument, but they seem to reach some sort of agreement. The officer doesn't offer his name, but he speaks English, the kind of English learned in life rather than the classroom. He tells me that he understands the problem and invites me to follow his jeep. I ask the two soldiers if they're happy with that, but they just point their eyes back towards the officer and shrug their shoulders. I take that as a 'Yes' and fold up my map.

As I climb back onto the Tiger the officer tells me that I shouldn't be too alarmed by the distant explosions. Today the army are playing 'War-Games', but they're shooting the Chinese today, not the English. Before I can ask anything more, or even tell Adam what's happening, the officer slams the door of his Uaz jeep and is racing off into the sand.

The track is sand, but thankfully the uppermost surface is compacted and although it's rough, we somehow manage to avoid bogging down and falling off. The officer drives the jeep like a maniac and I wonder if he's trying to show-off for our amusement, or if he's simply running for all of our lives. The explosions seem to have stopped, but maybe they're just being masked by the sound of the bike's engine and not hearing them is no less scary. It's by far the worst ground that we've ridden on so far, but speed is probably our friend and the Tigers just seem to growl and get on with it.

We follow in the speeding jeeps tyre tracks for almost half an hour and I begin to realise just how out of shape I've become. Not that I was ever particularly fit, but keeping the Tiger upright takes every ounce of my energy and I'm sweating like a pig in a sauna. I want to slow down, but the jeep driver is the only person here who knows where we're going. I don't want to lose him and accidentally wander into a more dangerous place, so there's no option but to try and keep pace with him. Adam's dropping back and I try to keep both the jeep and the Tiger in sight, but the distance between them is growing. If it comes to a choice then I'll have to choose Adam, but thankfully that's a decision that I never have to make.

With my last remaining morsel of energy, I crest an old revetment and land at the side of a gloriously paved highway. The officer is already out of his jeep looking hot and relieved. He approaches and grasps my hand almost shaking my arm from my body. His smiles a huge smile and passes his hand quickly across his shaven head while making the sound of what I assume is a whizzing missile. He's laughing, but he's also shaking like a leaf and that makes two of us. He points a little way down the road and tells me to be careful, because there's a police checkpoint just around the corner. He waits until Adam arrives, shakes his hand and then heads away in the opposite direction along the M5 Motorway. Adam whips off his helmet, wipes a river of sweat from his brow and asks what the hell has just happened. I don't know what to say. I'm really not sure what we've just done, but we're alive and we've found the road that we were looking for, so it can't all be bad.

As we head towards Samara and then Ufa, the road surfaces are gradually deteriorating. The roads are not impassable, they're just much less predictable and the traffic is slightly more suicidal. The people drive like there's no tomorrow and seeing the number of roadside memorials, for many of them that clearly became true. We stop at a tiny roadside shack for lunch and I get to practice the latest additions to my Russian vocabulary; 'borsch', 'kleb' and 'yesto', which I think translates to soup, bread and fried eggs. My translation may not be correct, but whenever I say it, that seems to be what they give us. It's simple food, but it's really quite delicious, especially when you're hungry. As Adam wipes the remaining yolk from his plate, I pay for the meal and then stroll outside for an after-lunch smoke. I know nicotine isn't healthy, but it just compliments everything else that I shouldn't really do in life.

Stamping out the butt and considering lighting up a second, I notice a collection of professional looking rally vehicles joining the highway from a small side road. They're heading in the same direction as us, so it would probably be rude if we didn't investigate further. We set out in pursuit and an hour later catch up with them when they stop for lunch at a tented Catering Camp.

The trucks, cars and bikes are all competing in the 'Rally Trans-Oriental' and we've bumped into them between stages. Our Tigers are parked together alongside a pair of competition KTM's from 'Team No Sponsors', and to the general public, our own motorcycles don't seem to look too out of place. I talk with a couple of guy's driving a huge Kamas truck, and they suggest that we should join them as 'Team Poor Circulation'. Of course they're joking, but we agree to ride along with them until they turn south and start heading towards their next competitive stage in Kazakhstan.

Here on the roads in Russia, most people will wave at us and 'honk' their horns as we pass them, or more usually, as they pass us. Quite a few will even stop their cars ahead of us, wave us down and offer us food and vodka at the side of the road. It's just something that happens several times each day and we've become quite accustomed to it. It's fun and it's friendly, but what we experience now takes that attention to an entirely different level.

We leave the catering camp following a group of competition motorcycles and the big Kamas truck. The bikes soon disappear into the distance and we're only just managing to keep pace with the truck. This section of road is designated as being 'Between Stages', but for Adam and I on the Tigers, it feels closer to flat-out racing. Through my freshly fly-splattered visor, I see cars heading towards us with passengers hanging from windows, snapping away with cameras and waving enthusiastically. Sandwiched between two amazingly loud trucks, we approach a police checkpoint at twice the legal speed limit. The police officers have blocked the side roads and are saluting us through.

Fifty extremely fast miles have passed, and above us a helicopter films our progress. A cameraman is hanging from the doorway and a waving arm behind him encourages us to respond in kind. People clearly think that we're part of the official rally and I'm more than happy to smile and wave back at them.

I'd like to think that the Tigers are comfortable at the pace set by the competition, and maybe they are, but as the road conditions start to deteriorate the competition starts disappearing over the horizon. The Tigers may be capable, but their riders are certainly not. It was great while it lasted, but all good things must come to an end. A few stragglers over-take us on a long downward straight and we see them turning south and heading for Kazakhstan. It's the point where our short but exciting union must end and their absence makes the road feel quite lonely.

We carry on eastwards but the new feeling of loneliness lasts for little more than a mile. A police officer who appears to be no more than twelve years of age, and wearing the widest rimmed cap that I've ever seen, has pulled us to the side of the road. He speaks very little English but a blind man could see that he's very unhappy with our actions. With the engine killed, I fumble for my documents and start mentally searching for be-lievable excuses.

Given our probable speed, I'm expecting the worst and I'm amazed when the young officer simply reaches out and politely shakes my hand. 'Wrong way Deutsch Man, Kazakhstan is this way'. He points his baton back down the road towards the point where the genuine rally folks had turned to the south. I don't think that telling him I'm English will help our situation, so I just smile and give him some story about visiting friends in the city of Ufa. He clearly doesn't have a clue what I'm telling him, but that doesn't seem to matter. He stalks around the Tiger inspect-ing all of its parts, but thankfully not in an official sort of way. I invite him to climb aboard for photographs but he seems apprehensive and keeps looking at his watch. He's probably worried that we'll fall too far behind the other teams and it's really quite touching that he cares.

Eventually he does climb into the saddle and satisfies his curiosity about all of the switches, but then looks again at his watch and tells me that it's time to go. I pat him on the shoulder and tell him that I appreci-ate his concern, but we really must go to Ufa. 'Yes, you told me already, but I am late for the end of my duty, goodbye Deutsch man'.

Last night we camped for the very first time in Russia. It was proper camping with tents and not the Russian version that seems to involve four walls and a roof. It felt good to be back under canvas again, liberat-ing and free of charge. The deeper we ride into Russia, the greater the distance there is between towns, and thus the more open ground there is for rough camping. I rode into a small forest and found a suitable spot that was far enough from the road to be safe, but close enough not to be scary. We pitched the tents, Adam lit a fire to keep away the mosquitoes and I cooked pasta that we washed down with cold beer. It turned out to be a relaxing night with no unwelcomed visitors and we'd both enjoyed a jolly good night's sleep.

Unlike hotels, camping doesn't offer the complimentary breakfast, so we were packed and back on the road shortly after dawn. We're making good progress on bad roads and the police interference since leaving Volgograd has all been of the positive kind.

As we cross into Asia for the second time on the journey, we meet up with five Polish riders on an assortment of motorcycles. I'd first seen them ride past the cafe where we were eating breakfast this morning, but this is the first opportunity that we've had to talk with them. They're heading from Poland down to Mongolia for six weeks of off-road riding and are celebrating their first entry into Asia by fashioning each other's hair in unusual patterns with a razor. I'm invited to join in the celebration but I politely decline. It's taken me forty years to lose this much hair and I really don't need any help with what little remains.

Adam also refuses a haircut, but he shakes my hand and welcomes me to Asia. He's talkative and happy, it's his first time outside of Europe and he's telling everybody how excited he is to be entering a different continent. It's good to see him this way, and it's not a day for bursting happy bubbles, so I neglect to tell him that we'd actually crossed into Asia when we'd ridden across Turkey.

We set out to ride with our new friends Michal, Pitor, Robert, Marcin and Burt, five guys who apparently met on an internet forum at the beginning of the year, and decided without ever meeting in person, to ride together on this great adventure into Mongolia. They have an assortment of motorcycles: Two Honda Africa Twins, a pair of Yamaha XT600's and unusually for an off-road adventure, a heavy shaft driven Honda NTV 650, the London courier's weapon of choice in the 1990's. The 'Polish Mission to Mongolia', as they call themselves, has arrived like a breath of fresh air and our day together is filled with hilarious activity. Between them, they speak many languages including Russian and English, and the first thing that they teach us is how to easily fill up our Tigers with fuel.

As night falls, I watch and take note as the Polish experts seek out suitable camping grounds. They choose sites that are close to villages, but not inside them. In the village, they seek permission to camp from village elders and if permission isn't granted, they move on to another location. It's an education for me and I learn that problems can occur if you simply arrive at a suitable site and camp without local permission, or even worse, you make your camp between two villages. Apparently, each village wants to lay claim to you as their guests, each village will guard you jealously, and if no prior agreement has been reached as to which village is your host, violence can actually break out. This sounds ludicrous, but they tell me that it's just the way that things happen out here. This is after all Russia, and not the Home Counties.

Once permission to make camp has been established, we're shown where to find drinkable water and firewood. Tents are erected and each member of their team seems to have a designated task. Two go collecting wood and start the fire, two start preparations for dinner and one goes off on his motorcycle to collect a fresh supply of ice cold beer. As the fire starts to smoke, it attracts the attention of the local children and they swarm around us outnumbered only by the mosquitoes.

They're fun kids, exactly the same as kids the world over. The bravest kid asks to ride on the back of one of the motorcycles, and then the others follow his lead. Within a matter of minutes, the five Polish guys are tearing around the field with screaming young pillions hanging on for their lives and loving every second of it. The remaining few kids stand looking at our Tigers, but they seem uncertain. The Tiger's aren't suited to this terrain, and neither of us can match the riding skills of the more experienced Poles, so maybe the kids are right to hesitate. I've no idea what the penalty will be for crashing a motorcycle and injuring one of the village kids, but you only live once.

I lift off my topbox, fire up the Tiger and two kids immediately jump onto the back. I won't say that I was ever confident, but the two kids weighed a lot less than my luggage and an absolute hoot was had by all. Nobody crashed, nobody died and we'd paid for the privilege of camping by distributing smiles.

All in all, it's been a perfect day of riding and we round off the night by drinking an unreasonable quantity of beer and sharing our stories. The beer runs out, and that's closely followed by the solitary bottle of vodka. Adam then remembers the several litres of Raki that we've carried with us from Albania and leaps into action. It's an action that tomorrow morning all of us will surely regret. Nobody died during the impromptu motorcycle racing on the field, but Raki is an entirely different kind of poison and I fear that an unforgettable evening, will sadly be forgotten.

Chapter 26:
Russia, Novosibirsk

We've been very fortunate to have fallen in with the five riders from Poland. For three days we've ridden long miles with these guys and spent three of the most memorable nights camping and drinking vodka around campfires in the forests on the edge of Siberia. We've helped them to fix punctures in the midday sun and eaten food in cafes that on our own, we might never have dared to order. They've taught us many valuable lessons about riding through Russia and prepared us well for the long journey ahead.

But sadly for all of us, the time has come for our paths to part. In front of a new and highly polished petrol station, we pose for final photographs and exchange contact details before they ride south towards Mongolia. It's sad to see our five new friends leave, and it's very tempting to follow them, but sadly our budgets and visas dictate that we remain here in Russia. We wish them all the very best on their mission to Mongolia, we thank them for their hospitality and hope that one day very soon, our paths will cross again.

'Please contact the nearest branch of your bank'. Ever since leaving England, this is something that Adam had worried would happen. The ATM on the outskirts of Novosibirsk has just refused to give Adam any money, but at least it's returned his Bank Card. Unfortunately, the nearest branch of Barclays Bank is probably back in London and visiting it isn't really an option. Adam hasn't taken the news well, but it's not the fault of the Sberbank Cash Machine and I doubt that swearing at it in English will help to resolve the problem.

I try to reassure him that it's nothing more than a temporary hiccup, something that can easily be fixed with a telephone call to Barclays Bank, but Adam's in no mood for listening. In London it's probably a little after nine in the morning, so I take Adam's phone, scroll through the contact numbers, and press 'Call'. A few seconds later I select 'Option #3' from the automated answering service. With the connection established, I pass the phone back to Adam.

While Adam talks to what I hope will be a real person at Barclays Bank, a heavily modified Toyota pickup truck draws to a halt in front of us. Fred and his wife Asi introduce themselves and explain that they're driving their mobile home to China from their permanent home in Switzerland. I explain why they've found the pair of us sitting here on the pavement on the outskirts of Novosibirsk and Fred just laughs. Apparently it's a problem that they both encounter often, something that every traveller experiences at least once on each journey, but that it's one of the easiest problems to fix. All it takes is a telephone call to the bank.

Adam's still talking to somebody at Barclays Bank, probably replying to security questions with specific names and numbers, but he's looking up at Fred, nodding his head and smiling. Hopefully that's a good sign and a temporary crisis has been averted.

Unfortunately Fred and Asi need to keep moving, they want to pass through Novosibirsk and find a suitable place to park on the other side of the city before darkness falls. As they drive away into the chaos of the city, Adam rises to his feet and puts away his telephone. Apparently a computer is accepting responsibility for temporarily divorcing him from his money, but Barclays Bank have assured him that within twenty-four hours everything will be functioning normally. Everything is once again rosey and it's time to move on.

Several hours, but not too many miles later, we stop at the side of the road and talk with Roland. Roland's a sixty-something cyclist from Germany who's making his way down through China into Hong Kong. Up until last year Roland had worked in Hong Kong, and when asked at his retirement party what he would do in his days of retirement he'd told them, perhaps drunkenly, that he was going to buy a bicycle in Germany and cycle back to Hong Kong. Perhaps they'd thought that Roland had been joking, but less than a year later he's already cycled more than half-way back towards them. Just as I finish filling Roland's cooking stove with fuel from the Tiger, Fred and Asi drive in to join us in their Toyota. We must have passed them somewhere in the automotive turmoil that was Novosibirsk, but I'm certainly happy to see them again.

It's getting late and as we're all travelling in the same direction, we decide to find and share a camping ground for the night. East of Novosibirsk, I skirt through the centre of a village and cross a bridge over a wide and free flowing river. On either side of the river there's a stretch of short grass that would be perfect for camping. Confident that it's the ideal location, I head back to inform the others.

After just a couple of miles I find Adam and the Toyota heading towards me. Before we've switched off our engines, Roland appears in the distance peddling like a man possessed. He's twenty years older than me and at least twenty times fitter. He doesn't bother to stop, but Fred points in the direction of the river and Roland keeps on peddling. With only one road to follow and the location of the campground obvious, I trust that the others will find it while I stop in the village to purchase supplies for the evening; pasta, tomato sauce and several tall bottles of ice cold beer. At home I'd probably have a list of individual dietary requirements for our new friends, but this is Siberia and if you choose to be picky about your food then you're probably choosing to go hungry.

On the grassy bank of an unknown river, at the edge of an unnamed village, but definitely somewhere in Siberia, Fred and Asi kindly cook dinner in the back of their van while we pitch our tents. We eat and we drink, and then we drink some more. The mosquitoes here are plentiful and they bite like absolute bitches. The repellent certainly helps, but it doesn't keep them all at bay. In the end the only answer is to drink lots of beer and let them have their hungry way.

As we laugh and joke after dinner, a car pulls alongside our tents and a man introduces himself as the local 'Chief of Police'. He's polite, speaks very good English and he's more than happy to allow us to camp alongside his river. Less than eight hours after saying goodbye to our Polish friends, the best Russian teachers that we could ever have hoped for, I'd forgotten everything that they'd taught me about the etiquette of camping in Russia. I feel strangely guilty for ignoring their lessons and embarrassed that we might have offended the locals here. Thankfully it seems that everything will be alright and the other's don't seem to have registered our faux pas. Adam's laughing and joking with Fred and Asi, and

Roland's already speechless from drinking far too much beer. We're all just happy strangers in a very strange land without a care in the world. It's not a bad life really.

At dawn this morning, a low mist hangs across the river and there's a magical stillness in the air. I move around taking hundreds of photographs and notice an old man wearing an even older jumper and ill fitting pair of trousers. He stands watching me, smiling and waving for me to come towards him. We talk for a few minutes but he speaks no English at all. Asi walks over to join us and I discover that her command of the Russian language is really rather good. The interestingly dressed stranger is a retired sailor who in his younger days had sailed the seven seas on a vessel called the 'Mariance'. Coincidentally, Asi believes that Mariance is also the name of the village, or the river next to which we're camping, but she's not quite sure which. The old sailor wants to give Asi some potatoes from his garden and as the others rise from their beds, he gives us all a guided tour of his small wooden home.

Everything within the house is beautifully tidy and clean, he's a man who takes pride in his home. He doesn't have much of anything, but everything that he does have has its own specific place and photographic reminders of his recently departed wife are everywhere. He's proud of his house, proud of his naval past and now proud to add a Poor Circulation pin badge to a small board on his kitchen wall containing memorabilia from his own distant travels. I notice a framed picture of Vladimir Putin and I point to it with a raised eyebrow. The old sailor smiles and raises a thumb and proudly speaks his name: 'Putin'.

Back in Sochi I'd suggested that Putin was a friend to Russia's oligarchs, the people he'd supported to develop business and who in turn supported his Presidency, but my subsequent experiences in Russia suggest something entirely different. Putin seems to enjoy a level of universal support that would make any Western leader turn green with envy. His support seems to come from every level within Russian society, including a middleclass that I thought hadn't even existed, and even from this old sailor here in Mariance. I don't pretend to know much about Putin or the politics of Russia, only what I've learned from the BBC, but what I've found here is certainly not what I'd expected to find.

As we prepare to leave the old sailors home, I peer over a small fence at the edge of his garden and I'm shocked by what I see. It's a small meadow of cannabis plants, not yet in bud, but well on their way towards it. As the others return to the tents, the old sailor opens a gate and invites me to take a closer look at his secret little garden. I'm not an expert on Siberian marijuana, but the plants look young, immature and too tightly spaced for their own good. He shrugs his shoulder and lets out a gentle sigh, as if he's telling me that they're menacing weeds that he simply can't control. He bends down and carefully pulls several plants out by their roots. At first I wasn't sure if he'd known what his apparently accidental crop really was, but as he pulls several more plants out of the ground, I sense that he's 'thinning' his crop rather than 'destroying' it.

Then from a small potting shed in the corner of the plot, he retrieves a small packet and hands it to me. I put it into my pocket and offer him one of my Turkish cigarettes in exchange. He takes one from the pack and sniffs it before placing it carefully in his shirt pocket. He then smiles quite mischievously, and takes the rest of the pack from me. Of course the old devil knows what he's growing here, and he's just made his first deal of the day. This is Siberia, a hostile place where even old sailors must need distractions during the long months of winter.

Once again, we find ourselves saying goodbye to new friends long before we really want to. We move out leaving the old sailor behind us, all heading east but at very different speeds. With a few relaxing miles under our belts, we stop at a small roadside cafe and order our usual breakfast; five eggs and five thick fingers of dry bread. Sometimes we get different amounts of each, and sometimes we get exactly what we think we've ordered, but always it's delicious and fulfilling.

Our time with the Polish riders and the Swiss couple, seems to have given Adam new confidence, and over breakfast he tells me that he wants to lead the next section of the ride. The choices of road out here are few, so navigation is relatively easy and Adam knows that exactly twelve miles east of this cafe, we'll be stopping to celebrate a major milestone in riding life. It'll be the first time that Adam's taken the lead since leaving Austria, and I'm quite pleased that he's chosen now to do it.

With breakfast eaten and paid for, I follow Adam away from the small rustic cafe and start counting down the miles. We've both reset our trip metres to zero and I've promised to remind him when we get close to the twelfth mile.

Eight miles covered and four miles to go. I hope that the twelfth mile will arrive at the side of a beautiful lake with snow capped mountains in the background, or failing that, at the door of an all day bar with red velvet curtains, chrome poles and a host of beautiful dancing girls.

Ten miles covered and two miles remaining. There's no sign of human life ahead of us, so I can probably forget about red velvet curtains and beautiful dancing girls, but there's still the slight chance of a beautiful lake appearing at the side of the road.

Eleven miles covered and one mile to go. I move closer to Adam's rear tyre and sound my horn until he responds. I see his face flash in the mirror and he waves a single finger, one mile to go.

Eleven and a half miles covered and it's time to start slowing down. Sadly, there's no sign of that beautiful lake, just miles and miles of spindly silver barked trees and open grassland in every direction. It might sound supremely silly, but it feels like I'm waiting for a birthday or Christmas to arrive and as each portion of the last mile clicks down, I get more and more excited.

At twelve miles I can see absolutely nothing of photographic interest to mark my milestone but as I look ahead, I can see Adam disappearing into distance. Has he forgotten to stop? I slow down to walking pace before the trip metre can race to 'Thirteen' and pull the camera out of my pocket. I hold it high above my head and start taking photographs of myself.

The thirteenth mile clicks onto my trip metre and I've now ridden a total of one million and one miles on motorcycles in my lifetime. The moment that took forty-five years to arrive has passed without ceremony. I've got photographs of the moment, but not the photographs that I'd really hoped for and I doubt that I'll ever reach two million miles.

One million and fifty seven miles into my lifetime journey, Adam pulls into a filling station for gas. I pay the girl in the kiosk and fill both of the Tigers before returning to collect my change. It works, the Polish riders have taught us well. Instead of guessing how much fuel we'll need, I now deposit 1,000 Roubles at the counter and say with a charming smile: 'Priviet, Anglian niyet Russian, dva motorsykle, dupulna'. I'm not entirely sure what this phrase means, but it seems to work an awful lot better than our old system.

With the Tigers refuelled, I sit on the grass and relax with a smoke. It's one of my Turkish cigarettes, but I could really use a joint right now. Adam seems to have found something of interest at the opposite side of the large forecourt, as far away from me as possible. When we'd first pulled in for fuel I'd asked Adam why he hadn't stopped to mark my millionth mile as we'd agreed, and he'd told me that he'd simply forgotten all about it. I know that it was my one millionth motorcycle mile and not his, but if the boot had been on the other foot he would have found me standing on the road ahead of him with the video camera rolling and in the absence of champagne, a chilled bottle of beer at the ready. I know we're different people, but I honestly didn't think that any two people could be quite as different as this.

I enjoyed our time together with Ruslan and Semyon, and then the Polish guys and Fred and Asi, not just because they were great people to spend time with, but because in a way they shielded me from Adam's increasingly dark moods. It feels that when we are with other travellers, apart from being a little shy, his actions are quite normal, but when it's just the two of us together, then all bets are off. I'm sitting here on the side of the road hoping that he'll change, but I think that what I'm really hoping for is another Samaritan to ride to my rescue.

We're now somewhere to the east of Kansk and riding along deeply rutted sand roads. The surface is dry and loose sand and with every bone shattering mile the invisible ruts seem to be getting deeper. I've let a little more air out of our tyres, and that certainly helps, but this morning there's another problem. My Tigers developed an intermittent fault that keeps cutting-out the engine. I'm not sure if it's an electrical fault or a fuelling problem, and I should really investigate, but it's far too hot and I'm way too lazy to start unpacking the Tiger out here. I'll live with it until we reach Irkutsk and fix it before riding out to Lake Baikal.

When we stop to brew coffee, I notice that Adam's chain guard is loose at the rear end. On closer inspection it seems to have snapped, exactly as mine had done a few days earlier. Aside from the as yet unidentified intermittent fault on my Tiger, in nine thousand miles, the chain guards are the only failures on either of our motorcycles. It's obviously a weak point on the Tigers, but if that's the only weak point then I'll be a very happy man indeed. Fortunately it's also an easy thing to fix and within a few minutes, we're ready to start rolling again.

Just as we're about to pull out onto the road, a tall German rider arrives on a BMW R100GS and introduces himself as 'Rick'. He seems like a fun guy, he's very talkative and he asks if he can tag along with us until darkness arrives. I've absolutely no idea how many miles it is from here to the visible horizon, but aside from the three of us and a whole lot of short tufted grass, I can see absolutely no other living thing around us. Of course Rick can tag along with us. Without taking a vote, Rick decides that he'll lead and shoots off into the distance.

I follow Rick and try to keep sight of his BMW ahead of me and Adam's Tiger behind. For two hours we ride as if attached by a lengthening piece of elastic. The road surface isn't good, in fact I'm not sure that you could really call it a 'Road', it's mostly just a sand track liberally littered with potholes that could swallow a fully grown Tiger. It's exhausting for riders and bikes, but Rick's determined pace is exactly what we need. We're riding through land where there's precious little to see and at least this way we're covering more miles than we would ever cover on our own.

It's starting to get dark, or rather the light is slightly less than it had been, and that suggests that it's probably eight or nine o'clock in the evening. We've crossed so many unmarked time zones that it's difficult to work out what time of day it really is. While contemplating what the actual time might be, I've neglected to keep a watchful eye in my mirrors. Adam's disappeared and I pull over to wait. A minute passes and there's still no sign of him, so I turn around and retrace the route. A few miles back down the track, I find the black Tiger parked awkwardly at the side of the road and Adam lying down on a large pile of sand.

At first I think that the Tiger's failed, or that he's fallen off and injured his back, but thankfully he's just exhausted. A few minutes later Rick arrives with a flourish on his Dakar Rally specification BMW. It's time to look for somewhere to camp for the night, and Rick volunteers to go searching. It's a good offer, and I'm almost tired enough to accept it, but I've seen the way Rick rides his BMW and fear that he'll find a campground that's impossible for novices like us to reach. I leave the two of them together and ride off in search of a suitable and accessible site

Adam and Rick are impressed, I've done well and I'll admit that I've even surprised myself. Behind a line of trees, I've found a beautiful meadow of deep grass and wild flowers, far enough from the road to be invisible, but close enough to allow access for our Tigers. We pitch our tents, Adam and Rick start the mandatory fire that suppresses all but the hardiest of the mosquitoes while I cook pasta with oregano and a mild chilli sauce. We wash it down with large bottles of unfortunately warm beer and we talk about our various motorcycling adventures.

It's now early morning, probably four o'clock, and I'm wide awake and trying hard to breathe in silence. The moon casts shadows of dancing trees across my tent, but there's something else moving out there and it doesn't have leaves or roots. I can hear panting, heavy breathing, and every now and again, a very low growl that lasts for several worrying seconds. Whatever it is, it's moving slowly between our tents. The one thing that I definitely can't hear now is snoring, and if the animal outside is what I worry it might be, I hope that Adam and Rick are hearing it too.

It has to be a bear, and although we'd joked about meeting one somewhere here in Siberia, now that it's here I'll openly admit to being scared. It's around the tents for several minutes, minutes that feel like hours, but eventually it must get bored and wanders away into the forest. I could unzip the tent and check, but I'm not totally stupid. I'm dying to take a piss, and I've got a suitable receptacle inside the tent with me, but I've no idea if bears react to the scent of urine, and now's not the time to find out. I'll cross my legs and wait until morning.

As I brew coffee and wait for Adam and Rick to emerge, I expect both of them to laugh at my bear story, but they don't. They'd too been woken by its growling, they'd heard exactly the same things and had been just as terrified as I'd been. It's great that we've encountered the famous Siberian Bear, but unless all future bears arrive wearing blue duffel coats and prefer the taste of marmalade sandwiches to humans, then all of us hope that it's an experience that won't be repeated.

Chapter 27:
Russia, Irkutsk

We enter the city of Irkutsk shortly after eight in the evening, and it's just starting to rain. The black clouds and lightning have been following us for the last hundred miles and our good fortune with the weather is finally coming to a stormy end. Our plan for Irkutsk is to use Rick's 'Lonely Planet Guide' to find a cheap hostel for tonight, spend tomorrow morning arranging a Mongolian Visa for Rick, and then in the afternoon we'll all head out to Lake Baikal for a few days of relaxation.

We've reached Irkutsk a week ahead of schedule and even more surprisingly, I'm still running a few shillings under budget, so under the circumstances a change in the weather conditions isn't really the worst thing that could have happened. I seem to have spent most of my life riding in and around London, often in bad weather, but nothing could ever have prepared me for riding through Irkutsk in the rain. It's the heavy kind of rain that we seldom see in London, the drains here don't cope well with the deluge and the hazardous potholes and raised manhole covers, or in some cases a lack of manhole covers, are now invisible beneath the flood water.

Using a sketch map of the city and Rick's GPS, we find the first hotel on our list. It looks to be cheap and clean, but the receptionist insists that my Russian Visa is invalid and refuses to let us stay. It's probably more likely that she objects to having three dirty wet bikers soiling her premises and to be honest, I can hardly blame her for that.

A few miles away, we find the second hotel where the only available room is a little on the small size for the three of us. However, it's only for one night and the price is right, so we can probably live with the size. We decide to stay, but a glance at my passport results in a familiar response. My visa is not in order and not only can we not stay at the hotel, but the receptionist must inform the police, immediately. I'll say without fear of contradiction, that I've had warmer welcomes at worse hotels than this, but a meeting with the police isn't something that I'd planned for this evening.

We're standing on the pavement in the pouring rain wondering which way to run, when a car pulls alongside: 'Can we help you?'. It's a young couple who speak very good English and from the moment that we say 'Yes', they're busy on their mobile phones trying to find us a berth for the night. I feel it only fair to tell them that the two previous hotels had noticed a problem with my visa and had refused to allow us to stay. They look at my passport, talk together and then begin telephoning again. Five minutes later, we're following their car to a hotel in the 'Business District' of Irkutsk. When we arrive we're warned that this hotel normally charges by the hour and that under no circumstances should we ever walk outside of the hotel during the hours of darkness. For good measure, they add that it might get a little noisy during the night, but I've already guessed what sort of hotel this is. It's the kind of hotel that doesn't want to look at any of our passports, and that's fine with me tonight.

We're currently checking into the finest no questions asked budget brothel that Irkutsk has to offer, but at less than £20 per night for three beds, secure parking for the bikes and hot radiators on which to dry our soaking clothes, as far as I'm concerned it's the best hotel in town.

By the time we've unpacked our bikes and laid our clothes out to dry, it's already close to midnight. We settle down for a decent night's sleep, but sleep is something that none of us gets. It's surprising how doors and corridors can be built to make so much noise performing the functions for which they were designed. It's a boisterous night of raised voices and endless banging, and I haven't even mentioned the beds yet. Looking on the bright side, we probably still slept better than any of the girls who are staying here.

After what sounded like a very busy night in the brothel, I enter the bar area in search of my early morning coffee. It's shortly after eight in the morning and there's more signs of life than I'd imagined there'd be at this hour. On the main table, nestled between empty beer bottles and overflowing ashtrays, a large open strongbox is overflowing with paper money. As I waltz in and greet them with a cheery English 'Good Morning', the girls just casually glance in my general direction and then return to whatever they'd been doing before I'd bounced in to disturb them. Their smiles are polite but weary, and are in stark contrast to those of last night when I'd probably been viewed as a potential client. I pour myself a glass of strong black coffee and stand in the corner of the room watching the girls file their nails and discussing the previous night's transactions.

Without warning, the external steel door swings open and the girls wince as the dark and claustrophobic room suddenly fills with sunlight. In the open doorway I can see the silhouettes of two broad and purposeful figures, figures that completely fill the narrow entrance. The two men enter the room, the muzzle of the first assault rifle pointing towards the floor and the second towards the ceiling. Neither of the black clad men is smiling and my coffee has suddenly developed ripples across its surface. I can't control the shaking of my hand and I really can't remember ever coming this close to actually shitting my pants. Caught somewhere in the void between intrigue and cowardice, I'd normally choose cowardice, but I'm standing in the corner and there's absolutely nowhere to for me to run to. I decide to stand my ground and eventually hold out a cautious hand in the direction of the two burley men, 'Priviet'.

A moment's silence is followed by a lightening flash of teeth. My hand is taken and clenched in a vice like grip: 'Deutch man, motorshikl?' The conversation is brief, and I quickly understand that their real interests lay elsewhere in the room. I take my coffee and decide that now would probably be a good time to visit our motorcycles outside in the yard.

I'm relieved to be out of the room and Rick soon joins me with the question: 'Did you see them?' Yes Rick, I most certainly did.

Once we're all wide awake and fortified with more coffee, rather than disturbing our motorcycles, we call a taxi and travel into the city under dark skies and more torrential rain. The roads are totally flooded, vehicles are making progress where they can, but the pavements are knee deep in water and the roads are even deeper. It's hard going for the taxi and I'm thankful that we we're not riding the Tigers.

We're dropped off on Karl Marx Street and head for the Mongolian Embassy where Rick hopes to obtain his visa. They won't accept Rick's money, and payment for the visa must be made through a particular branch of Sberbank in the city. We head off and find the bank in question, but there they tell us that they can't complete the transaction. They direct us to a second branch of Sberbank, and they direct us to a third and finally to a fourth. Each branch of Sberbank states that it's only at the next branch where such a transaction can be successfully completed. The wild goose chase that they send us on is an absolute pain in the arse and in desperation, we return to the first bank. Amazingly, we now find that the cashier who'd originally refused Rick's transaction, is now more than happy to complete it for him.

After paying the appropriate amount of money, we take the receipt back to the Mongolian Embassy, but we've arrived a few minutes too late and it's closed. We smile into the security camera, wave papers and money, and finally a returning employee allows Rick to enter. The visa will be ready for collection tomorrow.

We try to avoid the rain and dive into the nearest café for warmth. Across the large room, above the heads of several diners, I see two waving hands and beneath them the beaming smiles of our Swiss friends, Fred and Asi. It's our third accidental meeting with them and over good coffee we share stories and arrange to meet again at seven this evening for dinner. With time to kill, we explore the markets of Irkutsk and stock up on smoked sausages, fresh fruit, herbs and spices before moving on to an internet cafe. It's dark inside the cafe, the computers are old and teenagers playing annoyingly loud action games are occupying most of the booths.

We read emails and update our blog's as best we can between computer crashes and power failures. There are several emails wishing us well and one particular message from my daughter Hannah. She gives me the news from England, the activities of her best friends, the latest cool bands that I ought to be listening to, a shopping list of things that I should really try to bring back with me and news that my house in England has burned down. It's clearly a case of teenage exaggeration, somebody has probably burned some toast in the adjoining apartment, and as for the latest cool bands, I honestly haven't heard of any of them. It feels good to be back in touch with the world again, but as we head towards our dinner with Fred and Asi, I realise that there's a problem.

My wallet is missing from my jacket pocket, and my telephone, and my camera. I return to the internet cafe, which is now busier than ever, and I explain the problem of the 'missing' items to the manager. He looks concerned, but he's found nothing that could possibly belong to me. I point to the security camera mounted high on the ceiling, but apparently it's only for show and won't really help me. He asks if I'd like to report the theft to the police.

The wallet was the false wallet that was actually designed to be stolen, so there was very little in it. The camera was cheap and I'd already transferred most of the photographs onto my laptop, but the cell phone is slightly more complicated. I think I've got most of the important telephone numbers backed-up on my second phone, but so far in Russia my second phone has failed to find a signal. After last night's problems trying to check into the hotels, I feel that the less contact that I have with the police, the better. Anyway, if nobody got robbed then it wouldn't be a proper adventure, so I tell the manager not to bother.

I finally arrive at the cafe and we walk with Fred and Asi to a restaurant called 'Camelot'. It's a strange mock plastic castle where we enjoy what I think they call a 'Medieval Feast'. Whatever they call it, we wash it down with an unknown quantity of German beer and unanimously declare it to be absolutely delicious. We linger for as long as we can, not just because we don't really want to say goodbye to Fred and Asi for the third and probably final time, but because outside it's once again pouring with rain and Irkutsk is swimming. We draw straws to see who'll go and find a taxi to take us back to the brothel, and I lose.

I go out into the street but unfortunately, there's very little traffic. While I'm waiting for a taxi to come into view, I bump into a young couple from New Zealand who are travelling towards Europe and are currently feeling lost in Irkutsk. They know exactly where they are, they're just 'lost' in the sense of trying to understand their experiences here in Russia. They're looking for somewhere to eat, but they're nervous about entering restaurants where they might not know what food to order and they're frightened of talking to strangers. They're talking to a scruffy tee shirt wearing Englishman standing out in the pouring rain whilst trying to wave down a nonexistent taxi to take him back to a brothel. How much stranger do they think people get? I invite them downstairs to join us, but they decline. They have very little money and in a familiar sounding twist, they're worried about using cash machines here in Russia.

I feel sorry for them, they're fresh out of college and are supposed to be enjoying the most amazing holiday of their lives before returning to New Zealand and commencing a life filled with the tedium and traumas of a career. I give them 1,000 Roubles, point them in the direction of a cheaper cafe serving European food, and wish them well with the remainder of their journey. I just hope that they can relax and let Russia into their hearts, because despite several incidents to the contrary, it really isn't a place to be feared.

In the absence of gunmen, I take my early morning coffee outside and try tracing the fault that's been plaguing my Tiger for the past three days. I'd like to claim that I find the fault due to my years of experience in maintaining motorcycles, but that would be wrong. I simply lift the seat and look down at the battery. Where a bolt and retaining nut normally attach the earth wire to its terminal, there's now just a vacant hole. A borrowed nut and bolt from the improvised mud-foot at the bottom of my side-stand, and ten seconds later the electrical problem is fixed, permanently. A job well done, but what an absolute idiot I am for not investigating the fault earlier.

With the Tiger once again purring like a kitten, we ride into Irkutsk and collect Rick's passport from the Mongolian Embassy. The Mongolian Embassy has done exactly as it had said it would do and Rick's visa has been granted, so we head north out of Irkutsk towards Lake Baikal.

The smog and congestion of the city quickly washes away behind us and the cityscape slowly turns to steppe. The rain stops and the sun begins to shine, but the route that we need to take towards Lake Baikal is closed for repairs. It's exactly what we didn't want, but this is Russia, so we simply swerve around the road barrier and continue heading north.

As we move closer to the Lake, the faces of the people are changing. They're becoming less occidental and more oriental, the roadside statues and the village names are also slightly different and I begin to notice the appearance of Shaman spirit trees all along the route. At one such tree I stop and tear off a strip of old tee shirt. I tie the strip around a branch of the tree and tip my loose change and a few cigarettes onto the ground.

These spirit trees are physical connections between this life and the lives of those who've passed before, those who are now spirits. Apart from the hundreds of cloth ribbons fluttering gently in the hot breeze, it's absolutely silent here and I feel a sense of calmness that's difficult to describe. I'm a man without religion, but I'm not without feeling, and I just know that Lake Baikal is going to be a very special and significant part of this journey.

Chapter 28:
Russia, Lake Baikal

We arrive at the terminal where the ferry will take us to the island of Ol Khon on Lake Baikal. The ferry terminal is another concrete jetty with an arrangement of two almost derelict cafes, a rough concrete ramp, and following the best traditions of Poor Circulation, the only ferry is just disappearing into the distance. It's not really bad news because it's only a thirty minute crossing and that should give us just enough time to eat lunch and find fuel before crossing over to the island.

Adam and Rick order grilled meats and borsch from the cafe while I ride up a steep and anonymous looking track where the restaurateur assures me I'll find petrol. The track doesn't convince me that I'll find fuel at the end of it, but I ride up it anyway. At a junction in the sand, I see a stooped old lady wearing a black dress and headscarf. She's herding three well behaved and rather handsome looking cows. I smile and ask 'Benzene?' She points to the right and I guess she knows the area, so with increased confidence I follow the track that she's indicated.

Over the years I've seen finer looking filling stations than the one that appears at the end of this sandy track, but I've never seen any with a view quite so stunning. I give money to the beautiful girl in the kiosk and fill the Tiger with 84 Ron fuel. It's not the highest octane fuel that I've seen here in Russia, but it's also not the lowest. People seem to worry about the quality of fuel that's available in remote areas such as this, but it really doesn't seem to be a problem. As you approach such out of the way places, the quality of fuel seems to gradually reduce and by the time you arrive in a place like Ol Khon, your motorcycle's probably accustomed to running on crap. The quality of fuel is not as big a problem as the absence of fuel, so whenever I see it, I buy it. The lowest grade that we've used so far is 82 Ron, which probably had the combustive qualities of a mermaid's fart, but the Tigers hadn't objected to burning it.

With the Tiger's tank filled to the brim, I collect my change from the girl in the kiosk and take a few minutes to enjoy the view. I look out across the mirrored surface of Lake Baikal and it's difficult to see where the lake ends and the sky begins. It's one of the most beautiful places that I've ever seen and well worth the nine thousand miles that I've ridden to get here. Lake Baikal is by far the deepest freshwater lake in the world, and contains more than twenty percent of the worlds fresh water, so maybe its remoteness is also its saviour. Any closer to mass habitation and I fear that man would be robbing its resources for industry and leisure. There's something very special about the colours here, they look too sharp and perfect to be natural. It's almost as if the view has been painted by humans, a representation of how the perfect lake should appear and it's far more beautiful than I'd ever imagined it would be. I take photographs with my newly purchased camera and hope that just because it was cheap, it doesn't mean that it's crap. Far below my scenic perch, I can see two figures sitting beneath the loose canopy of the restaurant. Adam and Rick are eating my lunch and it's time for me to go.

As we roll onto the ancient ferry, memories of our attempted exit from Albania come flooding back to me. I tell the story to Rick, but he's not particularly impressed. Rick's clearly a well prepared traveller, a traveller who knows his geography far better than we do. Although he's never been to Albania, he already knows that Lake Koman doesn't stretch all of the way into Kosovo and seems surprised that we hadn't also been aware of that geographical fact. He suspects that our level of research and planning is inadequate, and in beautiful Germanic fashion, he tells us so, but we still laugh.

Just like in Albania, this ferry is old. It has the same broken boarding ramp and has become another 'Roll-On' 'Reverse Off' vessel. This is something that we've become accustomed too, but the situation today is made more interesting by the number of cars boarding that are towing fully loaded trailers. Given the narrowness of the vessel, it'll be interesting watching them trying to reverse off at the end of the crossing.

The voyage to Ol Khon takes less than thirty minutes and the people aboard the ferry are silent. For the first time on this journey our motorcycles are ignored and the people quite rightly concentrate all of their senses on the surrounding lake and landscape. It's just an amazingly beautiful place. These people aboard the ferry aren't tourists, they're local's who probably make this journey on a regular basis, yet still they gaze in silence at their surroundings. It really is that captivating and nobody here is taking it for granted. The air is fresh and clear, the waters are still and there's a slight shroud of pure white mist that adds a certain mystery to everything. Even above the throbbing of the ferry's ancient diesel engines, there's a serenity that's impossible to translate into words. It reminds me of the most beautiful place that I've ever had the good fortune to visit, Dahl in Kashmir. Because of political unrest, Dahl is now a difficult place to reach, and Lake Baikal is geographically almost at the centre of Russia, but if anybody ever has the opportunity to visit either of these places, then their long journey to reach them will certainly be worthwhile. You can't possibly be disappointed with either of them and such experiences will last for a lifetime.

If we'd arrived here two months earlier we could have ridden the motorcycles onto the island, because Lake Baikal would still have been frozen. Ol Khon is connected to the mainland during the summer months by this ferry, and in winter by a road across the ice. In spring and autumn the island is totally cut-off because the ice is too thin for vehicles to safely cross it, but too thick for the ferry to cut through it. Watching the island come ever closer, I'm beginning to think that if you're ever going to be isolated from the world for several months of the year, then Ol Khon might not be the worst location to choose. But then again, this is the height of summer and in the colder months Siberia probably loses much of its charm, but at least the mosquitoes would be gone. Once again, they're eating me alive.

The road towards the ferry had been marginal, but the road away from the ferry is in a very different league. The tarmac ended sixty miles before we'd reached the ferry, and here on the island what started as manageable hard packed tracks has quickly turned to soft sand and gravel. The Tigers, and riders, are not best suited to these conditions and our progress is painfully slow. Adam and I are familiar with the theory of successfully riding motorcycles through deep sand, it's the implementation that we're struggling with. It's not easy, because when every instinct tells you that if you don't slow down you'll fall off, the only safe thing to do is to apply greater bursts of power to the rear wheel. The slower you ride the faster you sink and the harder it is to control the motorcycle. On the other hand, Rick's in his Germanic element aboard his BMW and doing his utmost to make us look like the amateurs that we clearly are.

After finding a small but remarkably well stocked market where I buy provisions for the coming days, we fall upon 'Nikita's Homestead'. Nikita's is a famous overland travellers resting place that's renowned for its beautiful views and late night vodka parties. The views we could live with but the parties we could probably do without. So, we search for a more isolated place where for at least a couple of nights, we can camp peacefully and undisturbed.

As we head out onto a grassy peninsula, the track turns to deeper sand running through low dunes and Adam's Tiger grinds to a halt. I search for better tracks, higher paths where the root system of the short grass partially binds the surface together. It works to an extent, but the further we ride out onto the peninsula the deeper the sand becomes. We hit a particularly deep patch and Adam backs off the throttle too quickly. His Tiger's tail stops wagging and the front wheel digs-in causing the bike to stop and then slowly topple over. The sand is beautifully soft and there's no damage to the bike, but it's clear that Adam's had enough fun for today.

He's twisted his knee in the tumble, and while he knows that there's no serious damage, he'sworried that a more serious fall could put an end to his journey. In the far distance we can see the silhouette of Rick's BMW parked high and proud on a grassy hill. I unload some luggage to make room on the Tiger's pillion seat for Adam, but he's already started walking and I sense that he needs some time alone. I'll ride to meet Rick, establish our campsite on the edge of the lake and then return to recover Adam's Tiger.

With the tents pitched on the most perfect unofficial camping site you could ever imagine, and with Adam resting safely beside his recovered Tiger, it's time to go and have some real fun. I remove the extra luggage from my bike and ride off to meet Rick who's already on the other side of the peninsula. Without the extra weight, the Tiger feels almost like a gazelle and we start having fun racing each other through the dunes. There's no way that the Tiger could ever match the BMW for agility, nor my own off-road riding skills match Rick's, but as a Despatch Rider I'm not averse to taking shortcuts. For the best part of an hour, we have the absolute time of our lives larking about in the sand like a pair of kids set free in a new adventure playground.

Then, just when I'm gaining in confidence and it's all going unreasonably well for England, I embarrass my Nation by cutting across a dune that's far too much for both motorcycle and man. The front wheel digs into the dune and I fly over the handlebars kissing the sand in front of my wheel. As I wipe my face and empty the loose sand from my crash helmet, Rick raises his thumb and claims victory for Germany.

The Tiger's buried beyond its wheel spindles in soft sand and with a cheery wave, Rick rides away into the distance. I push and I pull. I rev the engine and rock the bike, and I bury the Tiger even deeper. Defeated, for the moment, I sit down on top of the dune and light up a smoke. It's one of the best cigarettes of my life and I honestly wonder if I could have possibly become stuck in a more beautiful place than this. I sit for about thirty minutes without a care in the world and then a small black speck appears on the horizon. I assume that it's Adam, back on his Tiger and riding to my rescue. The minutes pass, the speck grows larger, but it's certainly not Adam.

A few minutes later, a long haired nameless Belarusian is offering me a cold beer from his pannier while he casts an eye over the buried Tiger. Between the two of us we could easily extract the motorcycle from the sand, but even without speaking we both know that we'll finish our beers before the Tiger turns another wheel. This is Ol Khon and any thoughts of urgency have been left behind us on the mainland. As we sit together silently contemplating life, Rick returns and demonstrates how I should have ridden across the dune. Unfortunately for Rick, the laws of physics are indeed universal and his BMW is soon buried alongside the Tiger. Also unfortunately for Rick, I've just finished drinking the last of the Belarusian's cold beers.

It's one of the most beautiful mornings that I can ever remember meeting. There's not a single cloud in the perfectly blue sky, no mosquitoes to bother me, and a small herd of cows are wandering slowly along the white sandy beach in front of my tent. I've brewed the first coffee of the day and sitting here, I feel like the only person in the world. In my previous life back in England, this was often the time of day when all of my problems had vanished, the time of day when I'd felt the most peaceful and relaxed. It was my 'Golden Hour', the hour before the rest of humanity would wake and start shovelling shit onto my day. Here on Ol Khon, those peaceful feelings seem to be magnified and I want this perfect piece of time to last for as long as possible. If there really was a God, then this place would be Heaven and death wouldn't be something to fear.

Eventually weary eyes emerge from tents, blinking in the blindingly bright sun and the real day begins. We drink coffee together and try to make a plan for our time here on Ol Khon. Rick and I want to stay here for at least a week, relaxing, eating, drinking beer and seeing more of this beautiful once in a lifetime island. Adam on the other hand, is already talking about leaving. Yesterday's fall seems to have affected him far more than I'd thought. Physically he's fine, but mentally he seems to be bordering on depression. The deeper that we've ridden into Russia, the further Adam seems to have retreated into an invisible shell. I'm increasingly worried about Adam's state of health, and even Rick's quietly expressed concern. But, aside from both of us giving Adam constant encouragement and Rick tutoring him in the art of off-road riding, we really don't know what else we can do to help him. Adam's body is here in this physical heaven, but his mind seems determined to dwell in an imaginary hell.

An hour into the real day and Rick and I decide to ride out in search of wood for the campfire. We don't particularly need any more firewood, but we also don't need too many excuses to go exploring here. Crossing the peninsula, we clown-about like teenagers until we arrive at the top of a very steep slope above an expanse of perfectly green grass. Once again, Rick decides to demonstrate the supremacy of his Dakar BMW over my humble Street Bike in its adventure frock. I watch with much amusement as he drops down the steep incline and enters an area of deep bog where the BMW comes to an embarrassing halt. He pushes, he pulls, he pants, and if I'd paid more attention during my German lessons at school, I could probably confirm that he swore.

After an appropriately long, yet diplomatically important delay, I manage to stifle my laughter and ride down to help Rick extract his bike from the mud, mud that's slowly swallowing his once invincible machine. For the past few days Rick has been offering his advice on all aspects of my life in general, and my lack of riding skills in particular. Annoyingly, he's usually been absolutely right, but now it's my turn to smile and offer a little advice of my own. I tell him that if a piece of ground in Siberia looks invitingly green and lush, then rather than being a football pitch, it's more likely to be a bog. I do believe that Rick actually nods his head in agreement.

We've spent three nights camping here above the beach overlooking Lake Baikal. Everyday I've cooked food that we've bought from the tiny store located just a few miles away from our camp. We've eaten local pasta, smoked sausages brought with us from Irkutsk with locally caught fish, and we've drunk countless bottles of beer and vodka that have been chilled to perfection in the freezing waters of the lake. For seventy-two glorious hours we've kicked-back and chilled-out like never before. After eight weeks of travelling this has been our first real break and I don't think that either of us had realised just how tired we really were. But all good things must come to an end and it's time to start moving.

In respectful silence, we take down our makeshift camp and load the luggage back onto the motorcycles. We've travelled more than nine thousand miles to reach this place and the views from this grassy peninsula have made every one of those miles seem worthwhile. It's probably the most beautiful place that Adam has ever seen, but on our way back to the mainland we have something even more spectacular to show him. It's a sight that will hopefully make him forget all about riding on sand and broken roads, a place so beautiful that the impact of it will stay with him forever.

Yesterday just to the rear of Nikita's Homestead, Rick and I had discovered a place that is beautiful beyond words. It's a lush grass slope running gently down towards a sheer cliff that overhangs Lake Baikal. A single tree stands upright against the force of gravity and it mirrors a tall white rock rising proudly from the still and pure blue waters. Towards the horizon, the blue of the lake blends perfectly with the blue of the sky and there's no visible meeting point. It's spectacular and mind blowing, a rare place where you can do nothing but stand still and admire the sheer wonder of nature.

In our respective lifetimes, Rick and I have been fortunate enough to travel to many amazing locations and to witness nature's splendour, but we both agree that the place we've discovered is the most beautiful of them all. Adam had stayed in camp yesterday and missed this spectacle, but we'd talked about it endlessly over dinner and promised to lead him there today. It's a place that we need to pass in order to return to the ferry, but from the actual road you can't see it, which is probably why we'd missed it when we'd first arrived here.

For the return journey today, Rick and I have worked out a slightly different route that will avoid the worst of the deep sandy tracks and make the riding a little easier for Adam. I set out at a gentle pace with Adam and Rick following. When we reach the unavoidable sandy areas, I ride through and then park my bike, walk back to Adam and then ride his Tiger through the deeper sand. It takes more time but we've got all day and nobody should be in any great hurry to leave this place. After an hour of riding, we finally arrive at the special place at the rear of Nikita's Homestead.

We park the motorcycles and invite Adam to walk with us up the gentle hill and to experience the amazing view for himself. Unfortunately, Adam seems to have lost all interest in seeing it. It's less than ten metres away from him, and if he stood up on his tiptoes he could probably see most of it from here, but he's simply not interested in walking the extra few yards. Rick explains at length exactly what he's missing, and that he'll probably regret missing it for the rest of his adult life, but Adam's decision is final. It's a disappointing response, but I haven't come all of this way to miss out on any of the good stuff, so Rick and I wander away and take one last look at the best reason in the world for travelling.

The mystical beauty of Lake Baikal

Chapter 29:
Russia, Chita

After leaving the beauty of Lake Baikal four days ago, making the adjustment back to civilization hasn't been easy. It's not really the people, the buildings, the traffic and the chaos that feel strange, but the constant noise that surrounds them. Ol Khon had been absolutely silent but I hadn't really noticed it at the time. It's only now, now that I'm back in the circus of life that I can fully appreciate just how quiet everything had been out there on the island. There'd been the very hushed sounds of nature; buzzing insects, mosquitoes, a gentle breeze and the occasional bird with its early morning song, but there'd been very little in the way of human noise.

Since leaving Ol Khon, the noises that I've heard have been created entirely by man, and I've just realised that those two forms of noise seldom live in harmony together. I suspect that the ideological answer would be for Mankind to stop trying to overwhelm Nature and instead, to adapt and learn to live and work more harmoniously together. But, with a world population of seven billion people and rising, and with demands on land and natural resources increasing at an exponential rate, I sadly doubt that such harmony will ever exist in my lifetime. Nobody has ever accused me of being an 'Eco-Warrior', but a few days spent relaxing at Lake Baikal has certainly changed my perspective on this world. I've no idea if the experience will affect the way in which I live out the remainder of my life, but in the future I'll certainly be more conscious of the impact that my own actions have on this amazing planet.

After riding away from Ol Khon, we'd headed towards an old Soviet holiday camp called 'Bolshoi Banet', located on the edge of a small lake to the south of Irkutsk. Rick had arranged to meet a stranger there, a man he'd met just a few days earlier via the internet, an English teacher named Spike. Rick's new Russian friend had invited us all to join him and his large group of English immersion students at their educational retreat on the lake.

The aging Soviet holiday camp reminded me of those old stalwarts of affordable British family holidays: 'Butlins' and 'Pontins'. Closed metal gates topped with menacing razor-wire and a well armed guard had greeted our arrival. Once inside the vast and sprawling complex, we'd found row upon row of long neglected, but never luxurious, communal dormitories. It was a strange place, a place that conjured up images of similarly dressed people performing compulsory morning exercise in very neat and precise lines. It was a holiday camp that suggested that holidays in the former Soviet Union were not taken voluntarily. But, despite the starkness of the physical structures, it turned out to be a fun day and night of activities. It was refreshing to spend time with a group of energetic and enthusiastic younger people who seemed to be interested in learning an awful lot more about absolutely everything on earth.

We'd joined in their many eclectic activities, shared their simply prepared meals and in the morning, I'd had my first experience of teaching English to students. Thankfully the students had all been attentive and polite, volunteers rather than conscripts, and they'd really given me quite an easy time of it. Despite my initial reservations, teaching English to kids and young adults is something that I really enjoyed doing and given the opportunity, I wouldn't hesitate to do it again.

Almost without exception, the young people that I've met here in Russia strike me as being inquisitive, open minded and ambitious, and that seems to be in stark contrast to my perception of similarly aged kids back in England. Granted, I suspect that the Russian youths that I've met are generally from the more privileged sections of Russian society, but they still leave me with a very encouraging feeling. I'd ridden away from Bolshoi Banet with a confirmed feeling of confidence, confidence that in the hands of the younger generation, the future of this vast country will be both prosperous and secure.

From the English immersion school, we'd headed east towards the city of Ulan Ude and with every mile the signs of civilization had diminished. The towns had become smaller, the distances between them greater and the traffic on the roads much lighter. The landscape had changed from forest to steppe, a vast expanse of grassland that stretched unbroken for as far as the eye could see. Riding across the Siberian steppe feels strange, not just because the road surface is always changeable, but because there are often no landmarks to aim for. The lack of any visual recognition points seems to make every mile feel a little longer than it really is, and for the first time on this journey I'd turned to my MP3 player for company. The music helped one mile to blend into the next, but when you see a signpost indicating recognisable towns with the distance towards them measured in thousands of kilometres, it's a reminder of just how many more miles you'll need to cover before reaching the far side of Russia.

For our last night together with Rick, I'd found a beautiful camping ground on the edge of a lake on the north side of the Trans Siberian Railway. Crossing a small free flowing stream, Adam had dropped his Tiger, but aside from a missing indicator there'd been very little damage to the motorcycle. Adam hadn't been injured in the fall and overnight at the side of the fire, Rick and I had managed to successfully dry most of Adam's clothing. In the morning, I'd returned to the stream and recovered the pieces of the broken indicator. Thankfully, it had broken from the motorcycle kindly and was relatively easy to reattach to his Tiger.

Later in the morning, we'd broken camp and waved farewell to Rick who was riding south for Mongolia in search of further adventures. It's been good for both of us to have Rick around for the last week. We'll both miss him, but I'm sure that very soon somebody else will ride accidentally into this journey, because that's what always seems to happen.

Following Rick's early morning departure, we'd skirted away from Ulan Ude and headed towards the city of Chita, a city that marks the beginning of the Amur Highway, our route to Vladivostok on the very edge of Russia. This morning Adam had volunteered to lead the riding, but I'm not sure if that was as a consequence of some newly found confidence, or from an overriding fear that since Rick was no longer with us, I'd just bugger-off into the distance and leave him. Sadly, on leaving Ol Khon, Adam and I had almost come to blows and Rick had jumped in to maintain the peace. It had been a nasty situation and although it's now behind us, I fear that for Adam, it's not yet fully resolved. Anyway, Adam's reasons for volunteering to lead the riding hadn't really mattered, he'd been taking the initiative and I'd been happy to just sit behind him all day and relax with the vast open landscape and my music for company. We ended the day covering an awful lot of miles, more miles than I'd ever planned to ride, but it became yet another day that ended on a rather sour note.

With limbs aching, rain falling hard and darkness closing in around us, I'd found a suitable camp site and returned to Adam who'd been waiting back on the road. He'd shaken his head, tapped a finger at his Garmin GPS unit and told me that it wasn't a good place to camp. Apparently, we'd been at an altitude of more than two thousand feet, an altitude that he insisted would see us freezing to death in our tents. I didn't have my own GPS unit to confirm the altitude, but I did have a map. Looking at the various contour colours on the map of Siberia, I suspected that two thousand feet was an altitude that we really ought to get comfortable with. It was an altitude that wouldn't really change until we reached the end of the Amur Highway. In fact, it was an altitude that we'd already been enjoying for at least the last two weeks of the journey and neither of us had perished in our tents. Adam had disagreed with me, he'd suggested that my map was inaccurate and had insisted that we pushed on until we reached lower ground. I'd smiled and told him that I'd follow his lead. I'd totally disagreed with his reasoning, but at least he'd been making a decision, and when it came to Adam, decisions had become a very rare commodity.

Night riding is something that I really quite enjoy, and a familiar environment can give you a very different experience after dark, but night riding on unfamiliar muddy roads is something that I could happily live without. We'd stopped several times at what appeared to be suitable camping sites, but every time Adam had pointed to the altitude reading on his GPS unit and charged on ahead of me. Something had changed within him, I didn't know what that 'something' was, but I'd never seen him so determined about anything and he was riding faster than he'd ridden at any other time on the journey.

At first, I'd silently applauded his new found riding confidence, but after several hours and too many near misses, it became clear that Adam had somehow crossed the invisible border from 'Confidence' into 'Recklessness'. The rain had stopped an hour earlier, but the unfinished road was waterlogged and littered with hazardous obstacles. After too many encounters with stationary objects in the road, and several missing bridges, I'd finally decided that I'd had enough of the craziness and had physically forced him to stop. Parked safely at the side of the road I'd checked my watch and noted that it was almost three o'clock in the morning.

I'd brought the riding to a halt on top of a newly constructed bridge, but the person that I'd found riding Adam's Tiger wasn't the Adam that I'd known. His body had been physically present, silent and unmoving with an ashen white face and distant wild eyes, but his mind had been away in some far distant world. Many things had scared me on the journey to that point; rough roads, suicidal vehicles, black bears and burley police officers, but nothing had scared me as much as what I'd found beneath Adam's crash helmet.

Beneath the bridge I'd found a small raised area of dry sheltered ground. I'd helped Adam off the motorcycle and walked him down to the relative shelter below. I'd sat him down on a large slab of broken concrete beneath the bridge, but still he hadn't moved or spoken. In turn, I'd brought both Tigers down to the makeshift camp and fired up the stove to make tea. The tea had warmed him and he'd started moving independently again, but it was clear that he'd suffered some kind of mental or physical breakdown. His head had been bowed in his hands, his body rocking slowly backwards and forwards and an ocean of tears had streamed down his face. I'd tried to comfort him, but I'd been entering into totally new territory and hadn't really known what to do for the best. I'd thought about calling the emergency services, or flagging down a passing vehicle to take us to the nearest hospital, but we were in Siberia, not Suburbia. There'd been absolutely nowhere to pitch our tents, so I'd unpacked his sleeping bag, placed it inside the emergency waterproof bivy-bag and encouraged him to climb inside them. It was far from perfect, but under the circumstances it was the best that I could possibly do for him.

It's now six o'clock in the morning and I've been woken by a passing herd of cows making their way towards an unseen milking parlour. Adam's sitting upright on the flat piece of concrete. It's exactly where I'd sat him down last night and his sleeping bag looks to be unused. He's shaking, I hope only from the cold, but his head is moving and he seems to be in control of his limbs. The Zombie of three o'clock in the morning has gone, but he's certainly no picture of health. Adam talks a little, he asks me if I'd slept, and I just nod. His still wide eyes tell me that he's not ready for conversation and I daren't ask him about the events of last night.

I brew tea and encourage him to drink it while I pack everything onto the Tigers and ride them back up to the road. If he can't ride his motorcycle then I'm not sure what I can do, but thankfully he seems to have regained enough control of his body.

I pull in at the first cafe on the road and over breakfast, Adam starts to talk, but he's not talking about his actions of last night. I want to know what had happened to him during those six manic hours on the road, and how he really feels now, but he clearly wants to avoid telling me. I suggest that as soon as we reach the city of Chita, maybe an hour or two further down the road, we should find a hotel and get some proper rest. Adam seems happy to do that and I hope that a comfortable bed and a good night's sleep will do him the world of good.

Early yesterday afternoon we'd arrived here in Chita and checked into the Hotel Tourist. Thankfully the receptionist hadn't taken exception to our mysteriously exceptional passports and we'd acquired a pair of single rooms for the night. It's a hotel just like all of the other Soviet hotels, but its quirks don't amuse me quite as much this morning. The Tigers are parked outside, packed and ready to go, but which direction Adam's motorcycle will take, I honestly couldn't say.

Yesterday evening I'd bought dinner for Adam and encouraged him to open up to me. Too many of our days have had bitter moments and ended on sour notes. So much so, that it feels as if this entire journey has been hijacked by the differences that exist between us. Adam had brushed off the events of the previous night and insisted that he'd simply been 'Acting the Fool'. He'd laughed-off any suggestion of a 'breakdown' and tried to convince me that he'd been absolutely fine, just cold and tired from a long day in the saddle. I hadn't bought his explanation, but I also hadn't felt brave enough to press him any further on the matter.

Having at last started talking together, and with both of us wanting to clear the air, at Adam's request I'd gently scrolled through a list of the problems as I'd seen them. Adam had listened intently and tried to explain the reasons behind many of his more unusual actions. He'd continued to avoid talking about the late night riding incident, but everything else he accepted and put down to a mixture of homesickness, inexperience and a fear of entering the unknown. One by one, we'd talked through each of the different issues and as the coffee had arrived, we'd drawn a new line in the sand, a new beginning for both of us. We'd left that restaurant smiling and talking together. It had felt good to be that way again and it had also felt as if a great weight had been lifted from my shoulders. However, before leaving that restaurant I really should have confiscated Adam's shovel. But unfortunately, I hadn't.

As we'd wandered towards the centre of Chita in search of a late night bar, the racist within Adam had resurfaced. There'd been no particular incident or encounter that sparked it, but within minutes of finishing our coffee and making a fresh start, the shovel was out and Adam was enthusiastically digging another hole. This time it wasn't the 'Ignorant Paki Bastards' who'd annoyed him but the 'Gormless Chink Fuckers'. Apparently, such people had been wandering around Chita in disturbingly large numbers and spoiling what might otherwise have been a rather pleasant location for him. It had been a throwaway statement that had come out of absolutely nowhere, and delivered in such a casual manner that I'm not even sure that Adam had been aware of what he'd said. But, just a few short minutes after being drawn, our new line in the sand had been permanently erased.

Arriving back at the hotel last night, I'd written an entry for my blog and hovered over the 'Publish' icon for a little longer than usual. I'd written the text while I was angry, and that's probably not the best time to write anything that's destined to be read by other people. Up until that moment, we'd kept all of our differences strictly between ourselves, and apart from Adam's parents, nobody outside of this journey had any knowledge of the problems that had existed between us. But angry and emotional, I'd vented my literary spleen and told the entire story, warts and all. The longer my finger had hovered, the more my anger had risen, and in the end my finger had finally hit 'Publish'.

This morning there are several responses to that entry on my blog, which is good news in the sense that somebody actually reads what I'm writing, but not quite so good in other ways. Our mutual friends are surprised by my report of what's happened, but they're encouraging me to see Adam safely through to Vladivostok. Other commentators are using other language, some supportive, some condemning, some aggressive and there are several comments that I've had to delete. Adam's updating his own diary and blog, and I'm sure that he'll tell his side of the story, if not now then later, but in less than an hour I'll be mounting my Tiger and continuing east towards Vladivostok along the Amur Highway.

Along with the road, the Trans Siberian Railway also runs directly through Chita, they both run to the East and to the West, so Adam has several options to choose from. I'm not angry with Adam, I passed the anger stage an awful long time ago, but sitting here in the hotel and reading back through my handwritten diary, I'm angry with myself. I've allowed the thread of our relationship to weave its way through the tapestry of this journey to a point where the original picture has been lost. I'm bored with sour notes and bitter endings to days, they're really pissing me off, and today those things will stop. I have no idea which direction or means of transport Adam will choose, but the second new beginning in twenty-four hours starts right now.

Chapter 30:
Russia, Amur Highway

I set the tripod at the edge of the road and move the dial on the camera to 'Timed Delay'. The overnight rain has stopped but the clouds that had carried it here are lingering just above my head. They feel low and heavy and squash the available light into a narrow band that stretches right across the horizon. It's amazingly bright, a light that encourages me to squint, but at the same time is dark enough to force the automatic camera to 'Flash'. I'm five kilometres outside of Chita, standing on a pile of sand beneath a road sign at the junction of the M55 and M58 motorways. The huge blue sign tells me that I'll find the city of Khabarovsk 2168 kilometres along the M58, or as it's more poetically named, the Amur Highway. I've taken more photographs than I could possibly need and packed away the tripod, but I'm reluctant to start riding. Khabarovsk should be the mid-point of this journey, approximately halfway around the world, but from here it's at least three thousand kilometres to Vladivostok and those distances feel somewhat daunting. It's a bloody long road and I'll be riding it for many days to come, so I'm in no great hurry to get started.

Research tells me that in 2005 the Amur Highway was officially opened by Vladimir Putin. It was the out-going Presidents departing gift to the Russian people, but other travellers tell me that the official opening ceremony was probably a little premature. The M58 Amur Highway is the final piece of a massive road network that links St Petersburg in

The Amur Highway begins. 3,000Km to Vladivostok

the west with Vladivostok in the east, making it the longest continuous road in the world. According to my map, the road clings to the border with China across the region of Amur, hence its name, and seems to be shadowed for most of the way by the Trans Siberian Railway. Eventually it will be a perfectly smooth four lane super-highway, but recent reports suggest that much of it remains unfinished. With Magadan Airlines filing for bankruptcy, and in the process making Magadan something of a terminal town for travellers, the Amur Highway seems to be my only real option for travelling east onto Vladivostok. So finished or not, I suspect that I'm about to find out the truth about this legendary road.

I'm following the map and compass, but as there's only one road to take, even I can't get lost. I'm riding east on beautifully smooth tarmac, it's only a single carriageway but at least it's fully paved. The forests seemed to end long before reaching Chita and the road ahead is surrounded by steppe. Gently rolling grasslands are broken by the occasional red and white radio mast rising into the sky and I see occasional cowboys astride small ponies surrounded by grass munching cattle. As if to confirm that I've taken the correct road, I see the first convoy of Japanese cars heading towards me and they're showing absolutely no respect for the speed limit. The cars that are imported from Japan and heading for sale in Moscow appear to be covered in thick beige coloured mud and I assume that it's an indicator of the road conditions ahead of me. I pass the occasional cafe and fuel station selling unleaded benzene rated in the high eighties and my confidence starts to rise. Food, fuel and tarmac, what more could any traveller possibly ask for?

The tunes on my MP3 player are randomly playing and I'm happy to sing along with them. Far in the distance a narrow plume of grey smoke appears and I watch as it rises from the land. It suggests that there's a village on the road ahead. For mile after mile, I watch as it draws closer and I've never before found a simple plume of smoke to be quite as interesting as this one. It's not a particularly unusual or beautiful plume of smoke, but from horizon to horizon it's the only other thing that's moving. A few miles closer and I can see that the smoke comes from a chimney on the steeply pointed roof of a small wooden house. It's surrounded by other wooden houses and they all look remarkably similar and built surprisingly close together. Individual houses seem to have been constructed on narrow strips of land adjacent to the road, but given the amount of land that's available out here I can't understand why they're packed so tightly together. Maybe I'm looking at them with English eyes, eyes that see them as being far too close for privacy and comfort, but those English eyes would be totally ignoring the conditions that must exist here during winter and the necessary sense of community that such conditions must encourage.

From the edge of the village I can see that each wooden house has its own small vegetable garden and a large pile of roughly chopped firewood. A small store stands in the middle of the village and seems to be the centre of all activity. The village seems to have been built around the store and maybe that's so that when the snow becomes difficultly deep, every house should still be within easy reach of it. Old people accompanying children and cows seem to be wandering to and from the store looking slightly over dressed for the climate. This might be early summer for Siberia but it feels hotter than London on a record summer's day. That's not a complaint, just an observation, because I'd certainly rather be here now than in December or January when it's forty below freezing on a warm day.

As that climatic thought crosses my mind, the village vanishes behind me. I can see it disappearing in my mirrors and looking ahead I can see exactly what I'd seen before the village had arrived, minus the plume of smoke. There's absolutely nothing but grass, road and sky ahead of me. It's something that I'd better get used to because I suspect that there's going to be an awful lot of nothing to see before I reach the end of this rather lengthy road. I turn up the volume on my MP3 player, The Clash are Rocking the Kasbah and in the absence of anything else to think of, I wonder what Joe Strummer would make of the Amur Highway.

I'd expected the small village to have a fuel station, but I hadn't seen one, and as all of the buildings had been lined up along the side of the road, if it was there then I certainly would've seen it. The village was probably ten or fifteen miles back down the road, but I'm just pulling into a filling station now. I'm not sure where the next village or town will be, but I can't understand why the local fuel supplies should contradict my theory on the close proximity of Siberian living, unless of course my theory is wrong.

I fill up the Tiger in the prescribed manner, collect my change from another beautiful girl in a kiosk, and then go off in search of the toilets. Russian toilets are quite an experience, and the heat wave that's currently sweeping Siberia doesn't make them anymore welcoming, so I walk around the block and take a piss behind them. As I return to the forecourt I can see a black spot heading towards me, a black spot with a dust trail in its wake. A minute later Adam pulls in on his Tiger. We're both continuing east along the only road that's available to either of us, but it's two separate journeys that will be joined at filling stations and rough camping sites. Filing stations because Adam still has an aversion to using Russian cash machines and campsites because I've promised his parents that I won't let him starve to death or get eaten by bears. It's not a perfect solution, and I'm certainly not going to protect him from bears, but I'm trying to make the most of these awkward circumstances.

Almost 200km east of Chita and I'm beginning to think that other travellers have exaggerated the condition of the roads out here. I guess challenging roads make for better reading, but the Amur Highway doesn't look like anything that ought to be feared. The tarmac hasn't been great, but it still qualifies as tarmac and I'm happy to ride on it all day.

I find a nice patch of grass at the side of the filling station, kick off my boots and slump down to enjoy a smoke. I look at my watch and try to work out what the correct time is. The clock behind the beautiful girl in the kiosk had said eight o'clock in the morning, but I know that it's a lot later than that. Many places seem to have their clocks set to Moscow time, but that's several hours behind me now. My watch tells me that it's one o'clock in the afternoon and that would be five hours ahead of Moscow, but by now I'm probably six hours ahead. Normally when you're crossing time zones, you land at an airport and the flight crew kindly inform you of the correct local time, but when you ride across them there's usually nothing there to help you. It doesn't really matter because nothing here seems to have precise opening and closing times, and even if they did, I wouldn't know what they were. It's more out of curiosity that I'd like to know what the accurate time is. Well, curiosity and the fact that there's precious little else to occupy the mind out here. One o'clock or two o'clock, it's time to ride on.

Just as I'm contemplating completing the Amur Highway within just a couple of days and dreaming of a welcoming bed in Vladivostok, the road sends me a well deserved wake-up call. The tarmac simply vanishes. There's no sign to warn me, just a dusty line across the road where the tarmac ends and the sand begins. It catches me by surprise and I hit the sand at speed, but the speed probably saves me from falling.

I stop the Tiger, ride back a little way and park at the side of the road. The sand road is the same colour as the slime that had covered the earlier convoy of Japanese cars, so although it's dry here I guess that further east it will probably be wet. I make coffee, light a cigarette and wait.

Sitting on a small pile of rocks, I run my hand through a patch of tall green weeds. The weeds are the same variety that I'd seen in the garden of the old sailor back in Mariance. It's marijuana and it seems to grow everywhere here, uncultivated, wild and free, and I suspect that it was originally cultivated to make cloth, hemp. Midway through my second smoke, the spot on the horizon becomes recognisable as a Triumph Tiger, so I stand out on the end of the tarmac and make like a human warning sign for Adam.

Thankfully the sand is a lot more forgiving than that back on Ol Khon and the going is relatively easy. I slow down the pace and keep one watchful eye in my mirror and one on the road ahead. It's the same road that we've been riding since leaving Chita, but suddenly there's traffic. It's not the dense traffic that I've encountered elsewhere in Russia, but when you've become accustomed to no traffic at all, a few vehicles an hour has a feeling of gridlock about it.

Moving east with me are construction vehicles and I take it as a sign of improving roads ahead. The construction traffic is slow moving and leaves a trail of dust in its wake, dust that obscures everything ahead of me. It's impossible to follow behind them in the wake of sandy fog, and it's scary to overtake them. Shortly after the road had turned to sand, it had also narrowed to a single lane. Actually, that's not strictly true. The boundaries of the road are as wide as they ever were, but the traffic using this road has created its own preferred path. The preferred path sometimes wanders from one side of the road to the other, avoiding water filled potholes that could swallow a small house, but generally it just carves a single gully straight down the centre. Overtaking the trucks requires a certain degree of faith, but thankfully not too much more speed. You bite the bullet and chose left or right, whichever looks to be the safest, accelerate out onto the secondary path and don't back-off the throttle until you're safely passed the slower moving vehicle. Sometimes it's easy, and sometimes you encounter road obstacles that you hadn't expected, but even more frightening are the times when you suddenly discover that you've been following not one but a whole convoy of trucks. Overtaking the first time is difficult, and the second time is a little easier, so by the time I reach Khabarovsk I should be an absolute bloody expert at it.

Travelling west towards me are an increasing number of suicidal Japanese cars making their way to Moscow and every few hours there's an unintentional game of 'Chicken'. We all want to keep to the centre of the single gully, the Japanese cars to avoid costly damage from stone chips and me to avoid falling off in the deeper sand to the side. It's a battle of wills and the main danger is that once you commit to leaving the passable central track, you hand over control of the bike to the contours of the road. If the oncoming Japanese cars decide to break away in the same direction, then things really start to get interesting. I've developed a strategy that so far seems to be working. I stand up on the bike, look purposeful, and refuse to give way to the oncoming vehicles. Thankfully, they usually do give way to me and so far I've avoided any unpleasant collisions. Having said all of that, the road's uncomfortable, and some of the deeper sand and gravel takes a great deal of concentration, but so far it's been an awful lot easier than many of the horror stories would suggest.

The days like the miles, all seem to be blending into each other. The ever changing road surface means that the riding is certainly never boring, but the most appropriate adjective that springs to mind is 'Repetitive'. Bone jarring potholes, a body mask of beige dust, blind overtaking and occasional games of 'Chicken' are repetitive things that I could happily live without, but there are certain repetitive things that bring Russia deeper and deeper into my heart. I'm in the centre of Siberia, one of the most remote places on earth, but every time I stop the Tiger, somebody usually arrives to say hello. Cars stop and the occupants take photographs, share their cigarettes and give me food to carry with me. The Russian equivalent of the 'Pot Noodle' seems to be a particularly popular nutritional gift. They're genuinely interested in what I'm doing and why I'm doing it, and I'm fascinated by their own stories.

Apart from the construction vehicles heading towards as yet unseen construction projects, and the Japanese cars that seem to be driving nonstop to Moscow, everybody on this road seems to be here for a very different reason; a new born baby in Irkutsk, a job interview in Chita, a wedding in Khabarovsk and a road trip for father and son. Everybody has a different reason, but those eclectic reasons have brought us together on this road, and the road itself has become a widespread and eclectic community of strangers. That's not something that happens on the M1 in England, but the Amur Highway is a very different kind of motorway.

One thing that these people do seem to have in common is the fact that they each try to complete their journey in one continuous drive, just like the Japanese car couriers, but for very different reasons. The Japanese car couriers race from Vladivostok to Moscow as quickly as they can. In Moscow, they sell the imported car for a tidy profit, sleep on the flight back to Vladivostok and then repeat the journey with another imported car. The more cars they can move during the short season when the Siberian roads are passable, the more money they'll make. Their need for speed means that along the Amur Highway, they don't stop for sleep.

The regular car and truck drivers also prefer not to stop on the Amur Highway, but they keep moving in order to avoid contact with what they simply call 'Bandits'. I'm not sure exactly what they mean, and I'm not sure that I really want to know, but so far I've seen nobody that I could describe as being a 'Bandit'. Real or imaginary, without exception, the people who share their food and cigarettes warn me not to stop, and under no circumstance to ever camp, until the Amur is behind me. I never contradict them, but I always thank them for their advice and store the information away in a file marked 'They Did Warn You'. It's a file that at the end of this journey will probably make very interesting reading, but hopefully it's a file that'll remain closed until the official end has arrived.

Ignoring the advice of my fellow travellers, last night I'd found a beautiful secluded campsite at the opposite side of the Trans Siberian Railway. It was way down a muddy track and across a small stream, but it had been

The small chapel on the Amur Highway

well worth the effort taken to find it. There'd been a glorious lush green meadow filled with thousands of wild brightly coloured flowers and encircled with trees. A fire had kept the mosquitoes away but apparently not the bears. It was the second bear encounter here in Siberia, heard but not seen, but just as scary as the first. I'm beginning to wonder if the word 'Bandit' actually means 'Bear' in Russian.

Tonight's final destination is again in a small clearing surrounded by trees. The fire's blazing and dinner is bubbling away on the stove, with Adam stirring the pot. Ponini seems to be our staple diet out here, small parcels of pasta containing a mystery filling. Sometimes it's potato, sometimes chicken and sometimes cheese, but you never know what it's going to be until you actually bite into it. It comes frozen in packets and although the packet probably lists all of the ingredients, I sadly can't read it. It's the first meal that Adam's cooked, in fact it's the first time that he's ever fired-up the stove, and I'd been surprised when he'd volunteered his services.

Earlier today the repetitive nature of the road was broken by the appearance of a small chapel in the absolute middle of nowhere. I'd stopped the Tiger, stepped over the sleeping dog that guarded the entrance, and taken a look inside. It was by far the smallest chapel that I'd ever seen. Inside, if I stood in the centre of the single room and held out both arms, there'd have been no more than a few inches between the tips of my fingers and the walls. There was actually very little in there for the dog to protect, just a small altar, a large cross and some painted religious icons. After my two-minute all inclusive tour, Adam had arrived and inspected the chapel for himself. Back at the Tiger, I'd brewed coffee and enjoyed a smoke in the early evening breeze. The door to the chapel had been closed, with Adam inside it. An hour later, he'd emerged smiling and confident, and it was actually Adam who'd located tonight's camping ground.

Since leaving Chita a few long days ago, beyond the small villages I haven't seen anybody who you could possibly describe as a 'Pedestrian'. I guess that makes sense, because this is Siberia and where the hell could anybody possibly be walking too or from? But, as Adam lovingly stirs the pot of ponini, a man stands motionless on the track just a few metres away from our well hidden campsite. I watch him from the security of our hideout, hidden in the foliage but with a raging fire behind me that somewhat compromises our location. He's dressed in military fatigues, carrying an old army rucksack and a walking stick fashioned from an old chrome umbrella. Inevitably, curiosity gets the better of me and I invite the stranger into the camp to share our fire, our coffee and whatever food we have.

His name is Alexander and he's pleased to meet a pair of fellow travellers. He accepts a mug of steaming hot coffee and a smoke before dinner. He asks if we've seen the old border crossing into China where there's a small orthodox chapel. I hadn't thought of it as an old border crossing, but I show him the photographs that I'd taken at the chapel and Alexander confirms that it's the right place. I tell him that it's no more than ten kilometres west along the road and Alexander nods. The small chapel is where he intends to sleep tonight.

We serve the ponini and sit around the fire to eat. Alexander is from Kazakhstan and proud of his heritage. He speaks very good English and his words are few but well chosen with long pauses for thought and reflection in between them. We ask very few questions and are content to simply listen to this old man's stories. Adam sits at Alexander's feet and listens intently to every word, his eyes focussed on the old man's gnarled and weathered features. Alexander talks of exploring the area north of Vladivostok and the island of Sakhalin by bicycle, and of encounters with black bears and Asian tigers. He tells of his time in the Atlas Mountains and of his youthful days on pilgrimage to Jerusalem. For the past ten years Alexander has been wandering the world on foot in search of something, but until quite recently he hadn't known exactly what it was that he was searching for.

Born in what is now a part of Kazakhstan, Alexander is now walking from Vladivostok to St Petersburg, where for the princely sum of just 60,000 Roubles, he'll receive a Russian passport and a small plot of land upon which he'll build a small house and grow vegetables. I ask Alexander about the legality of purchasing a Russian passport, but he just shrugs his shoulders and takes another cigarette from my pack. He looks around our makeshift camp and asks if we've encountered any bears. He advises that we hang our socks on nearby trees because that will mark our territory and any bears will be scared to approach, or perhaps Alexander has simply smelt our socks. He then turns to Adam and asks if he'd spent any time in the small chapel. Adam tells him yes, probably about an hour, and Alexander smiles. He tells Adam that the small orthodox Christian chapel has special meaning for travellers. It's a place that famously changes the lives of the people who enter it. Adam just nods his agreement.

As semi-darkness begins to descend, Alexander rises and tells us that it's time to start walking towards the chapel where he'll sleep for the night. I offer to take him there on the Tiger but he refuses my offer. He shakes our hands and leaves. I feel guilty for not insisting on taking him on the motorcycle, so I follow him out to the road, but he's absolutely nowhere to be seen. Alexander has literally disappeared into thin air and his departure is even more mysterious than his arrival.

As we sit drinking our last coffee of the day, Adam tries to tell me about his own personal experience in the small chapel. He can't explain exactly what happened to him inside the chapel, but he knows that he's finally found what he's been searching for: God. The mysterious arrival and departure of Alexander is somehow connected to that life-changing experience, but Adam can't quite explain how, or why. I don't know what to say to him, because I honestly don't know what 'finding God' really means. However, if it's something that helps Adam with his life, and his acceptance of different cultures, then I'm genuinely happy for him.

The mysterious Alexander sharing our campfire, food and cigarettes

Chapter 31:
Russia, Khabarovsk

This morning I've encountered several foreign motorcycles heading west across Russia. First there was Charlie Honner, a young Australian riding a BMW R100GS towards England where he'd found a new job and had decided to ride to work in a rather unusual fashion. We'd exchanged information about road conditions in both directions, shared useful contact information and then simply wished each other well. Then there'd been Yoshi, an older Japanese guy riding a Honda Africa Twin towards Finland. Yoshi had told me about Yuki, a young Japanese girl who was three or four days behind him on the road riding her small Suzuki Djebel. Yoshi had been worried about how she'd be coping with the road conditions and had asked me to keep a watchful eye out for her. We'd chatted for a few minutes and I'd replenished his empty water containers before waving him on his way.

An hour later I'd met Yuki riding her black Suzuki Djebel, hot on the heels of Yoshi. She'd been fun and confident, halfway through her second solo circumnavigation of the world and rapidly closing in on Yoshi, a prospect that seemed to excite her. I'd filled her exhausted fuel tank from my jerry can and she'd raced off along the road in hot pursuit of her countryman. 'Good luck Yuki'.

It's now late afternoon and appearing through the dust, I see a fully dressed Harley Davidson. It's parked at the side of the road and I pull over to see if the rider needs any assistance. As the dust settles I see a line of similar looking Harley's parked directly behind it. Within seconds I'm surrounded by the 'Korean Harley Owners Group'. There are seventeen motorcycles travelling in convoy from Vladivostok to Hamburg. We exchange stories and gifts and they assure me of a warm welcome if I should ever visit South Korea. They've been surprised by the poor condition of the road between Vladivostok and here, and they warn me to be careful. They've read press reports about the four lane super highway and ask me where it will begin. The news that I give them isn't good. It doesn't begin, because it doesn't exist, and what they've experienced so far is probably about as good as it's going to get. They look totally crest fallen. Two of their motorcycles have already succumbed to the rigors of the road and are now riding on the back of a support truck. I fear that before they reach St Petersburg on their low-riding Harley Davidson's, they're going to need a much larger truck. Unfortunately their news about the road conditions between here and Vladivostok isn't all that I'd hoped for, but at least Vladivostok is an awful lot closer than St Petersburg.

'A can of beans, some black eyed peas, a Nescafe on Ice, candy bar a falling star or a reading from Dr Seuss'. One man can only have so much fun, and after too many thousands of kilometres on loose sandy tracks, the Tiger bounces onto beautiful black tarmac. I celebrate the moment along with Michael Stipe. My singing isn't good, but my feelings are way beyond orgasmic.

Thanks to a seemingly invincible Triumph Tiger, I've survived the Amur Highway. Statistically it's the second most dangerous road in the world, but it's a very long road and if you deduct the number of people who've died because of boredom, its statistics would be far more comforting. Triumph said that the Tiger wouldn't make it, it was a street bike wearing an adventure frock, but they'd been wrong. The chain guards on both Tigers have snapped just above the rear wheel spindle, clearly a weak point, but thankfully that's been the only weak point and it was amazingly easy to fix. I've adjusted the final drive chains once, added absolutely no oil to either of the motorcycles and everything else has been trouble and maintenance free. The Tiger's a long distance lazy mans bike, and that suits me just fine.

Through the wonders of the world wide web, I'm aware of three different groups of riders travelling behind me on an assortment of motorcycles; KTM's, Yamaha's and BMW's, and it'll be interesting to see how those motorcycles have coped with the same road conditions. I'm hoping to meet them all in Vladivostok, where we'll arrange a group exit from Russia, but Vladivostok is still a thousand kilometres away and I don't want to start counting my chickens just yet. Instead, I'll concentrate on the here and now. The tarmac beneath my tyres isn't the best in the world, it's covered in gravel and pocked with craters, but at this moment in time it's by far the most beautiful piece of road that I've ever seen in my life. It feels smooth, safe, comfortable, and if it was wearing panties I'd probably be asking it for a date.

At the end of the Amur Highway stands the thriving city of Khabarovsk, the gateway to Vladivostok in the south. The last city experience was Chita, it was only a few days and a few thousand kilometres away, but it already feels like it was way back in a different lifetime. I'm amazed by high-rise buildings and neon signs, by people walking on pavements and music playing in the streets, by traffic and congestion, by traffic lights and policemen, trolley buses and the general chaos that separates it from the countryside.

I ride through the city in search of a room for the night, a place to wash away the dust and grime from seven days of off-road riding, seven nights of rough camping and the stench of smoke from the mosquito repelling campfires of Siberia. I look rough, I stink to high heaven and I'm covered from head to toe in thick beige dust. Independent hotels here in Russia are generally expensive, and here in the East they're also very rare. I eventually find the Hotel Tourist, another old Soviet hotel. The foyer greets me like a familiar friend and it will be absolutely perfect for tonight.

I try to check in, but once again there's a problem. In Russia there's always a bloody problem, but at least this time I get an explanation of what the problem is. My visa was last registered on the 5th of June in Sochi, the day after I'd arrived in Russia. Today it is the 9th of July and this raises both eyebrows and questions. Officially when travelling in Russia, you must register your visa in each city where you stay for three nights or more. I'd first registered on arrival in Sochi and then registered no more. I explain to the English speaking receptionist that since the 5th of June I've ridden across Russia, camping in the forests each night and riding a little further east each day. Now on the 9th of July, that long journey has brought me to her fine Hotel here in Khabarovsk. I forget to tell her that I'd spent several nights at the Hotel Tourist in Volgograd, but what she doesn't know probably won't hurt her. 'Niyet'. In Russia I always expect to hear the word 'Niyet' at least four or five times before receiving the required 'Da'. It just seems to be the Russian way.

The receptionist thinks that I'm telling her a very tall story, because nobody would ever ride a motorcycle across Russia, at least nobody who was sane. I point through the large window to the Tiger parked outside. A small crowd of people are circling it, waiting for me to return and to pose for more photographs. Maybe the sight of my newly found fan club has convinced her that I'm actually telling the truth and she allows me stay for one night, but I must promise to leave her hotel before ten o'clock tomorrow morning. 'Thank you very much, that'll do nicely'.

Every day here in Russia, amazing things happen, things that you'd simply never see at home. This morning, travelling south from Khabarovsk along a stretch of deep gravel, I passed a work crew who were attempting to rebuild the road. It was rough, it was difficult terrain and the Tiger was doing everything within its power to shake me from its back. Behind me I'd heard the sound of horns, loud and constant. I'd sat down in the saddle and looked back in my mirrors but all that I'd seen was dust. I'd stopped the bike and turned to see the drivers of the massive JCB's waving frantically and heading towards me. I assumed that something had fallen from the bike, so I'd dismounted and waited for them to arrive. The first driver to arrive had summoned me up to his cab, where he'd pulled a new and rather rude air freshener from behind his seat and presented it to me as a gift. As I'd climbed down from his cab several of his colleagues had been waiting for me with dried fish, fresh bread and of course, an abundance of Vodka. It was probably just a little after nine o'clock in the morning and the monster vehicle driving road crew had already been totally hammered. It seemed that reports of Poor Circulation's progress had been passed along the line and this particular road crew were the first to have been able to stop me.

We'd talked in two alien languages but the message had been very clear. They were very proud of Russia and had wanted to wish me well on my way towards Vladivostok. I'd sipped their Vodka, eaten their bread and dried fish and then as quickly as I'd entered, I was gone from their lives. In all of my years of riding around the UK this has never happened to me before. I just love the people of Russia who each day have given me something special to hold onto, something that always made me smile.

Vladivostok is approximately 765Km south of Khabarovsk, or about 440 miles, and that's probably a little too far for one day of comfortable riding. In fact it turns out to be a little too far for two days of riding.

The Amur Highway work crew sharing their early morning Vodka and beer

Perhaps it's that I'm road weary after the Amur Highway, or more likely, I just don't want my journey through Russia to come to an end. I'm taking my time, savouring every moment and stopping to chat with as many people as possible along the way. It's actually a very easy thing to do here in Russia because everybody wants to stop and talk. Nobody is ever in too much of a hurry to spend time learning about your adventure or sharing their own stories, and that is an amazing thing to cherish.

Tonight Adam is alongside me and we've pitched our tents away from the road along a rough mud track. We're close to the forest but far enough from the road so as not to be seen. Being so close to the Chinese border means that this road south, the M60 highway, has security points every few kilometres and border guards who constantly patrol the rivers and byways. Not wanting to attract their attention, it isn't possible to light a smoky fire and we sacrifice our blood to the mosquitoes and make the most of what will probably be our last night of rough camping here in Russia. The sun is setting over China to the west and we're quite literally in the middle of nowhere. Thunder rumbles in the distance as a storm passes over Vladivostok, but here at our camp to the north of the city we're thankfully dry.

A new thunder disturbs me, the thunder from the broken silencer of a Ural motorcycle outfit. It arrives unexpectedly out of the thick brush that surrounds our camp. As far as I can make out there's nothing but a few kilometres of forest and scrub between our camp and the Chinese border to the west, so where has the Ural come from? We quickly established that the two young men on the Ural speak absolutely no English, and for almost an hour they sit on their outfit looking at us, smoking my cigarettes and nodding. They each accept a cup of coffee and we all drink in silence. Anywhere else in the world and this would be a weird experience, but this isn't anywhere else in the world, this is far eastern Russia where such meetings are taken for granted. With the coffee finished, they simply hand me back the cups, kick their Ural into life, and vanish. It's just another reminder that here in Russia, the strangest of things are simply everyday occurrences.

Chapter 32:
Russia, Vladivostok

The sign at the side of the road tells me that Vladivostok means 'Lord of The East' and it will be our last real port of call here in Russia. Riding south towards the city, the settlements are starting to overwhelm the countryside and the traffic density's increasing. It feels like congestion, but it's not, it's just a huge contrast to the roads across the wilds of Siberia. The experience of rural life in Russia with its hospitality and dangers, its beauty and starkness, its marginal roads and amazing people is behind me, but I'm already beginning to miss it. Arriving in Sochi more than a month ago Russia had almost felt like a country too far, but once again a country and its people have dared to surprise me. Russia has embedded itself beneath my skin and I know that in the years to come, my itch to return here will certainly need scratching.

Once again we're holed-up in an old Soviet hotel, this time the Hotel Vladivostok. In common with the other old Soviet hotels it's huge and reasonably priced, but this hotel has actually been updated. Gone are the 'Floor Grannies' who guard the keys, gone are the obscure and antiquated bathrooms, gone are the mismatched linens and gone are the undersized bath towels. The Hotel Vladivostok would feel quite at home in any Western European city, but amazingly the room prices match those of its unmodernized siblings. The plan is to stay here for two nights and then to move out to The Box, a temporary home for overland travellers belonging to Vladivostok's famous motorcycle club, the Iron Tigers. Unfortunately, in keeping with the other Soviet hotels, they'll only allow me to check in for one night and not two, but they're happy for me to extend my stay by a single night tomorrow morning. You can take the quirks out of a Soviet hotel, but you clearly can't take the hotel out of the quirky Russian system.

The plan from here is to secure passage, as directly as possible, to North America, preferably to Anchorage in Alaska, but anywhere on the west coast of North America will do. Vladivostok Air is now operating a weekly flight to Anchorage but it seems that the Tigers might be too large for their cargo holds. Before leaving England I'd been reliably informed that shipping to America would take a minimum of six weeks, but I've now learned that sea freight can actually take less than three weeks. In the foyer of the Hotel Vladivostok we've met an English couple, Phil and Dot Spain. They're the first English people we've met since leaving Split in Croatia. Their 1980's camper van has just arrived in Vladivostok by ship from Seattle, and it's taken just over two weeks for it to get here. Tomorrow morning I'll meet with Yuri, an English-speaking shipping agent who's been recommended to us here in Vladivostok. If Yuri can do for Poor Circulation here what Ruslan and Semyon had done for us back in Volgograd, then anything is possible and America could be less than three weeks away. In the meantime I'll track down the Iron Tigers and spend some quality time doing absolutely bugger-all.

It's now Wednesday the 16th of July, the eighty seventh day of the journey and after three peaceful nights, we've moved out of the Hotel Vladivostok and moved into The Box above Vlad Moto, the motorcycle dealership and workshops of the Iron Tigers Motorcycle Club. Sleeping on their floor surrounded by motorcycles, drum kits and other musical paraphernalia, this has got to be the coolest gig in town, not to mention the cheapest.

At night when the workshop closes and the last mechanic or party reveller has gone home, we're left alone and have the run of the place until morning. Workshop, tools, tea, coffee, food, washing machine and a computer, everything that we could possibly need is here and free for us to use. At night I work on our own motorcycles in their workshop; changing brake pads, chains and sprockets, oil and filters, and if we're still sleeping when the staff arrive and open the shop in the morning, they just silently work around us. Can you imagine your own local motorcycle dealership providing this level of service for a pair of complete strangers?

Yesterday had been a busy day for the Iron Tigers here at Vlad Moto. A shipping container had arrived full of imported Japanese motorcycles, an assortment of street bikes, road cruisers and choppers. The day had been spent unloading them, assessing any damage and shoe-horning them into any space that was available. To celebrate the arrival of the new stock, in the evening there'd been a party with barbeque, beer and of course far too much vodka. It carried on into the early hours of the morning and several intoxicated club members had shared The Box for the night and my paracetamol this morning. In the early hours of this morning, as the vodka had been passed from hand to hand, everybody had taken their turn to tell a motorcycle related story. It had all been in Russian, obviously, and I hadn't understood a single word of it, but I was prompted to join in and Mikhail, the President of the Iron Tigers, had acted as my personal translator. This is the story that I shared:

'Asil was a Turkish boy who had two passions in life; Motorcycles and Travelling. Disillusioned with his life in Turkey and the prospect of completing a year of National Service in the Turkish army, he packed his motorcycle with all of his belongings and began his journey. He travelled all across Europe, through North and South America, down into the centre of Africa and eventually arrived in Mongolia. In Mongolia Asil discovered that his Turkish passport was soon to expire and visited the Turkish Embassy in order to have it renewed. Unfortunately, the embassy realised that Asil had avoided his compulsory year of National Service in Turkey and refused to renew his passport, unless he returned to Turkey immediately. Not wishing to complete a year in the Turkish army, Asil sought advice from his new friends in Mongolia. After much discussion it appeared that there was only one possible solution to his predicament. Asil should find and marry a Mongolian girl and then apply for Mongolian Citizenship and a Mongolian passport. The plan actually worked, he found a girl, they married, Asil received his Mongolian Citizenship and then collected all of the documents necessary to apply for his Mongolian passport. With a spring in his step he took himself and the documents to the passport office in Mongolia and waited patiently in line. Eventually his application was taken and inspected by an official, but the news that greeted him was not what he'd expected. Unfortunately Asil was now 26 years of age and as a Mongolian Citizen must complete two years of National Service with the army of Mongolia.'

For the coming weekend we've been invited to ride with the Iron Tigers up to the town of Usseriske for a weekend of camping and general merriment. Called the 'Ride to Work Rally', it seems to be an annual event where motorcycle clubs from across Eastern Russia gather together and have fun. I suspect that it'll be just like a British motorcycle rally, but slightly more Russian. I'm sure it'll be quite an experience and I hope I'll be able to remember at least some of it, but at this moment in time I'm suffering from a serious case of information overload. In my search for the most efficient way to leave Russia, I'm encountering an epidemic of disinformation. Everybody seems to know something about the best possible solution, but definitive answers are in extremely short supply.

What I now know with certainty, is that flying with Vladivostok Air is no longer an option. Two German riders were a little way ahead of us and they chose the seemingly simple route of flying their BMW's from Vladivostok to Anchorage in Alaska. The promises made to them had been good, but the actuality had been something slightly different. Their BMW's now sit on the island of Sakhalin and will apparently move no further until a rather large ransom, or 'local tax', has been paid. No other airline will fly us out of Vladivostok, so the only other option is to take a ferry to Japan or South Korea. Neither of us has bought the expensive insurance carnets required for entering Japan with motorcycles, so it appears that South Korea is our only option for a seamless exit. I've contacted Wendy Choi of Aero International in Seoul and she's currently compiling the information that should help us to make our final decision.

Aside from the two German riders that I've just mentioned, the other three riders who were behind us on the Amur Highway all seem to have vanished without trace. A Brazilian duo riding Yamaha's were last heard of leaving Chita, and a single guy riding a KTM had been last seen approaching Khabarovsk, but there's been no news on any of them since then. Our German friend Rick is now back in Chita, but heavy rain seems to have made the Amur Highway impassable. If Rick thinks that it's impassable on his Dakar BMW, then Adam and I must have been the luckiest guys in the world to have crossed Siberia with the weather on our side. Our blessings have been counted and we'll raise a few glasses to our missing comrades and hope that they'll all eventually arrive safely in Vladivostok where a warm welcome awaits.

The Iron Tigers promised sunshine for the weekend and it seems that their weather predictions are every bit as good as their hospitality. It's

Saturday morning and the sun shines brightly as we gather beneath their clubhouse at Vlad Moto. We'd been promised a small gathering and a convoy of bikes but this is beginning to feel more like Sturgis than Vladivostok. We follow line-a-stern behind the President and arrive in the city of Usseriske with a police escort through to the centre of the city where several other bike groups are waiting to greet us. It's impossible to count the number of motorcycles, but it's certainly a lot more than the promised 'few'. We're introduced to other chapters of the Iron Tigers and feel immediately welcome in their family. All across Russia our bikes had stood out from the Ural's and Jawa's that travel the roads and byways, but here with the Iron Tigers our own Triumph Tigers are simply unusual bikes with slightly smaller engines and a lot less chrome than the Japanese cruisers that they seem to prefer around here.

With another police escort, we travel onwards in larger convoy to an enclosed camping ground beside a river several kilometres north of Usseriske. It's a carnival atmosphere; different groups meet as friends and party long into the night to the accompaniment of live music and fireworks. The beer and food are plentiful and the stream of vodka never ending. Here there's none of the tensions and rivalry often felt at similar bike rallies in other parts of the world, it's simply carnival time for everybody. The general feeling of safety isn't too surprising when I see how seriously the Iron Tigers take their security. It seems that here in Usseriske it's only the Englishmen who don't carry guns.

As the sun sets across Eastern Russia, we're introduced to a young Kiwi girl by the name of Danielle Murdoch. Aboard her aging Honda 250, she's travelled alone to Russia from New Zealand, via Cambodia, Thailand, Lao and Vietnam. She'll go on to follow the Amur Highway to Ulan Ude and drop down into Mongolia before conquering 'The Stans' and onwards to London. Twelve months ago, having never before ridden a motorcycle, Danielle had decided to ride a bike across the world to London. On her journey she's conquered roads and overcome problems in the remotest of regions, challenges that would have brought Poor Circulation to a grinding and tearful halt. As with all bike rallies across Europe, there's a 'Long Distance Award' that's presented to the furthest travelled rider. With 20,000Km under our belts the award is presented to Poor Circulation, but we politely decline and pass it on to Danielle. Every one of this gutsy Kiwi's miles is worth ten or more of our own and she deserves it far more than we do. I can only hope that upon arrival in London, Danielle's welcome will be as warm as it has been here in Usseriske.

At some point last night, I can remember standing on the large stage surrounded by beautiful half naked girls and getting groped to within an inch of a happy night. After a British bike rally I'd know that it had been nothing more than a drunken dream, but I'm not in Great Britain and there's photographic evidence to support this morning's feelings of guilt. Apparently last night I also agreed to take part in another Russian rally tradition this morning. It seems that every time I've shown my map to a Russian man, he's highlighted three things of interest in the next town; the best bar, the best brothel and the best banya. The bar and the brothel I can understand, the former I'll frequent and the latter I'll avoid, but the banya was always something of a mystery to me. Now, the President of the Iron Tigers is inviting me to join him and his senior colleague in the banya, and I feel that it would be impolite of me to refuse.

I quickly discover that a 'Banya' is actually just a sauna, nothing more and nothing less. Here it seems to be a tradition, winter and summer, that men take banyas and then plunge themselves into a refreshing river. For an Englishman entering this domain, it's a huge leap into the great unknown. With my clothing removed I enter the banya and as the honoured guest, I'm immediately directed to the uppermost bench, the hottest seat in the house. Laying flat on my stomach, a clutch of branches with leaves still attached is dipped into cold water and then thrashed across my body. Just when I think that the fun is finally coming to an end, and that I've survived my first banya, they turn me over and start again. The traditional process takes several minutes and all of the time the coals are being stoked and more and more water is added to the furnace. I assume that they're testing my metal, so I hold out for as long as I can, but eventually I give-in to the heat and the thrashing.

It must only have lasted for ten or fifteen minutes, but when I exit the banya my head is light and spinning, my body bright red and tingling. The small crowd waiting outside point me in a specific direction and I walk clumsily down a wooden jetty and throw myself into the river below. 'Fuck me!' English rivers can be chilly, but they're positively tropical in comparison to this stream of Siberian melt water. The experience is painful, and one that I won't rush to complete again, but my coldness is nothing in comparison to my embarrassment. The chilled water has shrunken my manhood into something that resembles a shrivelled peanut, and I'm more than reluctant to climb out with so many people watching me.

System Failure. Information Overload. Re-Boot System. Ctrl Alt Del. Press Any Key to Continue. For eight days, misinformation and half-truths about the best possible exit from Russia have been sending me on nothing but wild goose chases. Here in Vladivostok it seems that nobody will ever say 'Yes', they only offer me 'Maybe', or 'Possibly' or 'Please call back tomorrow'. I've given up trying and returned to the solution that had been there from the very start. I've been back in contact with Wendy Choi at Aero International in South Korea, and Wendy is arranging for both Tigers to be shipped from the southern port of Bussan, to Seattle in Washington State USA. It's not the cheapest or fastest solution, but at least it seems that in South Korea they have a proper rule book and everybody's reading exactly the same edition of it. Sadly, the same can't be said for their Russian counterparts, smiling people who all seem to require money before suddenly changing the rules. That's not a criticism, just another observation, but I've now passed the responsibility to Wendy Choi, somebody who's far more capable of making the arrangements than I am. Now all that I have to do is to get myself, Adam and the two Tigers, safely to Soc Cho in South Korea.

The motorcycles will be dealt with in the port at Soc Cho and after handing over our cash and signing the relevant documents, we'll simply take a bus to Seoul. Wendy comes highly recommended by other overland travellers but she makes it clear that Aero International will only accept payments in cash. Adam's aware of this and although he's still reluctant to use Russian Cash Machines, he assures me that when the time comes, it won't be a problem for him to pay. We'll spend time exploring Seoul until it's confirmed that the Tigers have set sail for Seattle, and then go our separate ways. From Seoul, Adam plans to head directly to Seattle and then cross the northern states of America and fly home with his Tiger from New York. I'll leave from Seoul to Thailand before flying to Seattle and then riding down into California where I'll deliver the Special Package and spend some time with the family in Boonville. Once fully rested, I'll start heading towards the east coast and find an efficient exit back to London. We're both happy with the outcome and it should all be quite straight forward, but then again, I'm still in Russia where nothing is ever as easy as it should be.

The two missing Brazilian riders have finally arrived. They've come here to the Iron Tigers' workshop with one broken motorcycle on the back of the Vlad Moto recovery truck. Nothing too serious, just a snapped drive chain, worn rear sprocket, broken frame, bent inlet valves, crunched main engine bearings, broken exhaust manifold and a shattered rear hub. Apart from that, the Yamaha dirt bike seems to have coped

*My guardians for the Ride to Work Rally,
Andre and Hans of the Iron Tigers*

quite well crossing Russia.

The rider with the broken Yamaha, a bike supplied free of charge by his main sponsor Yamaha, is a confident young man by the name of Rodrigo. His quietly spoken companion doesn't seem to have a name, but he's employed as Rodrigo's 'Minder' for an around the world journey that started in Spain two months ago.

Even before Rodrigo's broken Yamaha is removed from the Vlad Moto recovery truck, the diminutive Brazilian is barking orders in very good English to the Iron Tiger's mechanics. Overnight the Iron Tigers have made a one thousand five hundred kilometre round trip in order to rescue Rodrigo and his crippled motorcycle. Their services have been provided entirely free of charge, and the little shit's showing them absolutely no gratitude or respect.

A third man arrives with several cell phones and a rather splendid looking notebook. This man turns out to be Rodrigo's 'PR Representative' here in Russia. He's the man who oil's the wheels of Rodrigo's progress across Russia, but clearly not his drive chain or engine. He flies ahead of the Brazilian arranging his hotels and generally keeping everything sweet in Rodrigo's beautiful world.

If I remain in close proximity to Rodrigo, one of us will end up requiring dental treatment, so I retreat to the Tigers and work on a more permanent fix for the broken chain guards. A fresh faced portly Russian stranger joins me and bends down to see what I'm doing, 'What a freaking asshole'. Fortunately he's not passing judgement on my engineering skills, he's just referring to Rodrigo's attitude and he introduces himself as 'Ivan'. In Excellent American English, Ivan tells me that he's a business associate of the owner of the Dong Chun Ferry Company, the company that will be taking us and the Tigers to Soc Cho in South Korea. Between fixing the chain guards and listening to further outbursts from Rodrigo, I don't really pay too much attention to what Ivan is saying, and when he mentions the possibility of 'free passage' to Soc Cho, I just nod and mutter a slightly uninterested 'thank you'.

According to legend, no trip to Vladivostok is complete without three things. Firstly a weekend bike rally and secondly a banya with a group of hairy bikers. As a reminder of the former I have a beautiful tee shirt and for the later, simply the memory and a few scars across my back. The third element to this triptych of wonders is a visit to the speedway stadium on 'Race Day'. In the hierarchy of Vladivostok pastimes, speedway seems to come second only to drinking vodka. The local heroes, 'Team Vostok' have until this season been the champions of all Russia. Today the new champions from Kiev, the pretenders to Team Vostok's throne, are the visitors.

I buy tickets for our friend Andre, Club Secretary for the Iron Tigers, and his beautiful wife Ulia to join us: Start/Finish line, centre row, the best seats in the house. Four tickets for the princely sum of $10. It's a party atmosphere, the alcohol ban is enforced as if it never existed and the girls in the audience significantly outnumber the boys. I've been to speedway meetings in England but this is very different. It's more like 'Fashion Week' in Milan and is as far removed from Ipswich or Manchester on a cold and rainy evening as you could possibly imagine. The MC is loud and judging by the reaction of his audience, funny and popular too. The visiting team from the Ukraine includes the reigning world champion and Andre suggests that they are in fact the 'Chelsea of Speedway', a team lacking in neither talent nor finances, just history and heritage.

The racing begins, I stand, I shout, I cheer along with the masses and become an instant supporter of Team Vostok. It's impossible not to become involved because the enthusiasm is unavoidably infectious. To complete an almost perfect evening, Team Vostok win by 60pts to 30pts and Team Vostok will once again be National Champions. Vladivostok will party tonight and the party will last until dawn, because that is the Vladivostok way.

It's the last hour of my last day here at The Box above Vlad Moto, and it's time to add my name and comments to the Iron Tigers Visitor Book, a book that already seems to include entries from every motorcycle traveller that I've ever heard of:

'As a stranger in a strange land I came to Russia. A land where the police opened my wallet but the people opened my heart. Here at Vlad Moto in Vladivostok I found Mikhail and the Iron Tigers, and for your generosity, friendship and support, I will always be grateful. Ride Safe. Geoff'

The invincible Triumph Tiger, down but not defeated

Chapter 33:
Russia, Zarubino

It's day ninety-four of the journey, 7:30am on Friday 24th of July and we're waiting impatiently at the Iron Tigers' workshop. This morning we're taking the ferry from Vladivostok to Slavyansk from where we'll ride the remaining few miles down to the port of Zarubino. We were supposed to leave here thirty minutes ago with The Architect, and several other members of the Iron Tigers who've insisted on escorting us to the docks. Our ferry starts boarding in thirty minutes, but we're waiting for 'Rodrigo Arrogantus'. Apparently, he's now decided that he'll be joining us on the ferry to Slavyansk.

The Brazilian has turned up late, and now he's issuing orders as if he himself were President. His motorcycle isn't perfect, but it's more than capable of making the journey. His Yamaha has been thrashed to death and the mechanics here have fixed his rear hub, turned him a new rear sprocket, fitted a new drive chain, welded and braced his broken frame and done everything possible to revive his ailing engine. A lack of oil and an abundance of neglect have created problems that required a large number of replacement parts, but those parts simply weren't available here at such short notice. The mechanics have done everything humanly possible to get him on his way this morning, but a permanent fix will have to wait until Rodrigo reaches Vancouver in Canada.

His Yamaha is packed and ready to go, but Rodrigo doesn't seem keen to ride it. He's suddenly changed his mind about joining us on the ferry to Slavyansk. Now, he wants the Iron Tigers to transport him and his Yamaha two hundred and fifty kilometres south to Zarubino from where he'll also take the ferry to South Korea. Hopefully, it will be a different ferry to the one that we'll be travelling on. Of course the Iron Tigers will take him to Zarubino on their recovery truck, because that's the kind of people they are. It's time for Adam and I to leave and The Architect apologises for the unexpected delay.

We're already at risk of missing our ferry, but some things are far too important to be ignored. I use a valuable minute of time to take the confident Brazilian to a quiet corner of the workshop. His fashionable ethnic scarf makes an excellent holding point and hard against the cold steel of a large tool locker, I offer Rodrigo several well chosen words of advice. I suspect that my words will have little lasting effect on the confident young man, but the Iron Tigers are far too polite to complain themselves. Rodrigo's riding around the world under the banner of 'Ride for Peace', but I suspect that without an adjustment to his attitude, in places of lesser tolerance than this it won't be 'Peace' that's breaking out all around him. As we finally ride out of the Vlad Moto compound with our motorcycle escort, I'm sure that I can hear Rodrigo calling out to those around him. 'People, People, where's my latte?'

Zarubino is a small town in the far south east of Russia and the main port of exit for journeys to South Korea. From here we'll take the overnight crossing to Soc Cho. I purchased the passenger tickets in Vladivostok for $200 each, but the tickets for the bikes will need to be purchased at the ferry, though nobody seems to know quite when, where, or even how much they'll cost. With no opportunity to camp, the overnight hotel in Zarubino is thankfully cheap, just $10 per night with hot running water. Admittedly, the hot running water isn't in my room, but for just one night it feels great to be sleeping in a real bed again. The ferry will sail at 18:00 hours tomorrow, Saturday 26th July. Customs clearance will be at 14:00 hours and boarding will commence at 17:00, which for Russia, all appears to be very precise and well organised.

My last night in Russia was a peaceful one. A comfortable bed in a quiet hotel had resulted in a good night's sleep. This morning I'm confident that I have enough energy to face the inevitable hurdles of Russian bureaucracy. In England you'll see many older buildings with several of their windows in-filled with brick. This was done back in the days when a

'Window Tax' existed. The more windows a building had, the greater the tax it attracted. Here in Russia they also have a Window Tax, a unique form of Window Tax that appears to exist at border crossings. At every window where you're required to present your documentation, a tax becomes payable.

At the first window I pay 200 Roubles for the privilege of taking the Tiger and myself out onto the dock. Out on the dock, I find another open window. Through this window I pass the princely sum of 2,600 Roubles for 'Customs Tax', plus an additional fine of 136 Roubles for failing to pay the customs tax in US Dollars. I'm then directed to a third window where a further 460 Roubles is withdrawn from my wallet. This time it appears to be an 'Exit Tax'. Thankfully, this time no fine is levied for paying the tax in Roubles, the currency of the worlds' largest country. Moving onto the fourth open window I wait for my boarding card, but as always here in Russia, there's a problem. Adam and I must return to the passenger lounge and wait. Somebody will come and attend to us shortly.

For some time now we've been aware of several riders behind and ahead of us along the Amur Highway. The Brazilian duo, Rodrigo and his minder, we've already met in Vladivostok. Another pair of Englishmen riding BMW GS's, have apparently been forced to turn back after accidents and mechanical failures. Dan, a solo KTM rider, has vanished without trace and a German duo who are also riding BMW GS's were last seen corruptly stranded on the island of Sakhalin. Bored with waiting for somebody to come and attend to me, I sit out on the concrete dock enjoying a relaxing smoke when two BMW GS's pull to a halt in front of me. They introduce themselves as 'Hans' and 'Volker', a pair of medical doctors from Germany on a journey around the world entitled 'The Ride of Change'. They'd been a few days ahead of us on the road but at the very end of the Amur Highway they'd been caught in a storm and had tried to ride through it. A branch from a tree had broken in the wind and crashed down onto Hans' helmet, piercing the shell and sending him to a hospital bed for several days. The Amur Highway had claimed another victim but thankfully this time both bike and rider were well on the road to recovery.

Hans and Volker give me news of Dan, the solo KTM rider who'd been catching us along the road before crashing. Dan is apparently now in plaster and resting in Vladivostok. Dan's bike, although seriously damaged, is being repaired by another Vladivostok motorcycle club. I ask Hans and Volker if they've met Charlie Honner, the BMW riding Australian heading west to start his new job in London. Yes, they've met Charlie but the news isn't good. A few days after meeting him, Charlie had fallen and was last seen nursing torn knee ligaments on the beautiful island of Ol Khon. That's not good news for Charlie, but I can't think of a better place on earth to relax and recuperate.

Hans then asks if I've heard anything from the famous Brazilian television star who'd also failed to conquer the Amur Highway. It had never crossed my mind that Rodrigo might actually be famous. Perhaps he's famous in a 'Hello Magazine' world, a world that I certainly don't visit, but I smile and tell them that while his motorcycle was still quite sick, Rodrigo himself was sadly enjoying the rudest of health. Judging by the misadventures of other riders, the Amur Highway might actually be a little tougher than I've given it credit for, or maybe I should just start showing our bulletproof Triumph Tigers a little more respect?

Three hours after being told that somebody would be along to attend to us, I'm been given the confusing news that both of our visas have expired. It's now the 26th of July and I know for certain that our visas are valid until the 28th of August, so I hope that they'll excuse me for looking just a little perplexed. The validity dates for the visas are stamped in our passports, clear as day and there for everybody to see. They're the only entries on any of our Russian paperwork that are written in both Russian and English, so these dates are the only facts of which I'm absolutely certain. After another short pause, an English speaker is found and the problem is clearly explained to both of us. Our Russian business visas state that we'll enter Russia not before the 1st of June 2008 and exit Russia not later than the 28th of August 2008, a possible period of ninety days in Russia. The problem seems to be that although it was clear that we'd be in Russia for a possible period of ninety days, the customs officer in Sochi had allowed our Tigers to enter Russia for only fourteen days. All of this information is apparently clearly explained on our customs declaration forms, but unfortunately, those forms are written entirely in Russian. The temporary import 'visas' for our Tigers had expired on the 19th of June and therefore it's impossible for the authorities here at Zarubino to allow either us, or either of our motorcycles, to leave Russia. We're to wait here for a little while longer, we're not to move, and a Customs Official will be along to deal with us. I'm not sure if I really want to be 'dealt with' by a Customs Official, but I do know that I need another smoke.

I sit back on the dock enjoying the calming effects of nicotine and watch as a diminutive but handsome young man barks orders to two of his subordinates, one of whom appears to be pushing a familiar looking Yamaha motorcycle towards me. Some days, when you really think that things couldn't possibly get any worse, Rodrigo shows up. We're far too involved in our own different worlds to acknowledge each other's presence, and that's probably the best thing for both of us. I'm already resigned to the fact that we won't be leaving Russia tonight, and it'll be a shame to say goodbye to Hans and Volker who we've only just met, but putting some distance between myself and Rodrigo probably isn't such a bad thing.

Adam still seems confident that we'll leave on tonight's ferry and he's moving between windows trying to open some doors. It's good that he's fighting the battle, but I fear it's a battle than won't be won today. The English speaking assistant who'd told us that a Customs Official would be coming along to deal with us, hadn't seemed so confident about an early escape from Zarubino. I fear that her reason for seeking a 'Customs Official' is that he or she is the only person who has the power of arrest. I'm not particularly worried about it because I know that at some point in the next few days we'll both be leaving Russia, hopefully together with our Tigers, I just don't know when or how much money will need to change hands before that happens. Looking on the bright side, we could have been stranded in far worse places than this.

At last there's some news. Our visa problems can be fixed, but we'll need to wait until Monday, possibly Tuesday, nobody seems to be sure which. The English speaking lady with the smile tells us not to worry, but the Customs Officer with the oversized cap isn't sure. Standing next to them, the lady without the smile is adamant that we should both be arrested right now. They can't agree and we must wait a little longer for a decision to be made regarding our freedom. A few weeks earlier I would have been angry and shouting at every official in sight, but now I honestly don't care. As the Dong Chun Ferry raises its ramp and prepares to sail towards South Korea without us, our situation is finally made clear. The good news is that although we are now technically 'under-arrest', so long as we promise not to leave Zarubino until after our court hearing, which will apparently take place on Monday, we are free to leave the dock. The bad news is the 'Court Hearing on Monday', which sounds worryingly official.

We're invited to appoint our own English speaking representative to appear alongside us in court, but if that proves to be difficult then the court will appoint one on our behalf. The English speaking lady with the

The amazing Triumph Tiger trying to leave Russia

smile understands that this really isn't our fault and apologises, the Customs Officer in the oversized cap seems disinterested with the whole affair and the unknown lady without the smile now looks like the cat that got the cream. I've no idea what will happen in court on Monday, but I hope to hell that that particular bitch isn't there to judge us.

From the balcony of the hotel that we checked out of earlier today, I watch the Dong Chun Ferry sailing out of Zarubino's harbour. Through the binoculars I can make out the figures of Hans and Volker standing on deck, probably with a chilled beer in their hands. Closer to the vessel's bridge, I'm sure I can see another familiar looking figure, a confident young Brazilian who's probably offering navigational advice to the captain of the ship. I buy Adam a beer and we raise our glasses to absent friends. We're still in Zarubino, but I'm sure that South Korea is no more than a small bribe away.

After spending two more comfortable but uneventful nights at the small hotel in Zarubino, we arrived on the port this morning and were ushered into the Customs Master's office to receive our official spanking. It wasn't really a court room, probably just the largest available office on the docks, but the procedure seemed very official indeed. We were treated as separate cases, were asked to give evidence in our defence and once all of the evidence had been heard, we were asked to await the courts verdict. Apparently being unable to read Russian isn't an acceptable defence, so we were both found guilty of the charges. The fine was 1,500 Roubles each, a lot less than I'd expected, and we had to sign documents in which we admitted our guilt and accepted that the courts procedures and decisions had been fair. Given the mitigating circumstances I'm not sure that 'Fair' is the most appropriate word, but we're free to leave on the next ferry to Soc Cho, which should be later this afternoon.

The Dong Chun Ferry is very good, it has space for two hundred cars but is carrying just three European motorcycles and riders. We've been joined for the journey to Soc Cho by mystery man Dan Honcuic, the KTM rider that Hans and Volker had also mentioned. Towards the end of the Amur Highway, Dan had been involved in a solo accident leaving his motorcycle broken and his shoulder badly dislocated. A local bike club had taken Dan under their wing, arranged for his medical treatment and worked wonders on rebuilding his motorcycle. Both bike and body are still suffering, but determined to continue onwards with the journey. The emptiness of the ferry gives me time and space to think, and two things become apparent. Firstly, I now know why the insurance agent at Sochi had only given us fourteen days of motorcycle insurance, because that's how long our Tigers should have been in Russia. He must have known that this was going to be a problem, but he hadn't told us at the time. Given what's just happened, I think that in comparison to arguing with the alcoholic asshole Customs Officer back in Sochi, breaking the law and paying the fine has been a far more pleasing experience. The second thing that I remember is Ivan, the portly Russian man who'd talked to me back at Vlad Moto, the man who'd claimed that he could provide us with free passage for the Tigers to Soc Cho. At the time I'd already bought and paid for the passenger tickets, but we still haven't been charged for the Tigers. Maybe Ivan had been exactly who he'd claimed to be and I now feel very guilty for not showing more appreciation at the time.

'Dosvedanya Russia'. Next stop South Korea, the twenty-third country.

Chapter 34:
South Korea

Arriving in South Korea feels slightly strange. It's not a place that I'd really considered visiting and embarrassingly, my only real objective here is to leave the country as smoothly and cheaply as possible. We've sailed on the Dong Chun Ferry into the port city of Soc Cho, arrived exactly on time and our entry into South Korea couldn't have been smoother. Within a few minutes of wafting through immigration, both of the Tigers have been loaded onto a flat-bed truck bound for the southern port of Bussan. We've handed over the keys to the logistics team of Aero International and arranged to meet their representative, Wendy Choi, in Seoul early next week to say thank you.

During the overnight crossing from Russia, I'd struggled with the question of what to do with the Special Package, whether to leave it with the motorcycle or to take it with me in my hand luggage. In the end, I've decided that while being separated from it for the next couple of weeks isn't ideal, the package and its contents will be an awful lot safer if it remains hidden onboard the Tiger. I hope that I've made the right decision, but it's done now so there's absolutely no point in my worrying about it.

Having waved a temporary farewell to our motorcycles, Aero International hand each of us a photocopy of the final invoices for their service. They're calculated in US Dollars and the total amounts are exactly what Wendy Choi had told us they'd be. We should now be handing over our cash to Aero International, but embarrassingly, that's not going to happen today. Just twenty-four hours before our planned departure from Russia, Adam had dropped a financial bombshell. He'd had the $1,250.00 in cash that he'd need to pay to Aero International upon arrival here in Soc Cho, but unfortunately that cash had still been sitting in his bank account back in England. I'd sat patiently waiting for an explanation, or the revelation that he'd just been teasing me, but neither of them had come. I'd seen Adam visiting Cash Machines on a regular basis in Vladivostok, but if he hadn't withdrawn any cash, then I could only assume that he'd simply been window shopping. I'd had to send an urgent message to Wendy Choi trying to convince her that we were trustworthy people and asking if it was possible to delay our payments to Aero International. Thankfully, Wendy had agreed and Aero International would deal with our motorcycles before any money had changed hands.

We've never met Wendy Choi but her level of trust was really quite astonishing. She'd gone out on a financial limb for two total strangers and that's not something that you'll see very often back in England. Without her support I'm not sure what we would have done, she's just made everything so easy for us and now it seems that our Tigers will actually set sail for Seattle long before we've paid for their journey. Thank you Wendy.

As we're leaving the docks, I see a German traveller who I'd last seen on Friday afternoon during our failed attempt to leave Zarubino. He's sitting inside his camper van in the bonded enclosure cooking lunch on his gas stove. He's currently unhappy with the world in general and Germany's 1949 Minister of Transport in particular. Unfortunately, in his otherwise perfectly planned travel itinerary, Klaus has overlooked a minor administrative detail and is now awaiting deportation back to Russia. For some strange reason back in 1949, Germany failed to sign the 'International Convention on Road Traffic' and to this day, German nationals are apparently not allowed to drive any form of motor vehicle on the roads of South Korea. Klaus is not a happy chap and in an attempt to cheer him up and remind him that things could actually be an awful lot worse, I recall the story of Asil and his failed attempts to avoid National Service in Turkey. Unfortunately Klaus seems to have reached the stage where clutching at straws has become a viable alternative to his current predicament and instead of laughing, he just asks me if marriage to a South Korean girl would be legally binding in Europe. I wish the unfortunate traveller well, but as he no longer has a visa to re-enter Russia, it looks like he might be enjoying his new surroundings for a little while longer.

South Korea was never a confirmed part of my original plan, but here I am and from what I've seen so far, it's certainly not the worst place you could accidentally visit. The people here seem to be friendly, the streets are amazingly clean and when darkness falls, the whole of Soc Cho becomes a wonderland of neon splendour. Tomorrow we'll take a bus to Seoul and find a reasonably priced guest house where we can rest and make plans for our onward journeys. The price of a flight from Seoul to Seattle is around $800, and it seems to be exactly the same price if you fly there via Bangkok, Kuala Lumpur, Taipei, Jakarta or Hong Kong. I'll fly to Thailand where I can kick my heels for a couple of cheap weeks before flying on to meet the Tiger in Seattle.

After a restful coach journey to Seoul, I find a guest house where the rooms are priced on the edge of our budgets but where everything seems to work, including fast wireless internet which I haven't seen for some time. My first impressions of Seoul are good, but not great. It seems to be a beautiful city filled with very polite people and anonymous looking new buildings, but for a major Asian city, the overwhelming impression is slightly dull. So far I've seen nothing at all wrong with Seoul; it's clean, it's functional and the public transport system works beautifully, it just appears to lack an Asian heart. In the markets everything has a price tag and the stall holders sit patiently waiting for your business. There's none of the usual hustle and bustle that makes other Asian markets feel so addictively vibrant. Everything is just a little bit too easy and gentle here, too finished, too shiny and slightly too new. Perhaps I'm expecting too much of Seoul but it just seems to have a very different atmosphere when compared to other major cities here in Asia.

Another thing that Seoul seems to lack are street names, they just don't seem to use them here. Instead, every particular building has a name and is found by knowing which sub-district of the city it's located in. I guess that it's something that you would accept as being normal if you lived here and spoke Korean, but we don't, and finding anywhere is always something of an adventure. So there I am, criticising a perfectly fine city, whining like an Englishman and ignoring my own good fortune, and then it happens.

It's the event that makes me fall in love with Seoul, the fissure that allows me to see beneath its seemingly conservative veneer and find its beating heart. Every city has one, but here in Seoul it's taken a little longer to find. Outside of an absolutely ordinary looking shopping complex,

I see two girls standing on small platforms directing traffic in and out of the car park. This in itself isn't unusual, but its traffic directing married with theatre, a peculiarly Asian form of theatre that you'd simply never see in the West. Music plays and the girls are dressed in borderline inappropriate costumes with short skirts and oversized white gloves. They're dancing and directing traffic in the style of Michael Jackson. It's a small thing, but I've never seen it before and it makes me start looking more closely at the people.

I wander into a building known as 'TM', which I think is the Seoul Tech Market. Eight floors of electronics neatly packaged in air conditioned comfort, a zillion square feet of techno-nerd-nirvana. The Tech Market should be a magnet for male nerds and a place where girlfriends are an undiscovered species, but here in Seoul it isn't. The floors are filled with cool looking people who have lashings of style and the only thick rimmed spectacles that I see here are fashion statements rather than fashion disasters. It's vibrant, buzzing with life and contains an eclectic mix of everything that's currently trendy in South Korea. As a man who struggles with cell phones and Microsoft Windows, the electronic gizmos don't really interest me, but here that certainly puts me in a minority of one. There are music systems, plasma screen TV's, computers, cameras, massive karaoke machines and a million other things that I honestly can't identify. The young crowd here are not just window shopping, they're buying, spending big and it all seems to be charged on plastic. I seem to be the only person here in Seoul who still uses paper money. For the first time since leaving Italy I feel like the poorest man in the village, and I probably am.

The more senior people of Seoul, who I guess are the parents of this technically savvy crowd here at TM, are conservative, polite and all seem to employ exactly the same tailor, but the 18-30 crowd have a unique culture of their own. It's as if everybody under the age of thirty here in Seoul has been sprinkled with fun dust and wears styles that are absolutely unique. It makes me feel old and unfashionable, which of course I am, but it also makes me smile and anything that can do that, is certainly worth loving.

After dark I find city streets with a very different atmosphere, a mirror image of the daytime seriousness of people going quietly about their business. The older crowd have vanished and the youths congregate in lively cafes and bars, they drink designer beer and skinny lattes and confidently sing along to the latest Korean pop songs. Something else strikes me as being unusual in Seoul, but it's taken me a couple of days to realise what that something is. The products and styles enjoyed by the people are almost exclusively of South Korean origin; Hyundai and Kia cars, Samsung electronics, Hyosung scooters and clothing by SPAO et al. I'd always thought that when it came to next generation cool, Japan had enjoyed the monopoly, but watch out Japan because South Korean K-Pop culture is amazingly infectious and it's closing in on your crown.

Tonight we're meeting Wendy Choi for dinner and every day since leaving Soc Cho, Adam's been visiting the bank and withdrawing the cash that he needs to give her tonight. He's also decided that rather than travelling to another part of Asia, he'll stay here in Seoul for another week before flying directly to Seattle. The main reason behind his decision to remain in Seoul is that we've met a couple of Australian riders who we'd first bumped into back in Vladivostok. Mike and Joe are riding their BMW R1150GS back to their native Australia and have proved to be excellent company for Adam. He still seems a little uncomfortable mixing with local people, so having Mike and Joe around him for the next week should make his stay a little easier.

Yesterday Wendy confirmed that the Tigers were onboard the Seattle bound vessel and had already set sail from Bussan, which is actually a couple of days ahead of schedule. Confident that the bikes have left South Korea, I've booked my own flight to Bangkok via Kuala Lumpur and then onwards via Taipei to Seattle. It gives me about eight days in Thailand and assuming that the Tiger arrives in Seattle on schedule, we should be reunited on August the 15th, the one hundred and seventeenth day of the journey.

Within the community of overland travellers, Wendy Choi has a reputation for being one hundred percent reliable and amazingly efficient. Those travellers cover thousands of miles to reach South Korea, but it's often the extra mile that Wendy Choi is willing to go that keeps their journeys rolling. So, I'm not at all surprised when she emerges from the subway station exactly on time. After formal introductions, Wendy leads us to a Korean restaurant where we enjoy a selection of steamed vegetables and meats that we boil and barbecue on a flaming dome in the centre of our table. Her English is excellent and we talk about the various travellers that we all seem to have met. Wendy is both charming and disarming and encourages me to try the Korean delicacy Kimchi, which I do. It seems to be a dish that combines fermented cabbage with garlic and chilli. It's difficult to describe the texture and flavour of Kimchi, but it's an experience that I'll probably never repeat.

The restaurant is busy and the chatter of excited diners makes it impossible to discuss business. So, after we've eaten Wendy generously pays for our meal and suggests that we move on to a quieter coffee shop where we can talk through the paperwork and finalise our business arrangements.

At what I assume to be the Korean equivalent of Starbucks, we find an empty table and Wendy guides us through the procedures that we'll need to follow when we arrive in Seattle. Her professionalism reassures me, every possible detail has been covered and absolutely nothing's been left to chance. Happy that we both understand the details and with all of our many questions answered, the two original invoices are passed across the table, one for me and one for Adam. I take the envelope that's been in my pocket since leaving Russia and pass it to Wendy. She doesn't open the envelope and count the money that's inside it, she simply slips it into her briefcase, signs my shipping documents, shakes my hand and then looks towards Adam. Adam reaches into his jacket pocket, pulls out his wallet and confidently offers Wendy, a fucking Credit Card.

Wendy looks embarrassed and Adam's eyes drop to the floor. He's probably looking for a nonexistent escape hole somewhere beneath his chair and if he finds it, I'll happily jump through it with him. In my life I've had many embarrassing moments, but none of them could hold a candle to this one. Wendy gently reminds Adam that she can't accept his Credit Card, only Cash, and after a suitable pause adds that she'd thought that he'd fully understood those terms. Wendy's claim that she'd 'thought' that Adam had understood the Cash element of the transaction is a fine example of Asian understatement. She's giving him an opening to explain his lack of cash and an opportunity to allow everybody around this table to save face.

Adam's aware that Wendy's probably enabled our motorcycles to sail towards Seattle by transferring her own personal money to Aero International, and that we're here tonight not to pay Aero International for their services, but to repay Wendy for prepaying our respective invoices. But, for reasons known only to him, Adam's now chosen to renege on that deal. I apologise to Wendy and tell her that I too should have reminded Adam to bring the required cash to tonight's meeting, and then we both wait for Adam to throw his own apology into the ring. But he doesn't, he simply raises both hands in a demonstration of surprise and declares that nobody had ever informed him that he'd need to pay Wendy with hard cash. Wendy's face looks like she's just discovered that the Tooth Fairy and Santa Clause are both myths, and Adam must think that we're both totally fucking stupid. I want to drag him outside and tear him a new arse, but that's a game that he's not willing to play right now. He refuses to move. I stand up, apologise to Wendy for being so disorganised, and excuse myself from the table.

Back in Khabarovsk, I'd thrown away the small packet of marijuana that the old sailor had given to me in Mariance, but right now, I really wish that I'd kept it. Cigarettes just aren't strong enough to calm me. I'm back at the guest house ripping the lining out of my jacket and leather jeans, gathering together every single banknote from my emergency fund. It's a mixture of US Dollars and British Pounds, but it's still not enough to cover Adam's debt to Wendy. I find some Russian Roubles and Korean Won, but on my way back to the cafe I still have to visit the Cash Machine for more money. I must be totally mad. I should let the idiot sink in his own stupidity, but I won't, and he bloody well knows it. Back in Vladivostok I'd given my word to Wendy that she'd get all of the money that we owed her, and although keeping your word might not be important in Adam's fucked-up little world, it certainly is in mine.

I've been gone for an hour, thirty minutes to collect the money and thirty minutes to calm my anger, and I find Adam and Wendy sitting at the silent table where I'd left them. I hand Adam the envelope and without a word of thanks, he hands it straight to Wendy. This time she counts the money and I try to explain the various currency exchange rates that should bring the total value of cash to the amount that Adam owes her: $1,250.00. With the embarrassing cash transaction at last completed, Wendy quietly signs Adam's paperwork and we escort her back to the subway.

As we walk towards the station I ask Wendy if she's had any problems dealing with our mutual Brazilian friend, Rodrigo. With an exaggerated shake of her head and shoulders, Wendy tells me about the endless nightmares the Brazilian and his team have caused her over the past week. I laugh, and console her with the fact that Rodrigo's now Korean Air's problem, but Wendy stops me in my tracks. 'No Geoff, Rodrigo has decided not to fly to Vancouver, his motorcycle is now sharing the same container as your motorcycle and you'll meet him again in Seattle'.

Despite failing to shield me from future contact with Rodrigo, Wendy Choi, the Seoul representative for Aero International, is an absolute angel. But, given our failure to follow her simple instructions I fear that she must think that Adam and I are a pair of absolute dicks. Clearly she's right, for many reasons, but I can only hope that our actions won't affect her generosity towards the travellers who will pass through her very capable hands in the future.

After leaving Wendy at the subway station last night, I'd asked Adam to explain his embarrassing failure to bring cash to the meeting. Perhaps unsurprisingly, he'd had no explanation to offer. He'd simply broken down in tears, apologised for his stupidity and thanked me for once again saving his bacon. He'd also promised upon his newly found God, and upon the lives of all those he loved, that he'd repay all of his debts before I departed for Thailand. Now, on the communal computer at the guest house, I show Adam an email that I've just received from Percy Goodwill, an Englishman living in Essex. Percy's language is quite graphic and as Adam reads through the scathing email his hands shake and his face looks ready to explode. Theatrically aghast at what he's just read, Adam can't understand why a stranger to both of us would ever write such vile things about me. In the email, Percy Goodwill declares that I'm a total bastard for abandoning Adam here in South Korea and that I've simply used Adam in order to complete my own selfish journey around the world. He goes on to say that without Adam's unwavering support at every stage of this journey, I would never have made it across Russia. Percy then informs me that far from being a racist, Adam's just passionately patriotic and that I'd do well to mirror his opinions and that I should take more personal pride in being English. After making certain deeply personal comments about my family, Percy ends his attack by telling me that I should be ashamed to call myself an 'Englishman' and a 'Biker'. As Adam reads the email for the second time, I gently repeat the name of its author; 'Percy Goodwill? Percy Goodwill? Why does that name sound so familiar?' It's a name that Adam really ought to recognise, but he's clearly ignoring my whispers. Adam's still furious about the personal attack from a stranger, and he's promising to respond to Percy's email with the truth, the whole truth and nothing but the truth. I'm not angry about the email, angers an emotion that I abandoned way back in Chita, but I'm finding it increasingly difficult to control my laughter. The email isn't at all amusing, but the fact that Adam's failing to recognise the name of his best friend in England is absolutely fucking hilarious. To the side of the communal computer, my own laptop is displaying a picture that I've just downloaded from Adam's personal Blog. It's a cartoon drawn shortly before leaving England, a depiction of Adam aboard his Triumph Tiger and below it a caption penned by Adam himself: 'Many thanks to Percy Goodwill for drawing this picture. Exactly as I'll look after the first day'. This can't be happening, I'm either dreaming or a smiling TV presenter is about to jump out from behind the curtain and scream 'Surprise!' I feel like a parent trying to prise a confession from a clearly guilty child, but it's a confession that's never going to come; 'Percy Goodwill? I've honestly never heard of the man'. Dad often used to say something that I never really understood; 'you can't push spaghetti son', and that makes it an appropriate saying right now, because I haven't got a clue what's going on in Adam's head.

I can't possibly take any more fun tonight, so I sign out of the email account and remind Adam that I'm leaving for Thailand at six o'clock in the morning. He nod's, he knows exactly when I'm leaving, but his face turns a guilty shade of red. He hasn't got my money, he's forgotten about his promise of yesterday evening. I look at my watch, it's already after midnight but there's a row of cash machines at the bottom of the street and Adam promises to visit them immediately. I offer to go with him but he refuses. It's something that he insists on doing by himself. He tells me that it's finally time for him to grow-up, to overcome his fears and to start acting like a man.

Last night I'd been exhausted, but my mind had been racing and sleep hadn't come. It's now five o'clock in the morning and I'm sitting on the small bench in front of the guest house, drinking my last cup of coffee, smoking a cigarette and counting my cash. I've got two £20 notes and just over 30,000 Korean Won, which all adds up to around £55. It'll be enough to get me to the airport at Inchon, but if I encounter any un-expected expenses then I'm probably screwed. I could run down to the bottom of the street and withdraw some money from my account at the cash machines, or later at the Airport, but now it's my turn to fear losing my cash card. I'm not usually worried about losing it, because I know that I'll be able to retrieve it from the bank the next morning. However, tomorrow morning I'll be a few thousand miles from here and retrieving an unreturned card would be slightly inconvenient.

Thankfully, Adam's woken early and he's handing over the money that he owes me. I'm about to count it, but he looks at his watch, picks up my bag and suggests that if I'm going to reach the airport on time, then I re-ally ought to start moving now. He's right, I am running out of time, but his insistence that I should leave straight away, and his sudden willingness to help me with my bag, makes me feel slightly nervous. I decide to count the cash, but it doesn't take long: 40,000 Korean Won. It looks like a lot of money and it sounds like a lot of money, but sadly it's not a lot of money. It's a fraction of what he'd promised to repay me this morning, and more in hope than in expectation, I look to Adam for another missing answer. Once again he seems to be short of explanations and as I've recently discovered, you really can't push spaghetti.

Adam's fear of using foreign cash machines means that I've funded large parts of his journey across Turkey and Russia. I've paid for the shipment of his motorcycle to Seattle and I've even paid for his extended stay at the guest house here in Seoul. Adam seems to think that all of that adds up to 40,000 Korean Won, or at today's currency exchange rates, £19. Bless him. With the gentlest of smiles, I return the money and tell him to go out and enjoy another free-lunch. It's getting late, we've reached the junction where our journeys will take their separate paths and it's time for me to move on alone.

The bus journey to Seoul's Inchon Airport gives me time to think, time to reflect on what's happened on the journey from England to South Korea. From the relative comfort of my apartment back in rural Essex, I'd anticipated certain difficulties to arise on the long road travelling east, and hopefully, I'd been prepared to meet them with most of the right tools and the determination to succeed. Some of those problems have indeed materialised, but rather than stopping this journey they seem to have enriched it. Almost without exception, when local problems have arisen, it's been local people who've stepped forward and helped us: Jack in Albania, Ruslan and Semyon in Volgograd, The Iron Tigers in Vladivostok and Wendy Choi here in Seoul. In that respect I'm aware that we've been amazingly fortunate to have met exactly the right people at exactly the right time. But, it's been the unanticipated problems that have really derailed us, and those problems have been entirely of our own making.

In Chris Scott's Adventure Motorcycling Handbook, he dedicates an entire section to the problems encountered by riders who choose not to travel solo. Unfortunately, that's a section of the book that we'd clearly overlooked. 'Knowing' a person and being 'Friends' with a person are very different things. Before setting out on this journey, I'd known Adam as a friend, but meeting a person for a couple of hours each week for a beer is very different to living hand-in-glove with them for several months on the road. Living together for twenty-four hours each day, and needing to constantly work as a team, the commonalities that underlined our friendship became invisible and our differences seem to have raced to the fore. I'll be first to admit that I'm not the easiest person to live with, and I could name a couple of divorce lawyers who'd happily support that statement, but Adam certainly didn't go out of his way to make things easy for me.

With the benefit of hindsight, during the journey's planning stage we should have spent less time investigating the road conditions across Russia, and far more time investigating each other. Hindsight's a wonderful thing, and although it's too late for Adam and me, hopefully others can learn from our experiences. Half of this journey is now behind me, but half is yet to come. Roll on Thailand and yet another new beginning.

Chapter 35:
Thailand, Bangkok

It's the 8th of August, the one hundred and tenth day of this journey and time for the new beginning that I'd promised. I've escaped from South Korea and arrived safely in Bangkok with all of my luggage and most of my loose change. I've breezed through Thai immigration, received my thirty-day no questions asked visa on arrival and withdrawn 10,000 Thai Baht from a Cash Machine here at the airport. I feel confident again, it really does feel like the beginning of an entirely new adventure and I'm back in control of my own destiny.

My test for any great city is that in order to really love it, at times I must also hate it. If a city can't evoke both of those emotions in me, then it's probably just a little bit too dull for my liking. Bangkok is probably my favourite city in the world, but after so many years away from here it'll take a little time to get reacquainted with its uniqueness. It's gone eleven o'clock in the evening and far too late to squander money on a hotel, so I jump on a public bus and head towards the city. I start picking out landmarks but the skyline looks different to the one that I remember and I'm not entirely sure where I'm heading. Once again I realise that I've arrived in a country without much in the way of a plan, and decide that the best thing to do is to jump off the bus when it stops close to anything that looks remotely alive or familiar.

A group of girls dressed in airport uniforms sit a few seats in front of me. Occasionally they look around at the scruffy European sitting behind them and break into fits of childish laughter. I've no idea what they're saying about me. I can speak a little Thai but my listening skills work at a totally different speed to their rate of chattering. I'm sure that they're not being rude, they're just being 'Thai'. Looking out of the window the only thing that I recognise are the fancy flickering lights of what I assume is the Baiyoke Tower, Bangkok's tallest building, which I think is in the Pathunam District where I know there used to be a clothing market and all-night street restaurants. Twenty minutes pass and somebody shouts to the driver. The girls stand up and the bus pulls to the side of the road. This looks to be a lively street with lots of people, so I jump up, grab my bag and immediately start feeling guilty. I realise that this isn't an official stop, the driver is just pulling over to drop off the girls and I'm stood behind them looking like a bloody stalker. I adopt my most disarming smile and try not to look like I'm following them.

Down on the uneven pavement, the giggling girls walk down the road towards the brighter lights of activity, but unfortunately that's exactly where I want to go. I'm already feeling like a pervert and I'm far too bloody English to follow them any further, so I wait for a gap in the traffic, and then make a dash for the opposite side of the road.

I find an all-night food stall that's busy with customers. I take an empty seat and look at a menu that's impossible to read. It's written only in Thai which to me looks just like washing hanging from an invisible line on laundry day. Admitting defeat with the written word, I just ask for something that I can almost pronounce. What I end up with is spicy minced meat, possibly pork, with basil leaves and boiled rice. It's spicy but delicious, and together with a bottle of chilled Chang beer, it's also reassuringly cheap. Bangkok's a city that's always alive, a true city that never sleeps, and that makes it a perfect place to explore, but a poor place to relax.

I sit quietly drinking alternative beers and coffees, watching the world pass by and waiting for dawn to arrive. Alongside me is a quite convincing Johnny Depp look-alike complete with pirate costume, and a rotating group of hyperactive taxi-bike riders in their fluorescent pink and orange vests. Anywhere else in the world and this would feel strange, but this is Bangkok. The taxi-bike riders speak a form of Thai that I can't even begin to understand. They all seem to have red eyes that seldom blink and they look suspiciously too wide awake for this early hour of the morning. These guys ride their scooters around this chaotic city at break-neck speeds ferrying passengers who have no time to wait in a slower moving taxi and I suspect that the redness of their eyes, and frantic speed of their chattering, owes far more to the effects of chemical stimulants than to any great enthusiasm for their jobs.

They ask about my riding jacket and with the liberal assistance of hand signals, we talk about motorcycles. It passes the time and it also plants a new seed of adventure in my imagination. What would it be like to spend a day in their shoes, or more accurately, a day in their sandals? Would being a taxi-bike rider in Bangkok be so very different from being a despatch rider in London? I scribble down a telephone number for one of the riders, a man called Sunthon who can speak a smattering of English, and I promise to call him in a few days time.

My plan for the day is to find a motorcycle, get out of Bangkok and head north to the town of Chai Nat. My first challenge here in Bangkok is to find a suitable motorcycle, and when I say 'Suitable' I'm not referring to the quality of bike. I don't really mind what bike I ride, but the motorcycle's got to come with very few questions asked because I don't have a Credit Card and I can't leave my passport for security because I'll need it when I arrive in Chai Nat. Hiring a motorcycle or scooter in any of the Thai coastal resorts is relatively easy, but in Bangkok such rental services are scarce. On a travel website I've found several references to a man called Mr Moriarty, an American expatriate who rents motorcycles to tourists here in Bangkok. But, what little information I have about Mr Moriarty is probably out of date and my emails to him have remained unanswered. I'll try to track him down and see if he can help me. Finding a single man in a city of ten million people might not be easy, but I do have a plan.

I open my eyes and a less than happy young lady is tapping my arm. I've fallen asleep with my head on the table at the all-night food stall. The other seats are now full of early morning diners and the girl's message is quite clear; I should buy something or bugger off. I look at my watch, it's almost eight o'clock and I must have been asleep for three or four hours. Under the table my rucksack is still there, nothing's been stolen and I decide that buggering off is probably the best thing to do.

Around the corner, I find the PJ Watergate Hotel and ask for their cheapest room. They ask me to pay an early arrival fine, but I refuse. I think that they'll eventually drop the additional charge and they think that I'll eventually give in and pay it. In the end we reach a compromise, I'll leave my bag here and return later in the day, when I'll take their room at the usual price. I use the bathroom in the lobby to wash, shave and change into tee shirt and sandals. I deposit my bag in the storage room, steal a map of Bangkok from the reception desk and set out on my mission. Across the road from the hotel I buy a pay-as-you-go sim card for my phone and 100 Thai Baht worth of airtime credits. I walk back to the food stall and while eating rice and chicken soup, I plan my next action.

By lunchtime, I'm at the Prasanmit University talking to a very bright but hyper-active English student called Ae. She drives a hard bargain, but at least she seems to understand my strange requirements. Her English is excellent, but it's clear that it was learned in a classroom rather than out on the street. It's all very correct and proper. She's fun, she won't sit still and insists on punctuating my plans with niceties such as lunch, but I'm the piper and my 500 Thai Baht entitles me to call the tune. She's telephoning every known motorcycle shop in Bangkok and asking if they can point me in the direction of Mr Moriarty, but sadly they've either never heard of him or they're trying to protect his privacy. After several bottles of water and an hour of unproductive calling, Ae hands back my phone and tells me that it's an impossible task. She certainly doesn't sugar the pill, 'I believe that this idea is really rather foolish'. Sadly, I tend to agree with her and randomly calling motorcycle dealerships is getting us absolutely nowhere. 'Internet'. Ae insists that despite my earlier protests, she can probably track him down more quickly using the internet.

My laptop's already connected to the University's wireless system, so I find the link to Mr Moriarty that I'd first discovered back in Seoul. Ae studies the page for a moment and looks slightly puzzled: 'Why don't we call this telephone number?' I look at the page and sure enough, the link provides a telephone number for the illusive Mr Moriarty. Ae picks up the mobile phone and begins tapping in numbers: 'For an Englishman, you are really not very smart'. I can't really argue with her, I just wish that she wouldn't be quite so direct.

At three o'clock in the afternoon, I'm in an unfamiliar district of Bangkok looking at an even more unfamiliar motorcycle. The badge on the fuel tank tells me that it's a 'Phantom' and the engine casings say 'Honda', but I've never seen one before and have absolutely no idea how big an engine it has. It's a cruiser style of motorcycle with high looping handlebars and a low slung seat that probably puts all of the weight on your arse. It's not ideal, but for a document free transaction it'll be absolutely perfect for me. Mr Moriarty is happy to help me, he hands me a map of Thailand then looks at the beautiful Ae and gives me a wry little smile.

He's probably seen many a wide-eyed tourist in the past and assumes that our relationship is something far more than it actually is, but I assure him that it isn't. I should be so bloody lucky.

By seven o'clock in the evening, I've dropped Ae safely back at her University, retrieved my rucksack from the PJ Watergate, apologised to them for not taking one of their fine rooms and secured a bed in a hostel with safe parking for the Honda, all for the reasonable sum of 400 Thai Baht. Overnight I suspect that the Honda will be slightly more secure than its rider, but tomorrow's a big day with an early start and a journey on roads that I fear almost as much as the Amur Highway.

It's Sunday morning and I hope that a combination of the day and the early hour will help me to avoid the worst of Bangkok's traffic. Thankfully the Honda is an easy motorcycle to ride, but after so long riding on the right, returning to the left side of the road takes a little getting used to. I easily find my way onto an unpronounceable road that takes me all of the way to the unmistakeable Victory Monument. Twice around the massive roundabout before I'm certain of which exit I need to take, and then east towards the old airport. Navigation is now reasonably easy, I'm following the line of crumbling concrete pillars known locally as the 'Hopewell Towers'. It's miles and miles of phallic pillars built for an overhead transport system that was abandoned in the late 1990's and now stand as ghostly monuments to financial stupidity. In the West, these embarrassing reminders of incompetence and corruption would have been removed and the land reclaimed for other projects, but this isn't the West so everybody just ignores them and drives around the problem on a daily basis.

The Hopewell Towers don't appear on my road map, but the roads that they follow are clearly marked. Unfortunately most of those roads are toll-roads and overpasses, neither of which I can legally use on a motorcycle. Unfortunately, all maps are drawn from an aerial perspective, but I'm on the ground looking upwards at the roads that I need to follow. It's not really difficult, just little distracting and in a few short miles I've realised that if I really want to stay alive, then my attention should really be focussed on what's in front of me and not what's above me.

On the major arterial roads, motorcycles should travel in the far left lane, the hard-shoulder, but there seems to be as much traffic heading towards me as there is travelling with me. After meeting several other scooters and two speeding taxi's coming the wrong way down that lane, I've decided to ignore the rules and take my chances with the masses out on the open road. I have the route planned out in my head and the Thai place names committed to memory. I've found Highway 1 and from here I should slip seamlessly onto Highway 32 heading towards the ancient capital of Ayutthaya and then onwards to Ang Thong. Then it's a simple matter of finding Highway 311 which will take me directly into Chai Nat. It's a two hundred mile journey that should take me no more than four hours to complete, but if the roads are labelled with Thai names and not numbers, then I'm probably screwed.

Brimming with confidence and an amazing feeling of freedom that only seems to come when you're riding alone on a motorcycle, I twist the throttle wide open and enjoy the rising sound of the Honda's baritone exhaust note, but sadly there's no change in its speed. The Honda just lopes along at the same old pace and refuses to go any faster than 100kph. Confused by a rising road that I'm not sure if I can legally use or not, I take a wrong turning. I stop and practice my classroom Thai with a group of resting taxi drivers. They look at my map as if it were a forbidden book of dark spells. They laugh at my attempts to communicate, they each point in a different direction and they each have a strong and conflicting opinion about which direction I should take. In short, aside from an abundance of smiles, they remind me very much of London's Black Cab drivers.

It's frustrating, the map had made it all look so easy, but the map had been produced with car drivers in mind and doesn't account for the scenic route dictated by riding a motorcycle. But eventually, I find the right path out of the city. The buildings are becoming lower, Bangkok is vanishing behind me and I'm finally making progress towards the ancient capital of Siam, Ayutthaya. It's hot and humid, thirty-four degrees and this is the middle of the rainy season, but thankfully today there's no rain. My clothing is soaked, the little Honda is too slow to allow the air to flow through the material and cool me and I need to keep drinking water to avoid dehydration. At one stop, I inspect the Honda's engine and see on the side of its single barrel, 199cc. For what feels to be a very heavy motorcycle that's a mighty small engine and this journey could take a little longer than I'd expected.

Reaching the moated city of Ayutthaya, I find that at the end of every road they seem to have conveniently placed a temple complex for me to explore. I'm literally spoiled for choice, it doesn't seem to matter which road I choose, at the end of it, or somewhere along its length, there's something to stop and admire. Within a couple of hours I've visited two

The beautiful ruins of Ayutthaya in Thailand

such temple complexes both dating back to the 14th century. If that's the 14th century as I know it, then that makes the temples six hundred years old. However, if it's the Thai 14th century then they're eleven hundred years old because although it's now 2008 in Europe, it's 2551 here in Thailand. However old they are, the temple complexes are beautiful, busy with people yet still very peaceful and relaxing. To an outsider like me, the influences around these complexes seem to be both Buddhist and Hindu, two religions that I'd always thought of as being totally separate but which seem to share many common factors that live in harmony together here.

Entering the temples provides a stark contrast to the chaos of the road and inside they're mysteriously cloaked in tranquillity and even the air feels cooler. Thanks to a liberal scattering of bilingual information boards, I soon learn to differentiate between the different styles of architecture and see clear evidence that harmony hasn't always existed here. At one temple that I visit, the heads of every Buddha image has been removed, some quite cleanly but most very violently. I believe that these vandalised images are Siamese and had been decapitated by invading Burmese armies at some time in the late 18th Century, but who's 18th Century I'm not entirely sure. I'm also not sure why the Burmese had been so pissed with the Thai's that they'd decapitated and destroyed so many of their mutually respected images, but one day I'd like to come back here with time on my hands and find out much more about it.

According to my map I'm still almost fifty kilometres from my destination, the Sappaya Hospital on the outskirts of Chai Nat. I'm confident that I can make my way across country using road signs in the same way that I'd done back in Russia. On main roads here in Thailand the signs for major towns are written in both Thai and English, but away from the main roads it seems to be strictly Thai for the villages, a language that I simply can't read. This means that I do an awful lot of stopping to confirm my direction, but in this climate that's certainly not a bad thing. Every other rider on these roads is wearing a tee shirt, shorts and flip-flops. As they pass me, which they all seem to be doing, they look in astonishment at my fully armoured jacket and CitySprint vest and probably assume that I've recently landed from Mars. I should strip down and ride like the more comfortable natives, but the habits of a lifetime spent despatch riding are very hard to break. So, I'll just suffer the discomfort and keep reminding people that I'm really rather English.

I'm running late and I encourage the Honda onwards along the narrow back roads. I need to be at the Sappaya Hospital before three o'clock, but due to navigational challenges I've ended up on the wrong side of Chai Nat. The kind people who I've just asked for new directions have drawn me a helpful map. It's a map that's been scribbled on a sheet of A4 paper and it looks frighteningly similar to the map that was drawn for me by different kind people less than half an hour earlier, a map of false promises that had brought me in exactly the wrong direction. With just minutes to spare before the staff of the Sappaya Hospital's Emergency Room are due to finish their duties for the day, I see the first road sign for Sappaya. There's no time to stop and dry myself down, no time to cool off and drink some much needed water or to make myself look slightly more presentable.

I ride the burning Honda into the hospital and park, probably quite illegally, in front of the Emergency Room doors. I turn off the ignition and remove my helmet. Nurse Wipa Klampeng is standing in the electronic doorway, face held in her hands, jumping up and down and screaming excitedly in Thai. I see her colleagues massing behind her, straining to see the reason behind the commotion. Westerners are probably quite scarce in these parts, but a visit from Poor Circulation is a big surprise for all of them. I climb up from the bike and Nurse Wipa Klampeng places both hands together beneath her chin and bows her head once, 'Sarwadee Ka'. I reach to the back of the Honda and pull a sadly crumpled tube from beneath a rubber strap, flowers that I'd purchased back in Ayutthaya. I try to remember the words that I really ought to have practiced along the way: 'Suk san wan ghert Wipa'. Happy Birthday.

Chapter 36:
Thailand, Chai Nat

In the early stages of planning this journey, I'd foolishly assumed that all things would be possible. Looking at my world atlas, I'd yearned to ride through China, Myanmar, Vietnam and Thailand. Information on crossing the borders had been sparse and somewhat confusing, but I'd heard on the travel grapevine that entry into Myanmar might be a possibility. In order to discover the truth, a friend had put me in touch with a Thai doctor who'd recently worked with refugees on the border between Thailand and Myanmar. Through the wonders of the Internet, I'd traced the doctor to a small hospital on the outskirts of Chai Nat, the Sappaya Hospital. Our initial communications had been difficult, he'd probably assumed that I was crazy and my rudimentary command of Thai had been an equal match for his English. So, in order to avoid confusion, or to confirm my insanity, he'd asked an English speaking colleague to act as our translator. That translator was Nurse Wipa Klampeng. Sadly, my naive hopes of venturing through more of Southeast Asia had been cruelly dashed, but a new friendship had been born. Until reaching South Korea, I hadn't known if a visit to Thailand would be possible, with or without the Tiger, but here I am, happy with my lot and confident that I've made the right decision.

I've been installed in Room 230 at the Thannee Princess Hotel here in Chai Nat, and to the best of my knowledge I'm the only guest staying here. After being introduced to the medical team at Sappaya Hospital, Nurse Wipa Klampeng had driven to the hotel with me following behind and struggling to keep up on the Honda. She drives her Toyota Vios like many other Thai's drive everything from tractors to buses. It's as if they have the nine lives of a cat, and in a way they probably do, because they're Buddhists. For Thai's, this current life is a temporary stepping stone towards the next, so if they live this one in a good and helpful manner then they'll have an even better life in the sequel. It's actually not a bad concept and probably accounts for the Thai people's happy disposition, but being an atheist with a close understanding of mortality, I'll ride at my own pace and hopefully make my one and only life last for as long as I possibly can.

On first sight, I'd worried that this hotel would shatter my budget, but I hadn't accounted for the fact that this is rural Thailand. I'd handed over my passport to the beautifully moody receptionist and agreed on a tariff of 700 Baht per night. At around £14 I'd thought that is was a fantastic deal, but Wipa had thought otherwise. She'd gently moved me to one side and instigated her own negotiations. Wipa had risen to her full height of five feet and no inches, faced the receptionist with a glare and let loose with a torrent of dialogue that was far too fast for anybody but another native Thai to understand. For a full minute they'd exchange verbal blows with neither of them blinking. I hadn't existed, it was a war of words and I'd been the powerless observer. Then, a switch had been thrown and normal smiles had returned. The two girls had negotiated a lasting peace and a reduced tariff of just 500 Baht per night.

I'd showered and changed while Wipa had waited downstairs in reception. By the time I'd returned, Wipa and the moody receptionist had buried the commercial hatchet and were apparently now like sisters. As if the annual monsoons had been her own fault, Wipa had apologised for the current rain shower and taken me to dinner on the banks of the Chao Phraya River in her Toyota. It was a floating restaurant, wooden planks lashed to plastic drums with an overhead canopy of recycled vinyl advertising banners. The food had been amazing, but one particular whole fish steamed with garlic, bamboo shoots and chillies had been the hottest thing ever to enter my mouth. Spicy food I enjoy, but much to the amusement of everyone around me, that innocent looking fish had burned beyond my imagination. Thankfully, the beer had been cold and after fifteen minutes my mouth had finally returned to earth, but I'll be much more careful in the future. If the Thai's refer to any food as being 'Spicy', then to a Westerner it's probably inedible. When the bill had arrived and Wipa had gently tried to pay, I'd placed 500 Baht onto the plate and received change. In fact, I'd received an awful lot of change and it gave me confidence that Thailand is exactly the right place for circulating poorly.

Today we're visiting the place that made Chai Nat famous, the National Bird Park, but there seems to be everything here but birds. I'm here with Wipa and a couple of doctors from the Sappaya Hospital, but so far I've only seen a few peacocks, a group of birds that I can't identify and some concrete statues of white headed eagles and multicoloured cockerels. Wipa tries to explain: 'The park is very beautiful but unfortunately there are no birds, because we have bird flu'. She says it with the warmest of smiles making it impossible for me to know if she's joking or not. Deeper into the park we do find some living birds and the hospital group laugh hysterically at every one of them as if they were the funniest things they'd ever seen. I'm not particularly impressed with the selection of birds on display, but my guides are totally infectious. Having walked along every path within the park, and photographed every bird, flower and leaf, we arrive back at the gift shop and sit eating ice cream.

A small group of smartly dressed students are looking in my direction but seem too nervous to approach me. After several minutes of exchanged glances, an older girl who I assume must be their teacher, walks over and asks if I would be kind enough to talk with her students. I agree and I'm immediately surrounded by a giggling inquisitive mass of late-teen interrogators. With their quite lovely teacher acting as referee, they fire their prewritten questions at me and I answer each of them in turn. Where am I from? Why am I in Thailand? What do I like about Thailand? Will I return to Thailand? What is my job? Who are my friends? Am I married? As I answer each question, the questioner writes down my answer in their notebook and the teacher points to the person who should ask the next question. After thirty minutes, the questions are exhausted and the happy students move back to their own table. I talk for a few more minutes with their teacher and she thanks me for being so generous with my time. I tell her that her students should visit England, and I probably suggest that she should come with them. She laughs, and reminds me that they're 'Thai', so even if they could afford such a wonderful journey, they'd never be granted the necessary visas. She's probably right, on both counts, and it's another reminder that I'm a very lucky boy.

By accident of birth, I'm British, and that gives me unhindered access to ninety percent of the world, and that's a privilege that ninety percent of the world's people don't enjoy. One day the borders of the world will be open, just as they are across Europe for Europeans, but that's probably not going to happen in my lifetime. The bright and happy students here at the National Bird Park will remain in Thailand, watch the Hollywood movies, read the European magazines and live their lives believing that the grass would be greener on my side of the fence. The grass isn't any greener in the West, it's just cut in a slightly different pattern, but it's a shame that they might never get to see that for themselves. As we talk, my guides from the hospital are whispering between themselves and giggling. They seem to think that I'm flirting with the young teacher, and they're probably right.

Back at the hotel, Wipa asks why I can't stay any longer in Chai Nat, why I must return to Bangkok on Wednesday. 'Wednesday is too soon, Chai Nat would be a beautiful place for you to stay, or maybe Khon Kaen would be better for you'. I don't understand, so I ask Wipa what Khon Kaen is. With eyes filled with equal measures of life and mischief, she tells me that Khon Kaen is a town just like Chai Nat, but that it's famous for dinosaurs and beautiful teachers. She hands me a slip of paper with a name, 'Nid', an email address and a telephone number neatly written in English. 'Teacher from Khon Kaen thinks you are handsome, mak mak'. I'm surprised and touched, but I try to explain that I need be back in Bangkok on Thursday morning and while I'd love to spend more time here, and it must be said also in Khon Kaen, I simply can't. She seems doubtful, 'Why do European's always hurry hurry hurry hurry?'

With the medical team on duty last night I'd been left to my own devices, and that had involved a substantial quantity of beer and food. A knock on my door at eight o'clock this morning drags me from beneath an amazing power-shower and I find not a maid, but Nurse Wipa Klampeng wearing a huge smile and carrying a rather large package. Her diminutive size allows her to slip beneath my arm and enter the room before I've had time to invite her in. I'm told to change quickly, to wear the shirt that she's brought for me in the package, a shirt that was bought for the festival of Songkran and was never designed to blend in, not even here in the famous Land of Smiles. She vanishes behind the door of my wardrobe and emerges a few seconds later wearing my motorcycle jacket and crash helmet: 'Ooh, too heavy'. The jacket that she'd confiscated on the first evening, on the false premise that she would have it cleaned, is now covered in embroidered patches representing each of the countries that I'll visit on this journey. I'm amazed, it's a fantastic thing that they've done for me and I thank her, but she tells me that it's nothing. I ask her to turn around while I get dressed but she just drops down onto the bed and plays with the sunshield on the crash helmet. 'I'm a Nurse, I know English boys are not different to Thai boys, quick quick quick'.

I'm not sure what happened to breakfast, it seems to have been by-passed in favour of lunch, which was really quite delicious. Wipa taps me on the shoulder and tells me to pull over. Once off the motorcycle, she leads me into a hair salon and insists that they make me handsome. Nurse Wipa Klampeng isn't a girl to disappoint and I fear that 'handsome' is an unachievable dream, but thankfully the hairdresser's in charge of all of the sharp objects in the room. Thirty minutes later, apparently it's not quite 'handsome', but Wipa tells me that it'll have to do. I need to look my best because I've got a date with her mother, and that's a twist that I hadn't seen coming.

An hour later and I'm lying in a hammock strung between two trees, mango and banana I think. I've met Wipa's parents and they're delightful people. They seem to lack her enthusiasm for life, but they're rice farmers and I guess that thirty years spent working in the paddy fields probably knocks a bit of the fun out of you. My memories of rural Thailand are of people and buffalo working in the fields, but today it seems to be tractors. It's not quite as romantic but I'm only the tourist around here and don't have to do the backbreaking agricultural work myself. Parked in the driveway of their newly built Western style home are two brand new Honda scooters, a recent model Isuzu D-Max truck, Wipa's own Toyota Vios and a rather beautiful bright orange tractor.

When I'd ridden through this region twenty years ago, I'd seen none of these trinkets, just small groups of people, probably families, bent double in the rice fields beneath the burning sun. There's been a dramatic cultural shift here and although the size of the individual paddy fields has remained unchanged for centuries, in recent years the distribution of their ownership has completely transformed. The small individual plots have been purchased by the more economically savvy farmers and rice farming now seems to happen on a much grander scale. I'm not entirely sure if that's good news or not, and I do wonder what became of the families who'd sold those smaller plots of land when prices had still been relatively low. Wipa interrupts my thoughts and shouts that I should be careful of the Green Vipers, because they're very painful and poisonous. I quickly pull my feet off the ground and really don't feel like snoozing anymore. 'Green Viper doesn't live on ground stupid, it lives in tree'. The hammock has suddenly lost all of its charm. I really don't like snakes.

This evening I had a farewell dinner with the medical team from the Sappaya Hospital. Again it was on the banks of the Chao Phraya River and I certainly hope that the good people of Chai Nat are sleeping safely tonight, because it seems that the entire Emergency Room team left that restaurant incapable of walking. I know that none of them were supposed to be on duty tonight, but I just hope that none of them gets called into the hospital to deal with a major emergency.

I'm now sitting with Wipa watching the river flow past and listening to the giant carp jumping for the food pellets that we're throwing for them. Earlier in our action packed day we'd visited the temple where back in April Wipa and her medical colleagues had had two Buddhist amulets blessed by the monks in order to bring good luck for the journey. Adam and I had worn these amulets throughout the journey and given our easy passage across Russia, it's difficult to argue against their effectiveness. Today at that temple I'd 'Made Merit' with the monks by donating both food and money. I'd given them fruit that I'd picked from her parents garden and fish and rice that I'd purchased in the market on our way to the temple, and in return the monk had blessed me. I'm not a Buddhist, but the small ceremony had felt good and I'd walked away with what I can only describe as a peaceful and spiritual feeling. If I had my own religion then it would probably be somewhere to the East of Paganism, and I'm not looking to change that, but if I were, then maybe Buddhism would be well worth investigating. It feels calming, gentle, forgiving and accepting of other faith's, including atheists like me, and maybe one day I'll start scratching its surface and see what I find.

Wipa asks me if I liked her temple and I tell her yes, it was a beautiful place and I thank her for taking me there. She smiles, and asks me if I would take her to St Pauls Cathedral in London. I'm about to say yes, but before I can open my mouth she answers her own question. 'You can't, because English people do not like to share, you are not the same as Thai's'. She's absolutely right, but she's preaching to the choir.

It's time to say goodbye to Wipa, but it isn't easy. We're both quite drunk and 'Goodbye' feels awkward, but it must be said. I flag down a taxi to take her back to her room at the Sappaya Hospital and decide to walk back to my hotel. My time in Chai Nat has been all too short, but then that's true of many places that I've visited on this journey.

Shortly after dawn, I make my way out of Chai Nat on the road heading south towards Bangkok. The little Honda now feels like home, I miss the power and comfort of the Tiger but this little cruiser is beginning to grow on me and when I ride it I feel relaxed. Unfortunately I don't think 'relaxed' will be the word that I'm using tomorrow when I meet my new friends in Bangkok at seven o'clock in the morning. It seems that Bangkok taxi-bikes start operating rudely early.

In Bangkok, my day starts badly and threatens to deteriorate. Perhaps it's something that I've eaten, or more likely it's just a case of first day nerves. Right now, the tiny bathroom in my guest house feels like the most comfortable place on earth and I don't want to leave it. I can't imagine how drunk I must have been when I'd arranged to do this, but on a brighter note, at least it's not raining.

I've arrived at the wooden platform where the taxi-bike riders spend their downtime waiting for new jobs, and I hope for my sake that today the 'downtime' will be plentiful. I'd met Sunthon at the all-night food stall on my first night in Bangkok and together we'd discussed the benefits of being paid to ride motorcycles on a daily basis. Admittedly, Sunthon had been far more enthusiastic about his role as a Taxi-Bike than I was about being a Despatch Rider, but although our cargos and work places were poles apart, there were many similarities in how we earned our respective crusts.

Sunthon introduces me to his colleagues and to a man who seems to be their unofficial leader, the Top-Dog on their circuit. Unfortunately he can see a major flaw in my plan to spend the day working as a Bangkok taxi-bike. It's not my inability to speak or read Thai, or even my lack of street knowledge, but I don't have a permit to work, no licence to carry passengers and therefore no insurance to do their job. I think for a moment about how these guys ride their scooters around this crazy city and wonder what insurance underwriter would ever take on such an obviously high risk. Whatever the answer to that question might be, I'm clearly not going to be able to work as intended. To be honest, at the breaking of this news a warm sense of relief washes over me and for the first time today, my urgent need for a bathroom disappears.

A huddle is quickly formed with much chattering and gesticulation, a huddle into which I'm not invited. But, after several minutes a verdict seems to have been reached. It's impossible for me to legally carry passengers or packages on my Honda, but if I still want to understand their jobs then I'm more than welcome to ride along shadowing them for the day. And so it's decided that although Blue88 can't become a fully fledged Bangkok Taxi-Boy, he can at least tag along for the ride. It's agreed that I'll follow the first bike to secure a paying passenger and we'll simply see how it goes from there. Game on.

The next bike to secure a passenger, probably more by design than default, is Sunthon. It's a large lady of indeterminate age with an overly short skirt, high heels and a permanently becoming smile. She mounts Sunthon's scooter side-saddle, the passenger crash helmet crooked into her elbow and into the traffic they shoot.

I've been caught off guard, struggling with my ignition key and looking for somewhere on the Honda to hang my bag of iced tea. I speed forward in pursuit of Sunthon and encounter my first major difficulty. With its oversized mirrors, my Honda's twice the width of his scooter. I figure that today I'll be more concerned with where I'm going than where I've been, so I turn the mirrors inward and struggle on after him. It's hot and humid, not yet eight o'clock and already my skins burning beneath an unseasonably cloudless sky. I find gaps in the traffic that make the hairs on my neck bristle with fear, but by the first set of traffic lights I'm back alongside Sunthon and determined not to get separated again.

Here in Bangkok at each major set of traffic lights there's an electronic signal that counts down the seconds to the changing of the lights: '45, 44, 43 ... 6, 5, Go'. It's always motorcycles first, always just before the green and invariably it's a racing start. This time I anticipate departure and manage to tuck in behind Sunthon through the next set of green lights. His passenger is looking back at me, holding her hair in place with one hand and constantly waving with the other. With both hands occupied in what to her are important tasks, she's not holding onto anything except the crash helmet and I honestly worry for her safety. Without warning, Sunthon shoots down a narrow side street to the left and I'm forced to take a minor detour around a food cart in order to make the turn. As I accelerate along the street, Sunthon vanishes right along a track that seems to have no obvious entrance and I have to stop and try to work out exactly where he's gone.

When I eventually catch them, the lady with the overly short skirt has already dismounted and is making her way into an office building. At the top of the stairs, she stops, turns around and gives me an exaggerated wave. I've no idea if she knows what's actually happening or why I've been trying to follow her. Perhaps she thinks that I'm stalking again. A two kilometre journey has taken approximately six minutes including lengthy stops at traffic lights. I'm soaked to the skin, my bike jacket is trapping in the heat and the air vents are useless against the fierce heat of Bangkok. With a knowing smile Sunthon hands me his own bag of iced tea and I'm far too thirsty to politely refuse.

Beneath another tattered canopy on the edge of another large and hectic market, we rest and wait with other riders in an unofficial line. The other riders are eager to understand why I want to do this job today. Perhaps they think that I'm some kind of adrenaline junkie, but then they don't see this job as being in any way dangerous or exciting. To them it's simply a job that feeds and houses their families. I try to explain that I do a similar kind of job back home in London and that I want to understand how their jobs differ from my own. That's actually not true, but it's the easiest thing to tell them. If the truth were really told I'm only doing this because of a promise made to Sunthon at a time when alcohol had seriously increased the size of my balls. They don't really understand what I'm saying so in the end we do a strange man-thing that professional riders around the world will probably understand. We start comparing accident scars and it's a game that they win hands down.

As the day draws on, the jobs really start flowing and I'm criss-crossing the city chasing different riders as if our bikes were attached by an invisible length of string. The down-time is scarce and at every opportunity I eat refreshing hunks of watermelon and drink giant bags of iced tea laced with small bottles of the local 'M150' energy drink. My jacket is now riding passenger on the empty pillion seat because thirty-four degrees of wet heat has trumped my desire for crash protection. With a passenger safely dropped at Bangkok's highest hotel, I'm back with Sunthon again. He's trying to finish a story that he'd started telling me earlier this morning, something about my leaving party that's apparently happening tonight at one of Bangkok's most happening bars. It's my leaving party, but the taxi-bike riders seem to know an awful lot more about it than I do. Before he has time to finish, we're at the front of the informal queue again and collecting another passenger.

I follow him out onto the main highway where he executes a swift u-turn between the concrete dividers, straight into the arms of a waiting motorcycle cop. His cool mirror shades and immaculate uniform remind me of the seventies television show 'CHiPs', but this cop isn't smiling. He's unimpressed by Sunthon's illegal manoeuvre and even worse than that, I'm next in line for a ticket. Sunthon's off his bike and handing over a fistful of documents for inspection. A frantic conversation is taking place between them but Sunthon seems to be doing most of the smiling. I'm panicking, I've absolutely no idea if I'm riding this bike on legal documents or not. I didn't check before I'd ridden away from Mr Moriarty, or more correctly, I hadn't really wanted to know. Then I see it, the unmistakeable movement of a trained hand passing an open pocket and depositing a slip of coloured paper. Sunthon puts on his crash helmet, returns to his scooter and motions for me to follow him. A donation to the cop's retirement fund has assured our freedom and we're mobile once again.

We've now completed a full circuit of this area of Bangkok and returned to the platform where it had all started earlier this morning. For Sunthon and his colleagues, the day is only halfway through, but my day of following them must sadly end here. My Honda needs to be returned to Mr Moriarty in readiness for my departure to Seattle tomorrow morning. I say a fond farewell to Sunthon and his colleagues who've chaperoned me throughout the day and promise to meet them all again later this evening. I'm hotter than I've ever been in my life, I'm wet, I'm totally exhausted and had I been carrying real passengers then I'd be approximately 300 Baht richer.

Today has been one of the most nerve racking and exhilarating days that I've ever spent on a motorcycle. I enjoy track days, I enjoy racing, I even enjoyed the Amur Highway, but shadowing a Bangkok taxi-bike for a day is in a different league to all of those.

To an outsider it looks to be quite hairy and scary, but it's not really that bad. In Bangkok half of the traffic is comprised of powered two wheelers, and every single person driving a car has at some time ridden a scooter. That combination of numbers of scooters and universal familiarity with riding them produces a level of awareness that you simply don't find anywhere in the West, and probably makes riding here a whole lot safer than is appears. Sure, each year lots of people die here in motorcycle accidents, but given the number of motorcycles on the road you're probably statistically less likely to have an accident here than you are in Europe. I'm happy that I've had the opportunity to ride with these guys today, but would I do it again? Not on your life.

Chapter 37:
Bangkok, Klong Toey District

I've checked-out of the guest house and returned the borrowed motor-cycle to the mysterious Mr Moriarty. Thankfully, he'd ignored the additional miles and recently added scratches and simply wished me well for the remainder of my journey. A speeding taxi-bike has brought me here to the Klong Toey district of Bangkok and I'm ready for whatever my new friends have in store for me tonight.

Sunthon's arrived here ahead of me and his optimism continues to impress. He calls this place the 'Elephant Bar' and throughout the day he's being trying to convince me that it's the perfect venue for my leaving party. I'd never planned on having a leaving party, or any other sort of party, but it seems that parties aren't optional around here. Today, riding together on the busy streets of Bangkok, Sunthon's been my guardian angel and this probably isn't the right time to start questioning his judgement. But, to call the Elephant Bar anything better than a hovel, is probably a compliment too far. Technically speaking, I doubt that it even qualifies as a building. Buildings usually have a permanent roof, a few solid walls and at least one door, but this is just an awkward patch of wasteland uncomfortably nestled between a pair of modern apartment blocks. In its favour, it does have a designated entrance, a recycled tin roof and a neon sign that's yearning for an introduction to electricity. When properly illuminated the sign will probably say 'Elephant Bar', but in tonight's sunset gloom it's just visually mute and informatively pointless.

Sunthon leads me inside and my initial impressions are confirmed. The floor's nothing more luxurious than compacted dirt that's been generously varnished with spittle and beer. Every time I lift my foot there's a distinct hesitation before my shoe reluctantly follows. It feels as strange as it looks but I'll at least give it credit for being green. Grasping for more positives, I look around at what little there is to see and settle on the multicoloured furniture that's neatly arranged down one side of the narrow plot. It's an eclectic mix of aging plastic patio chairs, randomly arranged around half a dozen industrial oil drums supporting makeshift wooden table tops. The uneven floor makes for a less than stable surface, and probably accounts for much of the spilt beer, but as furniture goes it appears to function reasonably well.

The actual bar is nothing more than a trestle table on wheels, roughly framed with bamboo canes and decorated with tightly woven strings of Christmas lights. The tiny coloured bulbs randomly flash and reflect from a dozen familiar looking bottles. The bottles claim to contain whisky, white rum and vodka from the upper end of the spirits world, and they might be genuine, but I really wouldn't count on it. This is Bangkok and seldom is anything what it appears to be. Given a shiny suit and a new pair of loafers, Sunthon could easily pass for a property broker, but he's not. He's just a Bangkok taxi-bike rider who wants the people who pass fleetingly through his life to leave him wearing a smile. For that reason alone, I can't help but love the guy.

At the rear of the plot, Sunthon shows me the bathroom facility. It's a singular feature and even by local standards is probably a destination of last resort. There's a hole in the floor that's roughly framed with an ancient ceramic foot-bowl and a rusty staining pole that favours function over form. There's neither a mirror for vanity nor tissue paper for comfort, but in the corner stands a drum of cold water and a plastic scoop. I suspect that they're used for the swilling of reluctant turds and the rinsing of soiled body parts, but I really don't like to ask. Whatever the purpose, it's certainly not a facility that I'll be taking advantage of tonight.

That's about all there is to see here and my whirlwind tour of the Elephant Bar seems to be complete. With a beaming smile, Sunthon looks for my approval: 'Dee mai kap?' It's a pointless question and he knows it. It's almost seven-thirty in the evening and darkness is closing in around us. It's far too late to make alternative arrangements and whoever he's invited to attend my leaving party has already been told where to come. Anyway, he'd had me hooked at the entrance where I'd seen the neatly written sign. My command of Thai isn't great but 'Draught Beer 40 Baht' I can certainly understand.

The owner of this bar, or more likely its 'Official Squatter', has taken the unusable and transformed it into the useful. Using little more than his own imagination and other peoples debris, he's freecycled a business that probably clothes, feeds and shelters his entire family. I like inventive people and when their creations provide me with the opportunity to get hammered in exchange for a few coins in my pocket, I tend to respect them all the more. His efforts won't earn him a place on Thailand's version of 'The Apprentice', but with the prospect of embarrassingly cheap beer and deliciously volcanic food from the street stalls on the pavement outside, it'll work for me tonight.

Having inspected the premises and come to terms with the rudimentary charms of the Elephant Bar, Sunthon introduces me to the proprietor. I don't catch his name but he's very clearly a working combination of boss, bar man and builder. He also turns out to be Sunthon's eldest brother and that fact really doesn't surprise me. In true Thai tradition, Sunthon's a nepo-socialist and firmly believes in the distribution of my wealth amongst his family. I can't blame him for that. This is Southeast Asia and that's just the way that things appear to work in these parts. If I've learned anything on the previous one hundred and fourteen days of this journey it's that if I'm not willing to accept the ways and traditions of others, then I really ought to have stayed at home.

While Sunthon enthusiastically directs the rearrangement of furniture to form a mini amphitheatre, I settle down to enjoy the evening ahead. As guests begin to arrive, mostly taxi-bike riders and their friends, large jugs of unbranded beer poured over hand chipped ice are delivered to the tables. Some of the guests arrive solo, some in pairs on a single scooter and one or two have even brought their fare paying passengers along with them. Each and every one of them greets me with the traditional 'Wai'. Hands clasped together in front of their faces, heads bowing low. When I'd met these people earlier in the day their hands had been a little lower and the bows slightly less pronounced, but now things are different. Tonight, there's much more respect in the air. I'd like to think that having ridden all day on the busy streets of Bangkok with these taxi-bike riders, they now accept me as one of their own, but I've got to be realistic. During the day I'd been nothing more than the hapless Englishman with absolutely no sense of direction, but tonight I'm the man who'll be paying for their dinner. Their respect hasn't really been earned, but it's about to be bought.

Everybody seems happy, and so they should. I know that the beer is heavily diluted with melting ice, but it's flowing in obscenely large quantities and nobody appears to be shy when it comes to ordering refills from the bar. Happy that most of the people are already well lubricated, Sunthon appoints himself as my official spokesman and tries to explain my motorcycle journey from London to Bangkok. Everybody listens intently, but I'm not sure how much of it they really understand. In order to explain things more thoroughly, and no doubt to give Sunthon an opportunity to sit down and drink more beer, I'm encouraged to show photographs from my laptop computer. The crowd gathers behind me and I scroll through countless pictures of the places I've visited, the people I've met and the things that I've seen. They ask me questions, too many questions. They're mostly questions concerning the material things and they're all asked far too quickly. 'How fast is your motorcycle? How much did it cost? Why didn't you buy a BMW?' I try to answer each question in turn, but they don't give me time and chaos fast becomes the theme of the evening.

Two mysterious girls arrive carrying small trays of food and after depositing them on top of an unoccupied oil drum, they squeeze confidently through the crowd and snuggle down on either side of me. I've absolutely no idea who they are, and I certainly don't catch their names, but they don't strike me as girl's who'd worry too much about details. Rum based cocktails appear in their painted hands and they begin quizzing me on the more important things in their lives. 'Do I have a girlfriend in Bangkok? Which country has the most beautiful girls? Would I like to have a girlfriend in Bangkok? How much money do I earn?' My honest answer to the all important income question has probably dashed their hopes of any long term relationship, but it doesn't dent their enthusiasm for flirtatiously tampering with the more sensitive regions of my body. Don't get me wrong, what they're doing is far more mischievous than obscene, and I'm genuinely flattered by their attention, but after a few months on the lonely road I've clearly become far more sensitive to any level of intimate human contact. They've absolutely no idea what affect they're having on me, or maybe they do?

I can sense Mom looking down on me, her best Methodist stare instantly rebooting my morality. I reach down and delicately remove the playful fingers and narrowly avoid a very happy ending. The girls giggle, pick up their empty glasses and wander away towards the bar.

It's been a very long night, but one of the most enjoyable nights of the journey so far. This evening has been about people, and apart from the brief picture show, motorcycles have taken a rear seat. I've met real people relaxing on their own territory and I've probably learned an awful lot more about them than they have about me. I've been given an insight into their lives and one particular discovery has intrigued me far more than others.

Most of the guys here tonight were taxi-bike riders and Sunthon is quite typical of their breed. On a good day, which I suspect is any day that doesn't end in a hospital or the mortuary, after covering expenses he'll earn around 500 Thai Baht (£10). In the not too distant past he would've happily ridden a smoky old nail, a rusting scooter cobbled together with little more than gaffer tape and hope, but in these days of 'Easy Credit' and 'Minimum Monthly Payments', he rides a shiny new Honda. He still lives in the area of his birth, the Bangkok district of Klong Toey, but Sunthon lives quite differently to his brother and parents.

This area was once Bangkok's largest slum and home to more than a hundred thousand people. I remember Klong Toey as a close quarter community of squatters who built their homes on other peoples' land using anything they could scavenge or steal, but along with everything else here in Thailand, Klong Toey seems to be changing beyond all recognition. The shanty dwellings are being systematically replaced by glossy apartment buildings and the local residents are clearly buying into the dream of home ownership. In a short space of time, perhaps too short a space, it seems that the aspirations of parents have become the expectations of their children.

These guys now live in million Baht apartments and ride fifty thousand Baht scooters, yet they earn little more than the local minimum wage. I don't for one minute begrudge them a decent home in which to live nor a safe and reliable motorcycle to ride, but I really do worry about how they'll pay for them. Easy credit is a slippery slope that I've descended before. It's one hell of a ride down but eventually you'll reach the bottom and the landing won't always be gentle. I fear for their financial futures, but I also understand that it's probably just their time to start enjoying the sparkling toys that we in the West have for so long taken for granted. Sunthon and his bar running brother are wearing very different shoes, but I know which shoes I'd feel more comfortable in at the moment.

Here in Klong Toey the times are rapidly changing and I can only hope that those changes are sustainable, because once the 'Credit Genie' is let out of its bottle, it's a very difficult beast to tame.

If the Elephant Bar had a clock, it would be telling me that it's time to go home. The battery in my laptop is exhausted, the bar's almost empty and apart from Sunthon, the remainder of the guests have ridden away into Bangkok's neon sunset. The two unnamed girls are huddled together in the far corner of the bar, chatting, examining mirrors and re-painting synthetic nails. Sunthon's asleep beside me, his arse pushed back on the patio chair and his head resting on folded arms. I should really tell him to go home, back to his wife and children where he belongs, but I don't have the heart to wake him. I've settled the reasonable bar-bill and the bar owner, Sunthon's eldest brother, seems happy for us to linger. It's just as well because I don't have a bed to go to tonight and for all of its faults, the Elephant Bar's plastic seats are far more comfortable than the cold steel benches of Bangkok's Suvarnabhumi Airport. I've got an early morning flight to Seattle and it seems pointless spending money that I don't have on a bedroom that I'll probably never remember. The Elephant Bar is my home for tonight, and I've certainly slept in worse places than this.

I hadn't seen the young man entering the bar. Maybe I'd dozed off for a moment or perhaps he's a stealthy ninja assassin who dropped in through the ceiling. Regardless of how or when he'd entered, he's certainly making his presence felt now. Screams are ringing out and echoing back from the shabby tin roof. Wild animal screams that sound too highly pitched to be human. Fists and feet are furiously flying. The shorter of the two girls is already lying on the floor, perfectly still and worryingly silent. The taller girl is bravely standing her ground. Her head bowed defensively low, black silken hair performing an amazing fan dance, arms and fingernails wind-milling wildly. Despite the valiant effort, her slender frame and plastic talons are no match for the short but strapping ninja. She's lashing out like an anxious cat and he's grinning back at her like a loaded junkie. He's dodging her random blows and playing with his quarry. But then, he just seems to get bored with the game.

Punch. Punch. Kick. It's all over in three swift moves. Checkmate. She's down on the floor, lying next to her friend and there's nothing to be heard but the chilling sound of defeat: Silence. The battle has lasted just a few seconds but it feels more like minutes. I'd wanted to shout out for him to stop the assault, but the words just hadn't left my mouth. I don't know why I didn't move earlier. Perhaps it all happened so quickly that there was no earlier to mention. Now I'm moving, but it might be too late. His brutal mission is complete. He's making for the exit and there's no time to think.

The Elephant Bar is narrow, one way in and the same way out. As the ninja approaches my table, he scowls and points an angry finger towards me. He's probably telling me that it's none of my bloody business, and he's absolutely right. But he's also too late. I really don't mean to do it. I'm not a brave man, but I'm reasonably drunk and it's just something that instinctively happens. I swing around towards him and the edge of the closed laptop lands squarely on his chin. No warning shots. No opportunity for surrender. All that I hear is a satisfying 'crack' as two kilograms of plastic encased technology strikes hard against brittle bone. A knockout blow by Fujitsu Siemens and the girl beating ninja is finished.

Sunthon looks worried. He's leaning over me and saying something that I really don't understand. I've got a hundred different questions and no immediate answers. 'Why's he speaking Thai? Is he Thai? Can I speak Thai? Why is his tee shirt so red?'

There's a second man standing here and he looks an awful lot like Sunthon. I'm not seeing double, it's definitely two different men. Slowly the fog begins to clear and reality creeps in. I hurt so much that I couldn't tell you exactly where I hurt. The pain is just extreme and universal. Sunthon's not really helping and the whiskey that he's using to cleanse my mouth is stinging like hell. I stop him from playing nurse for a moment, and ask him to enlighten me.

Sunthon can't really answer my questions, he'd slept through the entire disturbance, but his brother can fill in some of the blanks. Apparently the ninja is a well known local thug, a full-time hoodlum and part-time lover of the tallest girl. Earlier in the evening they'd had a lover's quarrel, but I'm not to worry about that, because everything's going to be alright. Shortly after the battle she'd regained her composure, followed her violent boyfriend out of the Elephant Bar and was last seen at the end of the street sucking on his face and making all chummy. 'Good for them'.

Apparently, my confidence in delivering the perfect technical knockout had been slightly misplaced. The laptop had certainly struck its target, but the target had stood his ground and instantly retaliated. He'd knocked me to the floor and kicked me until I'd finally stopped bleating. Oh how I wish that I'd stopped bleating an awful lot earlier and saved myself some pain. But, much more than that, I wish that I'd finally learn to simply walk away from other people's shit.

I take the lint cloth from Sunthon and dab the area that hurts the most. It's my mouth. I must have bitten my tongue when the ninja hit me. It's throbbing like crazy and won't stop bleeding. Sunthon offers me the bottle of whiskey, insisting that it will help, so I take a reluctant mouthful and discover an entirely new level of pain.

I press a comforting palm to the side of my cheek and sense that the contours have changed. I've lost a bloody tooth. He's kicked one of my lower teeth clean out of its socket and my tongue probes the newly formed hole.

My temporary nurses look towards the floor, but the missing tooth is nowhere to be seen. I must have swallowed it. I start cursing the ninja for costing me a potential fortune in dental expenses, but Sunthon's brother jumps in to correct me. It probably wasn't the ninja but his tall and slender lover who caused my dental damage. Seemingly upset by my intervention, on her way out of the bar in pursuit of him, she'd paused and aimed several kicks at my body and face. It's not news that I'd expected to hear and recognising my new feeling of discomfort, mental not physical, Sunthon leaps to the defence of my waning masculinity.

Talking with the confidence of a man who has some experience, he suggests that given the girl's ample bosom and unusual height, it's quite probable that she wasn't actually a 'Girl'. His brother's nodding along with the statement. I understand that they're only trying to help, giving me an opportunity to save face, but it's the kind of help that I really don't need right now.

Having my teeth kicked out by a girl would be embarrassing, but in my defence I'd been unconscious when she'd attacked me. On the other hand, if Sunthon's claim is true, then earlier this evening while fully conscious and relatively sober, I'd thoroughly enjoyed being partially pleasured by an attractive man wearing a frock. All things considered, I've enjoyed more comfortable endings to an evening.

Tonight has taught me a valuable lesson, but I'm not entirely sure what that lesson is. Day one hundred and fifteen of this journey is now behind me, a fresh day is dawning and it's probably time for yet another new beginning. 'Mai pen rai kap' as they like to say here in Thailand: 'Go with the flow'.

Chapter 38:
Bangkok Airport

'Due to lack of interest, tomorrow is cancelled, let the clocks be reset and the pendulums held, cos there's nothing at all except the space in between, finding out what you're called and repeating your name'. The Kaiser Chiefs are doing their best to cheer me up, but it's really not helping. In the early hours of this morning at the Elephant Bar, I'd promised myself a new beginning, but here I am again, same old shit in a slightly different toilet.

Again and again, the China Airlines check-in girl had flicked through my battered passport. Sitting like a princess with perfectly painted face and couldn't give a shit eyes, she'd served the disappointing news with a well trained smile. Her statement had been quite clear; China Airlines wouldn't be flying me to Seattle today. As a matter of undisputable fact, she'd pointed out that my British passport didn't contain a valid visa for the USA. Allied to the obvious lack of visa, she'd then highlighted the fact that my China Airlines ticket was for a single journey, outbound only, no onwards element and certainly no return. In her opinion, I wouldn't be allowed to enter the USA and therefore China Airlines had no alternative but to refuse me access to their flight.

On today of all days, it wasn't the news that I'd wanted to hear. My good nature had been left behind at the Elephant Bar, along with a tooth, my dignity and far too much blood. I wasn't happy, so I'd told her that she was wrong. I'd reminded her that the passport she'd been holding was British, but that hadn't really helped my case. Unfortunately, she'd read the rule book and I clearly hadn't. With the human touch of a public service announcer, she'd informed me that I didn't qualify for the USA's Visa Waiver Programme. She'd explained the relevant equation in the simplest possible terms; 'No Visa and No Onwards Ticket equals No Flight'. My half-assed charm offensive had failed and from the start I'd been on a bureaucratic hiding to nothing. She'd been in the right and had become bored with my protests. I'd been wrecking her otherwise perfect day and behind me in the lengthening queue had been customers more deserving of her smile and patience. I'd had no alternative but to admit defeat and retreat.

The easy solution to this difficult problem is to buy an onwards flight out of the USA. All it would take is ten minutes on my computer and a credit card. Sadly, I don't have a credit card and the £500 loaded onto my pre-paid card has been used to get me this far. I've canvassed the various airlines here at the airport and the cheapest onwards flight will cost just over $1,200, and that's money that I simply don't have. At a travel agent I could probably get an onwards ticket for half of that amount, but because of the limits on my solitary bank account, it would take me two more days to withdraw that amount of cash from cash machines. The alternative solution is to visit the US Embassy and get a proper tourist visa. Unfortunately it's now a combination of the weekend and the Queen's birthday. All official offices, including The US Embassy, will be closed for the next three days. I can't wait that long, I've got a motorcycle to meet in Seattle and I'm already running late. I need time and space to think. I need a plan. I've got two hours before the flight leaves and I can't afford not to be on it.

Sitting on the cold steel bench my need for solitude acts like a magnet for the weird. I remove my earphones and learn that Nick's a vegetarian Virgo from deepest Surrey, who likes to talk. He's here in Bangkok at the end of his gap year, but a gap year from what I really couldn't say. He looks too old to be a student and too young to be taking a break between wives. He doesn't tell me and as I'm really not in the mood for chatting, I don't bother to ask. He's been in Thailand for the past two months but the skinny white legs hanging from neatly tailored shorts suggest that he's something of a stranger to Thailand's beautiful beaches. On the other hand, the heavy bags that underline his bloodshot eyes probably reflect a keen interest in Bangkok's eclectic nightlife.

Nick's waiting for his flight back to London but he really doesn't want to go. Bangkok's his new spiritual home and he shows me an ethnic tattoo to prove it. I smile and offer him my most insincere congratulations. The tattoo's written in Thai and seems to be a Buddhist prayer, but it could be absolutely anything. If the tattoo artist had taken a disliking to him, it could even tell the educated reader that Nick has an unhealthy passion for horny dogs. Whatever the tattoo says, he seems to be happy with it and I keep my own thoughts on the matter to myself.

I'm trying to think but he won't stop talking. He's telling me something about time travel and the opportunity to relive the past year with the benefits of hindsight and experience. He starts to laugh and tells me that time travel can't be possible, because if people could really travel through time then people from the future would be here with us right now. I've no idea if time-travel is even theoretically possible, but I disagree with his reasoning against it. I tell him that the only reason that people from the future wouldn't be here with us right now, is because 'right now' is just a little bit shit and probably well worth avoiding. He doesn't ask why I feel that 'right now' isn't the best time to visiting planet earth, but he seems to get the message that I really don't want to be talking. He pokes a hand into his man-purse and pulls out his passport and e-ticket confirmation. It's time to check-in for his flight. He smiles and offers his hand. 'It's been a pleasure to meet you, happy travels'. I take his hand and shake it enthusiastically. He doesn't know it, but he's accidentally solved my problem and I want to tell him that I love him, but I don't.

As Nick walks away, I scroll through the list of contacts in my phone. What I need is not a 'Flight', only a 'Ticket', and the two things are not necessarily the same, especially here in Bangkok. I remember the liquor bottles in the Elephant Bar last night and I'm sure that it wasn't 'Johnnie Walker' inside that square bottle with the red label. It was just the illusion of 'Johnnie Walker'. I call Sunthon and he seems to understand what I'm asking him to do for me.

In the last hour I've taken four calls from two people who I've never before met. Two were from a travel agent based in the Min Buri district of Bangkok and two from an unknown taxi-bike rider. The last call told me that the taxi-bike rider was waiting for me outside on the airport departures level. I look around and he's easy to spot. The bright fluorescent vest and puff of cigarette smoke rising in a no smoking area is a giveaway. The anonymous rider hands me a small brown envelope and I give him 2,000 Thai Baht and a healthy tip. As he walks away to wherever he's left his scooter, I open the envelope and carefully check the single document inside. It's exactly what I'd asked the travel agent to provide and my China Airlines flight leaves in just under an hour. The boys have done a fantastic job.

'Thank you Mr Thomas, you will collect your luggage in Seattle and as your flight is already boarding, please proceed directly to Gate 22A. Enjoy your flight and thank you for choosing China Airlines'. I walk away chuckling to myself. In a former life I must have been a really nice guy, because when I look at my boarding pass it says 'Seat 4A', and if I'm not mistaken, that means Business Class. Sunthon hadn't fully understood my request, but he'd certainly understood the urgency of it. I hadn't thought about the time that it would take a taxi-bike to come from central Bangkok to Suvarnabhumi Airport, but Sunthon obviously had. He'd used his initiative and contacted a travel agent in Min Buri, the district adjoining the airport. The travel agent had called me and fully appreciated my predicament. He'd been happy to help me, but only for a price. That price was 2,000 Thai Baht and for what that piece of paper has done for me, it's an absolute bargain.

The girl on the China Airlines check-in desk probably knew that my newly acquired British Airways e-ticket confirmation was a complete forgery, but she didn't seem to care. I've no idea how many rules have been broken today, but surely 'Rules' only exist to provide gainful employment for the word 'Exception'.

'Mai pen rai kap', go with the flow.

Chapter 39:
USA, Seattle

Arriving in America, I'd stood in the line at immigration control, presented my passport and been granted a ninety day tourist visa without any questions or referral to my onwards ticket. With only hand luggage to slow me down, I'd quickly found a shabby motel close to the Airport and there was one thing that I had to do before anything else. I had to eat food from a menu that was written entirely in English. American English would be perfectly acceptable. That might sound strange, but its two months since I've seen a menu where every dish was familiar and ordering a meal from it could be accomplished without reference to animal sounds or mime. I didn't for a moment think that the food in America would be any better or worse than the food that I'd eaten in any other country, perhaps with the exception of 'kimchi' in South Korea, but I just wanted to place my order and eat without having to think about it. Like a vegetarian returning to meat, I'd sat at the bar of a Denny's Diner and drooled over a laminated menu of dreams. I'd ordered and eaten a breakfast of crispy bacon, sausages, easy over fried eggs and hash browns, washed down with coffee and followed by pancakes with fresh cream and maple syrup. It had been absolutely delicious, everything that I'd dreamed it would be, but it's done now and I'm over it so I can move on with my life.

From the very beginning I'd convinced myself that America was going to be the easiest part of this journey, the land of plenty where nothing would be cheap but everything would at least be available. I'd flown out of Taipei in the early hours of Saturday morning, slept for almost eleven hours and arrived in Seattle late on Friday evening. Because of crossing the International Date Line, I'd arrived in Seattle before I'd left Taipei and my body clock is still in a state of total meltdown. I'm in a constant state of confusion and have only two desires, sleep and food.

In an attempt to further disorientate myself, I turn on the television and find that Team USA is now ahead of China in the medal tables at the Beijing Olympics. Last time I'd looked China had enjoyed a commanding lead over everybody, but on closer inspection I see that America uses a very different accounting system to the rest of the world, a system that puts the USA on top. I wonder if there's any arithmetic formula that could possibly show Team GB at the top of the medals table, but I very much doubt it. The TV in my room is bombarding me with two hundred and forty channels of twenty-four hour viewing. I find strange sports where it's the top of the fifth and somebody's trying to improve on a '5 & 2 record'. I'll be able watch the next game at 9pm Eastern Standard Time, but only if I subscribe to something known as HBO, and exactly what game or sport it is I'm not entirely sure.

In an unofficial advertisement sponsored by a local business consortium, I'm told that the current Governor of Washington State has voted 'For' fuel tax increases but 'Against' reducing the price of prescription drugs for the poor. Just as I'm thinking what a complete bastard he must be, Governor Rossi himself arrives on the screen and tells me that it's all fabrication, vicious lies designed to sully his good name. I also now know that I can buy a brand new Chevrolet with nothing down and monthly payments of only pennies on the dollar, but surely they have cents here in America and not pennies? Then I switch to Fox News and realise that America won't be quite as straight forward as I'd hoped it would be.

The Tiger will arrive in Fife, which is just south of Seattle, but according to my map Fife appears to be several miles from the coast and the bike is arriving on a boat. I have two telephone numbers to call but when I try them, both inform me that the numbers have been 'Temporarily Disconnected'. I have an email telling me that the Tiger will be ready for collection within the next few days, but I must first obtain a customs release form and ensure that all of my documents are in order. They'll helpfully explain the procedure when I telephone a third number provided in the email: 'We're sorry but the number you are calling has been temporarily disconnected'. Is everybody in America Temporarily Disconnected?

Things would be a little less frustrating if my laptop was working normally, but sadly it isn't. Clearly it hasn't reacted well to being used as a truncheon back in Bangkok and the screen constantly flickers on and off making it impossible to see or read anything. If I pinch the top of the screen to the outer casing it seems to stay illuminated for a few minutes, so I steal an industrial sized bulldog clip from the motel's excuse for a reception, attach it as described and the problem temporarily resolves itself. I find the website for Customs House Seattle, and call the number that's provided. This time it works and they tell me that in order to release the Tiger, I must bring my documents and credit card to their office. Assuming that everything is in order I'll be provided with a customs clearance form while I'm there. Hoping that they'll accept cash, I head into town and I'm immediately struck by the efficiency of Seattle's bus service.

The ride into central Seattle is amazingly cheap and is as far removed from a London bus journey as I can possibly imagine. There's no local jester sitting opposite me, nobody vomits down my neck and we'll probably arrive at the destination exactly on time. It's an absolute joy of a public transport system and hopefully one day all bus services will operate this way. Unfortunately there is a downside, but it's a downside that has nothing to do with the bus company. Seattle Customs have failed to update their website, they've recently changed location and I've arrived at the wrong bloody office.

Back at the motel, I fiddle with the bulldog clip and finally get another screen display. I ignore the emails offering me the temporary enjoyment of several million dollars from a sincere friend in Nigeria, several guaranteed solutions for 'erecti1e dy5function' (sic) and open a message from somebody called 'Dante's Dame'. I discover that Dante's Dame is the writing name of Colleen, a local biker here in Seattle. She's travelled extensively in the USA and Canada and she's a good friend of Burke Kron, a biker who I'd briefly met on my unsuccessful trip to the customs office this morning. I've never met Colleen before, but following a five minute conversation with her friend, she's offering me free use of her house for the next week while she goes away on business. Travelling around the world on a motorcycle is easy, even during the times when you don't actually have a motorcycle to ride, because strangers become friends and your support team of willing volunteers is endless.

Tomorrow I'll take my documents to the correct Customs House in the port area of Seattle, obtain my clearance forms and hopefully collect the Tiger from the bonded storage depot in Fife. I won't be in Seattle long enough to enjoy Colleen's kind offer, so I reply saying thank you, but sadly not this time. Tomorrow's the day when I start heading south on the Pacific Coast Highway, California 1, the road that Mom had wished that her and Dad could have ridden together on their own Triumph. This is America where everything is easy, so what could possibly go wrong?

American's love their automobiles, so much so that nobody ever seems to walk anywhere. If people don't walk, then I guess that governments don't need to spend precious tax revenues on pedestrian walkways. Customs House is now located on Harbour Island, I can see it and I could ride across to it in just a few minutes, but I just can't figure out a way to walk there. There's a beautiful road, but no footpath at the side of it and I'm sure that here in America they have a crime known as 'Jay Walking'. Eventually I find a cycle path on a flyover that crosses the island, walk along it and then find a hidden staircase that takes me down onto the island below. I'm on Klickitat Avenue, but I'm not sure which direction to take. North or south? I see a postman and ask if he knows the whereabouts of Customs House at 1021 Klickitat Avenue. With a smile suggesting that he's about to make me look like a complete idiot, he points to the building just ten feet behind me and the large sign above the double fronted entrance, 'US Customs Seattle'.

Inside the office, I introduce myself to the two immaculately uniformed officers. For some strange reason, they seem to be expecting me. We talk for a few minutes and I discover that the Brazilian rider Rodrigo has already been here. Over the past five days his representative has telephoned them several times an hour and not more than thirty minutes ago, they'd had the pleasure of meeting Rodrigo in person. He'd left an impression, an impression of great urgency and now that his business with them has been finalised, I swear that I can hear their sighs of relief echoing around the office. They ask me how my 'Race' around the world is going and I have to explain that Poor Circulation has more in common with 'Reclining' than 'Racing'. My papers are stamped, they refuse to accept any money and my new best friend Jennifer clearly explains the procedure for collecting the Tiger from the bonded warehouse in Fife. It all seems to be quite straight forward but when I ask about the probable release date, she drops a bombshell on my world.

The container carrying the Tiger had arrived aboard the vessel 'HJ London', and that particular container has been designated for inspection by the US Department of Agriculture. My face drops and Jennifer must notice my loss of colour and change in mood. She asks if that's a particular problem for me, and I just mutter that I'd hoped to start riding south as soon as possible. Jennifer promises to do everything within her power to help me start moving as quickly as possible and wishes me luck with the remainder of the journey. I thank her for her help, collect my completed paperwork from the desk and prepare to leave the office. Jennifer asks me to wait for a minute and busies herself on the telephone while I chat with other waiting customers and hope that they can't smell my fear. It's not the delay that worries me. I'm only worried about an agricultural inspection discovering the earth and ashes within the Special Package that's still onboard the Tiger.

A few minutes later the news is slightly better. Jennifer has contacted the Agricultural Inspection Team and encouraged them to move the container to Fife without delay. She doesn't think that it'll be a problem, because the container only holds three motorcycles and several million pairs of Korean made spectacles. Jennifer can't guarantee that an inspection won't take place, but she doubts that it will be necessary. My hope is that the faster they move the container the less they'll inspect it and the more likely I am to escape from Seattle and deliver the Special Package safely to Boonville. I thank Jennifer sincerely and begin walking back towards the city. A horn sounds behind me and another customer from the Customs Office pulls alongside in his car. 'Can I give you a lift Sir?'

Since arriving in Seattle, I've heard nothing from Adam, but a mutual friend tells me that he's staying with David, a traveller from Washington State who we'd met on the campground at Dubrovnik. Adam hasn't replied to any of my emails yet, but according to our friend he's doing fine, looking forward to crossing America and is relaxing for a few days before setting about retrieving his own Tiger. I've sent him instructions about the administrative procedure that he'll have to follow and hopefully seeing my mistakes will save him some time and avoid unnecessary journeys to nonexistent offices. I've wished him well for his onwards journey, whatever route that might take. I didn't mention money in my emails, but hopefully that's something that he'll resolve in due course and not something that I want to think about on the remainder of this journey because it's now time for me to start moving south.

After what's felt like a lifetime, the call has come to say that the Tiger is ready for collection. Under the first clear skies for a week, I've made my way to the bonded warehouse in Fife, just south of Seattle. I've handed over almost $200 and the crate containing the Tiger is now mine. Unfortunately, I only really wanted the motorcycle and many of those dollars have been paid for the environmentally sound disposal of the wooden crate that holds it. Armed with hammers and crowbars borrowed from one of the clerks, I'm about to attack the crate when I'm approached by a man asking me to keep the crate as whole as possible as he'd like to take it home and use it to build a garden shed. A deal is done, I get a refund of the disposal charge, my financial saviour pulls his truck alongside the crate and the careful dismantling operation begins. As elements of the crate slowly move into the truck, I can see more and more of the Tiger.

We've been apart for a total of twenty-four days but I turn the ignition key and at the first touch of the button, it growls into life. It's a sound that I'd almost forgotten, but a sound that makes me smile. I unhook the tank bag and open the secret compartment at its base. Hesitantly I feed in my hand and I'm delighted to report that the Special Package is exactly where I'd left it, unmolested by The Department of Agriculture and ready for its journey down to Boonville on California Highway 1. I quickly pull on my riding gear, return the borrowed tools to their owner and ride the bike down from the base of the crate. I've ridden the Tiger for twenty thousand miles around the world without having a single puncture, but that record has just ended. In my haste to release the Tiger from captivity, I'd overlooked a wayward nail in the base of the crate and I've just ridden straight over it.

Chapter 40:
USA, Pacific Coast Highway

I've spent almost a week in Seattle and quite embarrassingly, I've seen very little of the city. My days there had been hijacked by constant conversations with various authorities trying to get the Tiger released from federal captivity. Every day had been punctuated with the promise of 'tomorrow Sir', but sadly tomorrow had always been postponed until the next day. Now that's all behind me. I've plugged the puncture in the front tyre and replaced a headlight bulb that had blown on the ride down to Zarubino, the sun's shining and I'm heading south on Interstate 5. It feels great to be riding again, and although this Interstate is one of the most boring roads that I've ever ridden, it's probably the best possible reintroduction for both me and the Tiger. It's all very easy, I just choose a lane to ride in, sit at 65 mph and try to avoid hitting anything in front of me. I count down the exits to Tacoma and pull off the Interstate to find the Triumph dealership directly in front of me.

A stranger in Seattle had taken my details and contacted the Triumph dealership in Tacoma, and they in turn had invited me to visit them on my way south towards Boonville. After the warmest of welcomes from Robert and his colleagues, I drink gallons of Tacoma coffee and chat with passing customers. Triumphs have become very popular here in America and amongst the passing customers there's much interest in the Rocket III cruiser with its huge engine and gigantic weight, all frightfully American really. I look at the new motorcycles on display in the showrooms and discover that here in Washington State, a Triumph motorcycle retails for around half of the price that it would back in Leicestershire where it was built. I see a brand new Triumph Scrambler with a price tag of just under $7,000, or approximately £3,600, a motorcycle that would cost £6,500 from a showroom in England. Given the costs of shipping my Tiger to Seattle and the additional costs of retrieving it from customs, if I'm ever fortunate enough to do another adventure in America, I'll avoid all of the logistical and administrative headaches and just buy a motorcycle when I arrive here. The locals can't believe that we pay more for a Triumph back in England than they do here in America. They think that British riders are being ripped-off and ask why we don't make a bigger fuss about it. Of course they're absolutely right and as if to answer their question in a very English manner, I just change the subject. With nothing needing to be fixed on my Tiger and with a burning desire to reach the Oregon coastline by nightfall, the staff at Triumph Tacoma point me in the right direction and wish me the very best of luck.

The interstate is busier than it had been, the heat is intense and at the first opportunity I turn and head towards the coast. We find the beautiful Highway 101, pass through Port Angeles and back down to Aberdeen. Away from the manic Interstate, the temperature has dropped and we've discovered real motorcycle roads. Twisting and turning, rising and falling, these are roads the likes of which we haven't ridden since leaving Turkey way back in May. It feels good to be so close to the ocean, an ocean that we can follow almost all of the way down to Boonville. I can hardly believe it, we're on the Pacific Coast Highway and it's everything that I'd dreamed it would be. Any cares that I'd had have drifted away, Mom and Dad are chuckling away in the topbox and everything in life is good.

The speed limit here is 55 mph but on roads like this that's not a limit but more like a target for the brave and the foolish. We're enjoying this ride more than any other on the journey so far, it feels like freedom and I for one, don't want it to end. I stop often and take photographs of amazing ocean views and quirky small town streets, I brew coffee at the roadside and chat with those people who have the time and desire to join me. The people here are polite and seem to respect my personal space. They stand back discreetly watching and wait for eye contact and a smile before they'll approach. Most of the people that I talk to are fellow bikers and all seem to be slightly older than me. It's a weekday so perhaps the younger riders are all working and I'm just meeting the retired folks.

Poor Circulation

Back in England these riders would be categorised as 'Born Again Bikers' but I'm getting the distinct feeling that it's a term that's more appropriate here. Aside from an obvious devotion to the products of Harley Davidson their other common passion seems to be religion, and they're not shy when it comes to telling me all about it. Personally I'd rather talk about motorcycles and roads but that's not really a problem, I'll happily talk about anything with anybody. After the overwhelming friendliness across Russia, and the human claustrophobia of Bangkok, the stand-off politeness here has come as something of a shock to my system. It's not that it's better, and certainly not that it's worse, it's just different and will probably take a little time to get used to.

Along the coastal road my senses are constantly bombarded with beautiful scenery and as my stomach tells me that it's almost time to eat, I decide to make camp just north of the border with Oregon. I've been warned by a group of surfers that free camping on the beach is frowned upon and if I want to avoid any interfaces with authority, or 'Nazis' as the surfer dudes had called them, then I should wait until dark before venturing into the dunes on the Tiger. I stock up with food at a local market and cook dinner on a small grassy knoll at the side of a quiet road. By the time the pots are washed and repacked onto the Tiger, the sun is beginning to fall into the Pacific Ocean and I can wait no longer.

The small road to the beach that two hours earlier had been packed with the trucks and vans of the surfers, is now completely empty. The sand is quite firm but nowhere near firm enough for a 300 kg Tiger and its incompetent handler. Thankfully nobody is around to watch me as I struggle along the beach before turning left and wobbling further up into the sand dunes. I daren't risk the attention that a campfire might bring, but I pitch my tent in a west facing gully, open a cold bottle of beer and marvel at the amazing array of night time stars. I've seen the movies where they talk about 'Big Skies', but it's true. With no light pollution, the contrast between the blackness of the sky and the brightness of the stars is beyond words, it's something that makes you just want to lay back and watch it for hours on end. For the first time since Lake Baikal, I take the Special Package from the Tiger and lay it on the dune beside me. The security seal is unbroken, no moisture has entered and in contrast to everything else on the Tiger, it looks just as it had done back in London. I drink another beer and we look at the heavenly show above and the Tiger sparkling in the light of the moon. I think we're going to enjoy our time here on the Pacific Coast Highway.

I wake to the sound of the waves crashing onto the beach and a million gulls circling above my tent. I brew coffee and sit on the beach wrapped in my sleeping bag for warmth. It's bitterly cold, the coastline is shrouded in mist and apart from a few distant kite flyers, the beach is totally deserted. I should really take down the tent and move on before people begin to arrive and notice my illegal camping, but it's too beautiful a place to leave quickly, so I brew another coffee before making a move.

With the bike fully loaded I stumble down onto the beach and head back towards the road. The sand seems softer than it had done last night and the Tiger finds its own path through it. I just let it go where it wants to go and hopefully at some point we'll end up back at the road. It takes a while and the effort certainly warms me, but as the Tiger scrambles from the sand onto the gravel track, a police patrol car seems to be waiting for me. It's clear that he's seen where I've just come from, but he doesn't seem to be interested in me. I wave politely as we pass and he waves back. We roll back onto Highway 101 and within a few minutes cross the border into Oregon and a new day of adventure has begun.

Yesterday I'd thought that this road had lived up to my expectations, but I now think that it's exceeding them. Here in Oregon it clings to the coastline, rising and falling with the contours and around every bend I anticipate another magnificent view to admire and capture on film. It's more beautiful than the Adriatic coast road running down through Croatia and the surface is superior to that of Turkey's Black Sea road. It's green, it's lush and the rolling white mist makes it feel quite mysterious, almost as if the road itself has a soul. A few hundred meters out to sea, a blanket of thicker fog partially shrouds the massive rock formations that seem to stand in every cove along this coast. The mist is constantly moving and new rocks appear and vanish between blinks of the eye. I look all around and aside from the road itself, I can't see anything that's man-made, everything is natural and untouched by humans.

I'd been told that I'd encounter heavy traffic with recreational vehicles, caravans and trucks moving slowly in both directions, but thankfully they're scarce and the road is peaceful and quiet. I feel like we've got the road and the coast all to ourselves, there's nobody here to ruin our enjoyment, no crazy drivers to anger us, no slow vehicles to frustrate us. It's just me, Mom, Dad and our Tiger on a road that encourages us to keep on riding. Mom had never ventured quite this far north of Boonville, but this is certainly the road that she'd wished for and I've got an overwhelming feeling that we're all riding it together. We're moving enthusiastically but that's not something that I'm choosing to do, it's simply something that this road demands. It's smooth and it's progressive, the Tiger's seldom running on the centre of its tyre, constantly banking from left to right and then back again, always at a healthy speed. The salt air flows through my open visor and loosely zipped jacket. One minute it warms me and the next it freezes, my mind is humming but this road doesn't need a soundtrack, it's absolutely perfect as it is. The hours and miles pass, I haven't eaten, I haven't stopped for coffee and that for me isn't just unusual, it's unheard of. Usually I can't do anything without caffeine, but today I feel more alive than I've ever felt before. I'm in love with the world and perfection is too small a word for it.

We're heading south and pass through the town of North Bend, but yesterday I'd stopped to take photographs in the equally pleasant town of South Bend. I'm slightly confused, the Pacific Ocean is still less than a hundred meters to my right, the late afternoon sun is sinking towards it and my compass is usually accurate, so I'm definitely heading south. For some strange reason, North Bend is located to the south of South Bend. Maybe the two places are located in different states, or more likely they've just been named to confuse people like me. I stop to make a brew and end up chatting with several riders who are all heading down towards San Francisco. They look at the maps on my panniers and ask about the journey so far. I begin of course in England and to the accompaniment of intermittent responses of 'wow', 'awesome' and 'amazing dude', I bring the story to a close here in Oregon. I'm asked the first question and it makes me smile. This guy's funny, his face doesn't slip and it just goes to prove that American's do understand British humour. 'Wow, is Seattle really as cool as they say it is?' What I'd thought was a self-deprecating joke turns out to be a serious question and he really doesn't give a flying fuck about anywhere outside of America. It's a beautiful moment, but I guess it's one of those moments that you have to witness first hand to fully appreciate.

Leaving North Bend, we approach the town of Brandon and Highway 101 moves inland. The last twenty miles of coastline has been entirely shrouded in mist and it's sucked every degree of heat out of the air and my body. I could stop and add extra layers of clothing but if I'm going to stop then I might as well stop properly and make a night of it. I pull into an official campsite and they point me to the last available pitch. I seem to be the only tent amongst hundreds of caravans and recreational vehicles. I didn't expect the site to be so full and I've no idea where these vehicles have come from, because they certainly weren't travelling on our road.

I pitch the tent, strike up the stove, pull the ring on a freezing cold beer and sit down to relax. I'm camping in amongst giant Redwood trees, the tallest trees that I've ever seen and I sit there feeling like a Hobbit in an enchanted forest. The canopy blocks out most of the sunlight and shadows race around the ground as the branches dance in the wind high above my head. It's quite beautiful but it's also a little bit spooky. The soft floor of the forest deadens the sounds and it seems that everyone is whispering. I'm about to start cooking and as usual this seems to be a cue for people to come and talk with me. They're intrigued by the various names that are written on the topbox and panniers and I explain that they're the names of people who've donated money to my chosen charity, St Teresa's Hospice, or the names of motorcycling friends who've sadly died enjoying their pastime, or in most cases, their careers as London Despatch Riders.

Before long, there are twenty or thirty people around me, all asking questions, all wanting to know a million different things at the same time. A bundle of wood is dropped into the metal fire ring in front of my tent and two guys start lighting a campfire for me. A casserole dish arrives along with a plastic American sized dinner bowl and a spoon. There's a bottle of red wine from another couple and the loan of a folding canvas chair from their son and his family. As the evening draws on, tables arrive and more chairs for more people. Ice chests filled with cold beer, cartons of Ben & Jerry's ice cream, potato chips and various dips. A lot of my new best friends are talking in a language that I simply don't understand. It seems to be a language relating to technology and recreational vehicles and I get the distinct impression that these good folks would never leave home without a plasma TV, chest freezer and full satellite entertainment system. I'm receiving five star treatment from strangers in the middle of an Oregon forest so I'm not complaining, I'm just comparing the different approaches that we each have to outdoor living.

It's a great evening of fun, food, beer and laughter, but at ten o'clock, it's almost as if a bell sounds and everybody rises to leave. They gather together their personal possessions, wish everybody 'goodnight' and return to their own temporary homes in the forest. I finish my beer, douse the fire with water and climb into my tent. It's been a fantastic day followed by a perfect evening, and tomorrow we'll arrive in Boonville where our outward journey will end.

The amazing Pacific Coast Highway

Chapter 41:
USA, Boonville

We're still riding south on Highway 101. We haven't travelled far enough south to make any climatic difference, but the mist of the past two days has disappeared and it feels as if we've jumped into a totally different season. Yesterday, while riding in full leathers and boots for most of the day I'd been chilled to the bone, but today wearing just tee shirt and sandals, I'm burning like an Englishman in the sun. At home I'd never dream of riding anywhere without full leathers and protective armour, but here in California it just feels like the most appropriate thing to do. Without realizing it, we've entered California and my attitude to everything seems to have adjusted accordingly. There'd been no sign at the side of the road saying 'Welcome', the scenery hasn't really changed and the road is just as spectacular as it had been back in Oregon. But, the people here seem to be different. They look roughly the same as the people did back in Oregon and Washington, but the wiring in their minds seems to be configured quite differently. They're more open, they wave at us out on the road, they come over and talk to me every time we stop for a break and they seem to be aware of a world that exists outside of the USA.

At Trinidad Beach, I meet Jason, a surfer who drives an aging VW Camper and wears his ponytail comfortably. He calls me 'Dude' and wants to know more about Russia. He wants to flame up a pipe and share some of his home grown weed but today I'm riding, not smoking. He tells me that here in California growing marijuana is legal and if I obtain a letter from a 'Dope Doctor', I could grow an entire field of my own. I'm not sure if California really is that liberal or if Jason's just teasing me, but as I don't have a field in which to grow anything, then it doesn't really matter. Jason loves California but doesn't see it as being part of the USA. To him, California is an independent republic that's divorced itself from the other forty-nine States and apparently; 'for a dude like me', it's the only place to be.

A Toyota pulls into the resting point behind us. Troy and Ellen introduce themselves and for some reason insist on calling me 'Geoffrey'. They also decline an introduction to Jason's marijuana pipe but seem quite keen on introducing me to their God. Before long, another small crowd has gathered and plates of food are arriving from recreational vehicles that have quite clearly ignored the 'No Overnight Parking' signs. These folks all seem to be travellers and the questions that they ask are broad and quite worldly. As I recount tales of random meetings with various strangers in the middle of everywhere, I notice that Jason isn't the only pipe smoker here. It's really quite surreal, they'll happily smoke marijuana in an open public space, but when I light a legal cigarette they silently make me feel like a serial killer.

Before our arrival, these folks had all been strangers camping along the same short stretch of road, but now they're sharing jokes like long lost friends. It's nothing to do with me, I'm just the catalyst, but I think it has everything to do with being here in Northern California. Everybody just seems to be chilled and relaxed, less judgmental and certainly more world wise. I'm sure that a relaxed approach to the legality of dope has got something to do with that, but there's got to be something more to it. I'd like to kill more time with these folks, but we should really get moving. We've been on the road since six o'clock this morning, the map that I'm using is useless and I've seriously underestimated the distance to Boonville.

An hour has passed, we're fifty miles south of Trinidad Beach in the town of Leggett, California Highway 101 has morphed into California Highway 1 and this is the actual road that Mom had referred to. This road is narrower now, it's taking me through the giant redwood forests back towards the coast and the deep shadows of the trees has come as a welcome change in the burning heat of the day. For twenty-plus miles we head south towards Fort Bragg riding the most amazing stretch of road that I've ever ridden. I know that the story of Poor Circulation is littered

Navarro Beach, Mendocino County, California

with claims of 'World's Best Biking Road', and perhaps at the time of riding them each of those statements had been true, but today this little piece of utopia is simply beyond comparison. Here the tarmac is perfectly smooth and the direction is never straight. One moment I think that I'm back in the Black Forest of Germany, the next it's the Pass de Giovo into Italy and the next it's the beauty of the Adriatic Coast in Croatia. There's a decision to be made at every bend; to continue enjoying the ride or to stop and capture the view with my camera, but the riding wins every time.

This road is certainly special, a road with an abundance of quality. This very short stretch of a very long road features strongly in the final chapter of Robert Pirsig's iconic book: 'Zen and the Art of Motorcycle Maintenance'. This is precisely where Phaedrus, a character who'd dedicated his life and sacrificed his sanity searching for the meaning of 'Quality', is finally satisfied and set free. I don't pretend to fully understand Pirsig's book about a journey towards awareness, and hopefully I won't lose the remainder of my own sanity anytime soon, but if Phaedrus had been searching for 'Quality', then I can fully understand why he'd found it here on this road.

After the picture postcard town of Mendocino, we leave the main road and head down to the beach at Navarro. I love this wild beach where the sands are littered with the giant trunks of petrified trees that lay like randomly placed relics for as far as the eye can see. Over time, people have fashioned these ancient trees into amazing structures; play houses for kids, shelters from the burning sun and nests for young lovers. I park the Tiger and brew more coffee. There are a few people on the beach but maybe they sense that for us this is a private place and respectfully keep their distance. Boonville is less than twenty miles to the south of here, but the urgency of the past two days has gone. We don't want California Highway 1 to end, there's no hurry and this is a place where we all want to spend a little time alone with our thoughts and memories.

Behind the beach are several camping pitches with 'Honesty Boxes' for payment. The sites are all empty and I decide that it's a good place for us to spend our last night together under the stars. Tomorrow Dad will meet Alan and Torrey and his grandchildren Sam and Willow, but to-night it will be just the three of us. On Mom's last day in Boonville she'd come here to Navarro Beach with the family. They'd played in the flotsam structures, jumped through the waves breaking onto the shore, melted marshmallows on the open fire and watched the sun set into the Pacific Ocean. When she'd spoken in hospital of her final holiday here in Men-docino County, memories of that last day on this beach with her young grandchildren had been her fondest and it was a day that she'd wished could have been shared with Dad.

I'd woken late this morning and lingered until lunchtime. It wasn't the moderate hangover that had slowed me, but the place. I'll come back to Navarro Beach soon, along with Sam and Willow, but right now our tar-get is Boonville. We leave the coastal road and turn inland on California 128. I've ridden this road before and no matter how familiar it becomes, it's impossible to get bored with it. It winds through tall Redwoods that border the road and would make England's great Oaks look like little more than twigs. They're massive in both girth and height, but in parts they're also missing, a result of historical logging and the more recent de-velopment of vineyards. We pass the first sign for Boonville and instead of picking up the pace, I actually slow down.

For the first time on this journey my mind is been drawn to what will happen after Boonville. One hundred percent of my thoughts and nine-ty-nine percent of my planning have concentrated on getting us all to this place, and there's no real plan for leaving it. Boonville will mark the end of one journey and the beginning of another entirely different one, but exactly what shape the next journey will take I really don't know. People will no doubt ask about my plans, but I honestly don't know what I'll tell them. I'll think of something before I leave here, but in the meantime, together we'll keep enjoying the remaining part of this outward journey.

Poor Circulation

Boonville

It's the 1st of September 2008, the 134th day of the journey and we've finally arrived. Bay Creek Studio, 12831 Ornbaun Road, Boonville, California 95415; a two acre parcel of land and home for the past eight years to my brother Alan, sister in law Torrey and their two children Sam and Willow. To complete the inventory I should also add one family dog, three pigs all named George, two cows, two sheep, a pair of ducks, several chickens and now one Tiger, its' English rider and a pair of happy stowaways.

The welcome is warm and emotional, the home coming meal fantastic, the fridge is filled with beer and Sam and Willow even seem to remember who I am. They should do, it's only been nine months since I was last here, but what a nine months it's been. A lot's happened and many things have changed, but on this amazingly wonderful day, the family is finally united in Boonville.

After dinner, Sam and Willow take me outside and introduce me to the animals, some that I remember and some that have arrived more recently. We feed organic hay to the cows and the two orphaned sheep that the kid's have hand reared on bottles. The small garden gives us vegetables that we'll eat tomorrow and the large chicken house two dozen eggs, some for breakfast and some to be exchanged at the Farmer's Market for other locally grown produce. At just seven years of age, Sam's already a budding farmer. He shows me his growing crop of rather large rabbits. They're beautifully playful and as he proudly tells me, a little too chewy for the barbeque but absolutely delicious in casseroles.

The Family United

They're not totally self-sufficient here and Torrey explains that true self-sufficiency is an impossible dream. They still need money for mortgage payments, gasoline, telephone services and the like, but the more that they can produce and trade as a family team, the less time they have to spend working away from their homestead. It's a beautiful place on the edge of Boonville where together as a family they carve out a difficult lifestyle, but carve it they do. It's a lifestyle that Mom had seen and had known that as a farmer, Dad would have appreciated and applauded. I look towards the Tiger and swear that I can see Dad raising his giant farmer's thumbs and smiling. Mom and Dad are hugging each other in the topbox, tears running down their cheeks, mine too. Happy tears, there's no sadness here today, only joy, love and a certain feeling of relief. Somehow we've managed to achieve the seemingly unachievable and we're here in Boonville, together for the first time as a family.

With Torrey, Sam and Willow sleeping soundly in their beds, Alan and I sit drinking another bottle of the Anderson Valley's finest Pinot Noir and wonder what we should do next. On the table between us sits the Special Package that I've carried with me from England, and technically speaking, it's now been delivered to the intended recipient. Ordinarily I'd accept a signature, make a telephone call to the office in London and then start riding home. However, the usual etiquette for courier deliveries clearly doesn't apply here and neither of us knows what we ought to do next. At some point in time Mom and Dad's ashes, and the earth collected from the farm, will be scattered in the most appropriate place. But, deciding upon the most appropriate time and place is something that we'll do as a family when all of us are sober. In the meantime, we talk about the good old days and it's strange how the events that as kids had made us cry the most, now make us laugh the loudest. Growing up with four years between us we always seemed to view everything from opposing perspectives, but now that we're parents ourselves we seem to be sharing the same rose tinted spectacles. We still don't see eye to eye on everything but on one matter we're in total agreement, we've had the best parents that this world could possibly have given us.

Mom and Dad have travelled with me across Europe, Asia and into North America. After narrowly escaping an agricultural Inspection in Seattle, they'd ridden together down The Pacific Coast Highway to be with the family that Dad had never met here in Boonville. Mom's two outstanding wishes have been granted, but probably not in the way that she would have imagined when she'd mentioned them to me a year ago in Ward 32 of Darlington's Memorial Hospital.

'Blue88, empty Boonville ... Over'.
'Roger that Blue88 ...Return to London ... Out'

Epilogue

Delivering the Special Package to the family in Boonville had always been the primary objective of this journey, hence the title of this first book: Ashes to Boonville. But geographically speaking, Boonville was little more than halfway around the world and I'd soon need to start riding back to England. The second book in the Poor Circulation trilogy tells the story of that journey: *Homeward Bound*.

The small green sign on Highway 128 seemed to say it all: 'Boonville. Population 715'. By any standards Boonville was a small town and beyond enjoying time with the family, I'd always assumed there'd be very little to hold me there. However, when it came to attractions, Boonville was a town punching well above its weight. During a conversation with a reporter from the Anderson Valley Advertiser, I mentioned Ted Simon's name and the reporter nodded in recognition. I logically assumed that he'd read Jupiter's Travels, but he hadn't. Jupiter's Travels was something of a mystery to him, but Ted Simon certainly wasn't. 'I think Ted still lives here in Boonville, I'll give you his number'. There were seven billion people in the world, and the one person that I wanted to meet above all others had apparently laid down his hat in the tiny town of Boonville. Was the world really that small?

Although I'd ridden halfway around the world on a strictly limited budget, until reaching South Korea money had always been the least of my problems. Then, as I'd prepared to leave Seoul, everything had changed. I'd arrived in America with enough money in my bank account to complete the journey back to London, but my emergency reserves had gone. My financial safety-net had been taken away and I'd felt naked and vulnerable without it. With very little chance of recovering any money from Adam, before leaving Boonville Alan and Torrey stepped forward and restored my peace of mind. They refilled the hidden compartments of my riding jacket with crisp dollar bills and I rode away from Boonville with the happiest of memories and a determination to return there.

Leaving Boonville behind me, I headed across America meandering between National Parks and other places of interest. Some of those places I'd been aware of before leaving London, but many of them I simply stumbled upon by chance. The geographical splendour that I found was overwhelming, and although the distance between many of America's national treasures was vast, the strangers that I met in between them turned every new day into a new adventure.

As I continued to travel east, the financial establishment was collapsing all around me and I was discovering a country that was seemingly 'For Sale'. Every street had a Yard Sale and the roads were littered with U-Haul trucks. Young families were relocating, turning their backs on the American dream, abandoning their depreciating homes and returning to live with their parents. Each day I met new victims of the economic crash and each of them had a different story to tell. The land of the free was feeling more like the land of the angry, but despite these economic traumas, the kindness and generosity of strangers continued to amaze me.

'Yes We Can'. A new war cry was echoing across America, a war cry designed to unite a nation that was falling apart at its financial seams. Within coastal towns and at the centre of large cities, I found people inspired by Barack Obama's words, but in the more central areas of America I found exactly the opposite reaction. If it had ever existed, the political middle-ground had vanished and those opposed to Obama were declaring the end of civilization and threatening to run for the hills with their guns.

On the night of the US Presidential Election, Tuesday the 4th of November 2008, I arrived in neutral territory: Toronto, Canada. I took a stool at a local bar and watched as the election results rolled in. All around me was a vociferous and seemingly well informed audience, an audience that ignored the racial differences between the candidates and concentrated on their politics. In short, it was a very different audience to the one that I'd left behind me in the USA. As the hands of the clock rolled beyond midnight, it became clear that Barack Obama had clinched the Presidency and Toronto, and possibly much of the world outside, breathed a united sigh of relief.

Three days after the election, I arrived safely back in England with the trusty Triumph Tiger. The flight had been relatively painless and smooth, but as with many other aspects of the journey across North America, certain unexpected challenges had threatened to derail me. Once again, the kindness of strangers had enabled me to keep on moving and the England that I found seemed little different from the England that I'd left behind me six months earlier.

On Sunday the 16th of November 2008, I rode the Triumph Tiger into the car park of the Ace Cafe in Northwest London, and officially completed a full circle of the world. I'd ridden 28,000 miles through 28 different countries in 28 weeks. My original 'Rule of Twenty' had been shattered, but somehow I'd still managed to remain within my budget of just £20 per day. My daughter Hannah and many friends, old and new, were there at the Ace Cafe to welcome me home. It was another emotional day and a day that will never be forgotten, a day of intentional endings and accidental new beginnings.

After leaving the Ace Cafe, I'd ridden home to my old apartment in the village of Great Saling in Essex. The emails that I'd received from Hannah had indeed been accurate. While I'd been riding through the wilds of Siberia, the entire building had been destroyed by fire. Thankfully nobody had been injured in the blaze, and I hadn't owned the now derelict apartment, only the things that had been stored there. Aside from a suitcase containing items of family history and my loaded motorcycle, everything else in my world had surrendered to the flames.

Before starting out on the journey, losing everything that I'd owned would have absolutely fucked-up my day, but on that day, I could do nothing but smile. With even less baggage to hold me back and only limited resources to drive me forward, I started the Tiger, engaged first gear and set out on an entirely different journey. This would become the third unique stage of Poor Circulation, a journey into the unknown, a journey without an ending. I'd happily become *The Accidental Pilgrim*.

Printed in Great Britain
by Amazon.co.uk, Ltd.,
Marston Gate.